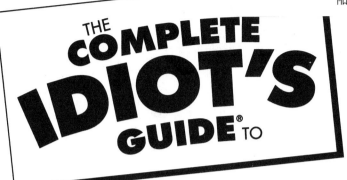

THE **COMPLETE IDIOT'S GUIDE**® TO

Elves and Fairies

by Sirona Knight

ALPHA

A member of Penguin Group (USA) Inc.

ALPHA BOOKS

Published by the Penguin Group

Penguin Group (USA) Inc., 375 Hudson Street, New York, New York 10014, U.S.A.

Penguin Group (Canada), 10 Alcorn Avenue, Toronto, Ontario, Canada M4V 3B2 (a division of Pearson Penguin Canada Inc.)

Penguin Books Ltd, 80 Strand, London WC2R 0RL, England

Penguin Ireland, 25 St Stephen's Green, Dublin 2, Ireland (a division of Penguin Books Ltd)

Penguin Group (Australia), 250 Camberwell Road, Camberwell, Victoria 3124, Australia (a division of Pearson Australia Group Pty Ltd)

Penguin Books India Pvt Ltd, 11 Community Centre, Panchsheel Park, New Delhi—110 017, India

Penguin Group (NZ), cnr Airborne and Rosedale Roads, Albany, Auckland 1310, New Zealand (a division of Pearson New Zealand Ltd)

Penguin Books (South Africa) (Pty) Ltd, 24 Sturdee Avenue, Rosebank, Johannesburg 2196, South Africa

Penguin Books Ltd, Registered Offices: 80 Strand, London WC2R 0RL, England

International Standard Book Number: 1-59257-324-X
Library of Congress Catalog Card Number: 2005922484

07 06 05   8 7 6 5 4 3 2 1

Interpretation of the printing code: The rightmost number of the first series of numbers is the year of the book's printing; the rightmost number of the second series of numbers is the number of the book's printing. For example, a printing code of 05-1 shows that the first printing occurred in 2005.

Printed in the United States of America

Publisher: *Marie Butler-Knight*
Product Manager: *Phil Kitchel*
Senior Managing Editor: *Jennifer Bowles*
Senior Acquisitions Editor: *Randy Ladenheim-Gil*
Development Editor: *Lynn Northrup*
Production Editor: *Megan Douglass*
Copy Editor: *Molly Schaller*
Cartoonist: *Shannon Wheeler*
Cover/Book Designer: *Trina Wurst*
Indexer: *Angie Bess*
Layout: *Ayanna Lacey*
Proofreading: *John Etchison*

Contents at a Glance

Appendixes

Contents

Foreword

The Complete Idiot's Guide to Elves and Fairies by Sirona Knight is a comprehensive book: It has something of everything connected to fairy lore, tradition, and legend. For the reader who wishes to know more about fairy tradition but is daunted by the wide range of books available (from heavily academic to speculative nonsense), this book will be a helpful guide. Sirona has created more than just "another" introduction to fairy lore; it contains many insights, practical suggestions, comparisons, and valuable reference sources. The delightful section on building a fairy or elven garden is, alone, worth the time spent buying and reading this book … and that is only one item from a wide range of contents and extensive research clearly laid out for us to enjoy. There are short, concise summaries of different cultural traditions, in which Norse, Celtic, and famous literary sources such as Shakespeare, among others, are clearly described for us. Through this book, we rapidly discover that fairy lore is not merely the whimsy of modern postcard art or the romance of Victorian sentiment, but has ancient and beautiful precedents in myth, legend, and folklore through the ages.

Sirona also describes in clear detail how our contemporary storytellers and their great modern works of magical fiction do not appear out of nothing. Famous writers from Tolkien to Rowling, she reveals, all drew upon existing fairy and mythological themes to bring us the stories that have been so successful in book and film. She reminds us how even *Star Trek*, that great mythic series from American television, has many connections to the imagery and tales of fairy tradition. Some years ago, I heard a revered teacher demonstrate, as an exercise in the power of myth and consciousness, how we could engage in spiritual meditations using *Star Trek* characters, so Sirona is both accurate and in very good company!

Another excellent feature of this book is that it has many practical suggestions and insights for coming into genuine communion with fairy beings. What we call "fairies" or "elves" (the origins of the words are explained in the book) have many names worldwide, among every race; they are the spirits of the land and water in our sacred living Earth. Sirona offers some simple and joyful methods for making contact with them, for inviting them, for building relationships with them. I consider this building of good relationships between humans and spiritual beings to be our true task in this world, a task that we have forgotten or rejected. The delightful suggestions and methods in this book help us to happily, and safely, fulfill that task.

Sirona's research, insights, and concise writing, combined with the easy-reading and clear reference layout, are informative, inspiring, and a pleasure to read!

I teach many classes on mythology, legends, and fairy tradition, in the United States and Europe, and for years, when people asked "What would you recommend for a complete beginner?" I have been stuck for a simple answer. Until now.

R. J. Stewart

R. J. Stewart is a Scottish author, composer, and musician now living in the United States. He has 40 books in publication, and is known as author and designer of the best-selling *Merlin Tarot*, which has been in print in many languages for 20 years. R. J. has written extensively on the fairy and underworld traditions, and on themes such as the medieval Welsh Prophecies of Merlin, music and meditation, magical arts, and creative vision. His books have been translated worldwide. He has also composed music for film, television, and theater, and made many recordings. In 1997 he was admitted to the United States as "resident alien of extraordinary ability," a category awarded only to those with the highest achievements in the arts or sciences. He teaches classes and workshops, and performs concerts, in many parts of the United States and Europe. Visit the Stewart website at www.dreampower.com.

Preface

As a small girl sitting beneath the blossoming apple tree in my backyard, it was easy to believe in the magic of elves and fairies. They danced among the flowers and shook petals into my hair. And they were always close by when I walked through a shadowy forest, watching me from atop toadstools and beneath ferns and giggling in my ear.

I grew up, left home for college and law school, lived and worked in a city, forgetting the elves and fairies that continued to play in our garden. Though I no longer saw them, they still perched on the fruits of summer, turned the leaves of fall golden, glided to earth in skirts made of snowflakes, and rode the breezes of spring on the backs of red-breasted robins.

Had those emissaries of enchantment, glimpsed from the corner of the eye and as real as anything in plain sight, been forever banished by the rules and reason of adult life? Is it idiotic to long for the magic with which they blessed our childhood? Or is the playful joy that we feel whenever they appear—now only in children's books or major motion pictures—a reminder of the heart's vast wisdom?

Elves and fairies show children what we have forgotten: that the world is alive with mystery and wonder. And with the slightest encouragement—opening this book, reading a fairy tale, feeling your heart leap in the presence of Nature's miracles—the power of imagination reawakens. Our spirits soar and the Fey reappear in earthy attire and gossamer wings, as makers of mischief and bestowers of blessings.

Fairies and elves have always been and will always be our guides to the numinous reality that permeates daily life. They remind us that the natural world is an outer expression of an inner grace. They are revelations of that holiness, spirits of Nature and realms beyond, messengers who carry our dreams to the stars we wish upon, give flight to the secret desires within our hearts, and assurance that no matter how dark the circumstances or obscure the path we are never alone.

Shape shifting with the seasons of the Earth and our lives, they appear to us in the forms that we need them to take. With pranks and undeniable presence they provoke elation and confusion, challenging our intimidated acceptance of modern life's bullying and opening us to boundless possibility. Letting go of what we have been taught to believe, we open to what is true. Behind the diminutive guise of sprites and Tinkerbells we discover the infinite power of ancient Gods and Goddesses.

Dancing between light and shadow, the Fey and all their cross-cultural peers remind us that our view of life as a perilous struggle between "good" and "evil" is instead an embodiment of divine love and delight. And so we need never be afflicted with anything more malevolent than mischief. Call them and they will come, reminding us that hope can grow wings, dreams do come true, and there is reason to trust in the unseen because, when we open our hearts, the realm we all share is Sacred.

Phyllis Curott

Pioneering spiritual teacher **Phyllis Curott** was honored by *Jane Magazine* as one of "The Ten Gutsiest Women of the Year," and is the best-selling author of *The Love Spell*, *Book of Shadows*, and *Witchcrafting*. She is a member of the Assembly of World Religious Leaders, a Wiccan High Priestess, and an Ivy League attorney.

Introduction

The elves and fairies dwell in our imaginations and in the magical gardens of our minds. They live in our very spirit, not just in books, fairy tales, or history. The fairy world is a crossroads where wisdom and whimsy remain constant bedfellows. It's a place of hope and fancy, where good prevails and the story ends happily ever after. This provides a positive contrast to modern life. It represents the fulfillment of our desires and the wistful longings of our hearts.

Fairy tales are the stardust of our imagination. Troops of enchanting water sprites and wood nymphs, fairies and elves frolicking in magical gardens and mystical forests, shoemaking, shape shifting, hiding crocks of gold, and singing rainbows into the sky, as well as riding swift horses laden with tinkling bells, and performing honorable deeds, are all part of the enchanting world of fairies. Their uncanny mischief, tricks, and bizarre behavior compel us to know more.

The elves and fairies live in the mountains, wooded glens, forests, groves, gardens, sylvan sanctuaries, creeks, springs, rivers, lakes, and oceans. They are the spirits of nature, living in a magical realm one step beyond the mortal world. And in the fairy world, like our mortal one, the polarities of good and evil both exist.

Stories of magical beings with supernatural powers who greatly affect the daily lives of people exist in all cultures around the world. In *The Complete Idiot's Guide to Elves and Fairies*, you will encounter and learn about the array of elves, fairies, and other magical creatures, and how they can positively influence your life. This book begins by giving you a basic overview of what elves and fairies are, and then moves on to fairy tales, folklore, and mythology, including modern fairy tales such as *The Lord of the Rings* and *Harry Potter*.

Elves and fairies provide a magic mirror into the human psyche, and therefore can help you better understand yourself. They act as change agents for personal empowerment, enrichment, and growth. As you learn all about elves, fairies, and magical creatures, you unlock the doors into your inner self. Also included in this book are exercises and techniques, such as planting a magical fairy garden, that make your process of self-discovery easier and more understandable.

The elves and fairies are very much alive and well in the modern world just as they were in the ancient world. It's time to chart a pathway to fairyland and open the doorway into their enchanted lands. Learn how they live, play, laugh, make music, dance, love, grieve, sleep, and dream. Listen to the language of the fairies and recite the prayer of the elves.

Let us go now on a magical journey, a voyage of discovery, by earth, sea, and sky. Within the many fairy tales of grace and fancy, we will explore the different kinds of elves and fairies, and all of their shape-shifting faces. The journey is guaranteed to stir the childlike wonder within you and strengthen your belief in magic!

How to Use This Book

To help you gain a better understanding of the many qualities of elves and fairies, this book presents the information in six parts:

Part 1, "Enter the World of Elves and Fairies," begins your adventure by introducing you to different kinds of elves, fairies, and other magical creatures, and the world where they live. Included is a sampling of fairy tales, folklore, mythology, and spiritual history.

Part 2, "Modern Elves and Fairies," continues your adventure by welcoming you to the world of modern fairy tales, including *The Lord of the Rings*, *Harry Potter*, and *Elf*. You will also become acquainted with modern fairy traditions, and how they use fairy magic in a multitude of ways to improve their lives and their connection to nature and the divine.

Part 3, "Habits and Habitats of Elves and Fairies," delves into the specific characteristics of various magical creatures, including physical attributes, how to find them, and how to meet them. Included are methods for attracting beneficial fairy energies and protecting yourself from the bad ones.

Part 4, "The Spiritual Aspects of Elves and Fairies," looks at the similarities and contrasts between humans and fairies and elves, including the question of immortality. Also in this section you will encounter the divine aspects of elves and fairies through rituals, meditations, and blessings.

Part 5, "Connecting with the Spirit of Nature," introduces you to Findhorn and other magical places that work with nature devas in order to produce some supernatural results. Included are instructions for planting your own fairy garden.

Part 6, "Exploring the Magical Powers of Elves and Fairies," is about connecting to the magical elf and fairy within you. Included are lists of foods, beverages, herbs, stones, and essences along with their magical properties and how to use them.

Extras

To add to your adventure into the magical world of elves and fairies, the following boxes are interspersed throughout the book. They contain interesting bits of information and insights, depending upon their heading.

Wizardly Wisdom

Here is where you will find information and tips that you can use to better understand elves and fairies.

Through the Ages

This is where you will find interesting quotations from famous people regarding elves and fairies.

Fairy Tales and Legends

These boxes contain pieces of fairy tales, myths, and folklore about magical creatures.

Magical Meaning

Here you will find definitions of terms to help you in your understanding of elves and fairies.

On Guard!

These boxes will caution you to be aware of or avoid certain things, including harmful elves and fairies.

Acknowledgments

Once upon a time …

There was a group of magical and brilliant minds that helped make this book a success. I would like to gratefully acknowledge the brilliant ones that made this book happen, the elves and fairies, especially Alvis, Oberon, and Titania; Randy Ladenheim-Gil (my senior acquisitions editor extraordinaire!); and Marie Butler-Knight (my empowering and supportive publisher). Many heartfelt thanks to the ones who made this book great, Lynn Northrup (the best development editor a mortal could ever hope to work with, who was certainly an elf in another lifetime!); and Molly Schaller and Megan Douglass (my marvelous, magical fairy lady copy and production editors!). And sincere thanks to my senior managing editor Jennifer Bowles, my product manager Phil Kitchel, and to everyone at Alpha Books who helped make this book magical!

I also want to lovingly thank my parents, in particular my terrific mother Betty and stepfather Allan, who were available to answer my every question about folklore and Shakespeare. And sincere thanks to my father John, who spent so much time when I was young enchanting me with fairy tales. Watermelon kisses to you! And to my kind stepmother Susan, who is an angel; my great-aunt Rose; and my 99-year-old grandmother Mabel. Thank yous and hugs to my family—Margaret, Dale, Angela and Jeff, Pat and Nancy, Paul, Richard, Alicia, Emily, Jason, Chrissy, and Jennifer. And many thanks and hugs to Katy, Stephanie, and Justin. Genuine thanks to Norman, Karen, Rick, and Jonesy.

I would also like to thank all of you who have brought magic into my life—Heidi Ellen Robinson Fitzgerald, Melissa Dragich, Donovan and Linda Leitch, Jeff Beck, Bret Lueder, Steve Vai, Ottmar Leibert, Michael McDonald, Brandon Boyd, Keb' Mo', Perry Farrell, Julian Cope, Meredith Brooks, Alan Stivell, Loreena McKinnitt, Maireid Sullivan, Crispian Mills, Jay Darlington, Ravi Shankar, Aine Minogue, Eric Johnson, Rick Rubin, R. J. Stewart, Starhawk, Patricia Telesco, Phyllis Curott, Swami Satyambranada, Sally Griffyn, Deepak Chopra, Jordan Maxwell, Michael Battista, J. Drew, Z. Budapest, Timothy Roderick, Mike Lewis, Skye Alexander, Marion Weinstein, Raymond Buckland, Raven Grimassi, Micki Bauman, David Hennessey, Adrianna Huseman, Dr. Steven Bannister, Neale Donald Walsh, James Redfield, Cynthia Larson, Zecharia Sitchin, Mark Victor Hanson, Margo Anand, John Perkins, Dr. John Gray, Chris Ahearn, Tony Clark, and Oberon; and many thanks to everyone at *Magical Blend Magazine*, especially my editor, Michael Peter Langevin.

I would also like to send magical and loving hugs to the blessed ones whose souls have passed to the Otherworld—Midnight, Blue Sky Happy, Missy Momma, Amber Amstray, G. W. Dog, Blue Sky Snoopy, and Shasta Daisy. May the helpful elves and fairies, God, and Goddess, bless, guide, and protect all of you, always!

And they all lived happily ever after. The end.

Trademarks

Part 1

Enter the World of Elves and Fairies

What are elves and fairies? Why do they continue to excite the human imagination through movies, books, and art? From the fairy tales your parents read to you as bedtime stories to the plays of William Shakespeare and more recently the works of J. R. R. Tolkien, J. K. Rowling, and artist Brian Froud, the magical world of elves and fairies provides a continual source for creative inspiration and personal enlightenment.

It's time to begin your adventure into the realm of these magical beings who throughout history have influenced the human psyche and helped people gain a greater understanding of their relationship to nature. In this part, we'll look at some traditional perceptions of elves and fairies in fairy tales and mythology.

Chapter 1

What Are Elves and Fairies?

In This Chapter

- Early ideas on elves and fairies
- A peek inside their magical world
- How they continue to excite the human imagination
- The different kinds of elves and fairies
- The extraordinary powers of other magical creatures

Do you remember seeing *Peter Pan* for the first time as a child? Toward the end of the story there is a scene where Tinkerbell's light is beginning to dim and Peter calls for everyone to believe in fairies. How hard did you wish for Tinkerbell to live? Stories describing magical beings and the wonders of their world have been told through the ages from the earliest peoples to the modern day. Many are the tales of elves, fairies, and other magical creatures who have helped or hindered the fortunes of humans who come in contact with them. Besides the array of traditional fairy tales, many renowned writers such as William Shakespeare, W. B. Yeats, Sir James Matthew Barrie, and L. Frank Baum have added to the volumes of literature about elves and fairies.

An example of a modern fairy tale is J. R. R. Tolkien's *The Lord of the Rings* trilogy, which is a classic tale of the bond between elves and humans. This bond goes back to the beginning of time. In Tolkien's trilogy, this bond had become strained. Aragorn, a human, brings about another alliance between the elves and the humans. He invokes the help of the elves in his quest to defeat the forces of darkness and fulfill his destiny to become king.

Many fairy tales allude to a time when the world of elves and fairies was very much a visible part of the human world. Through time, the human and fairy worlds dimensionally separated, only coming together at certain places, times, and events. Two of these times, May Day and Halloween, are still celebrated throughout the world.

Although no longer as easily accessible, the elven and fairy energy is still a power that you can call into your life when you need it. Like Aragorn, you can summon magical energies and unite ancient bonds. All you need is a basic knowledge of elf and fairy habits and habitats along with their likes and dislikes. The purpose of this book is to give you solid background in how to make your elf and fairy experiences positive and beneficial. (For the purposes of this book, I will be using the spelling "elven" rather than elfin or elvin. This is the literary adjective. It is also the preferred spelling of J. R. R. Tolkien, who was a medieval language scholar at Oxford.)

Elves and fairies are a natural expression of your inner being that includes your dreams, aspirations, and desire for something more in life than what's being offered. Elves and fairies beckon you to a world where anything is possible as long as you set your mind to it!

Magical Meaning

Elves are magical beings with extraordinary powers that are associated with natural settings. **Fairies** (also spelled *faeries*) are magical creatures with supernatural powers who embody the many aspects of nature and life.

The Nature of Elves and Fairies

The original depiction of the race of *elves* comes from Norse mythology. Created before humans, elves possess extraordinary powers and are associated with nature, particularly woodland and forest settings.

The way J. R. R. Tolkien depicts elves in his epic trilogy *The Lord of the Rings* is consistent with these Norse descriptions. Somewhere between mortal and divine, elves are anywhere from five to seven feet tall with catlike ears. They are said to be thin, strong, flexible, and quick. In early mythology, elves and humans forged an eternal bond that has remained strong through the ages.

The basic concept of *fairies* originates from Irish mythology. They were originally the ancient people of Ireland, who when defeated in battle became assimilated into the hills and natural features of the land. At first they became the Celtic gods and goddesses, but in time, they evolved into the many types of fairies described in folklore and literature. (You'll learn much more about folklore and mythology in Chapter 3.)

In their early forms, fairies were magical creatures that embodied the various aspects of nature and life. Often with supernatural powers, they are portrayed as being both helpful and harmful, depending on what kind of fairy they are and how you treat them. This is why when dealing with fairies it's good to be able to identify the kind of fairy, and what the proper etiquette is in asking for what you want. Give a fairy what it wants, and it will help you. Mess with a fairy, and it will hinder everything you do.

A Glimpse into Another World

The world of elves and fairies is always with you wherever you go, it's just that most times you don't see it because it is hidden by a veil that makes it invisible. At certain times of the year this veil becomes thinner and is lifted to the point where you can glimpse into this magical realm, often gaining insights into the problems of your own life. For example, during the full moon and on the seasonal festival days such as Beltane and Halloween, it becomes easier to commune with the fairies. (You'll learn more about these magical times of the year in Chapter 11.)

Folklore and literature abound with stories of people visiting the enchanted world of elves and fairies. Sometimes these encounters seem short, but in reality they can last years. This is because time in the immortal world of elves and fairies is not the same as in the mortal human world.

Because the world of elves and fairies parallels our own world, there is a continual interaction between their world and our world. Besides humans visiting their world, elves and fairies also move through the veil and visit the human

Fairy Tales and Legends
In the story of *Rip Van Winkle* by Washington Irving, the main character encounters a short, square-built old elf who takes him to a strange place where other elves are playing a game of ninepins and drinking from a wooden keg. He drinks some of the delicious brew before falling into a deep sleep that lasts for 20 years.

world. These visits are fully documented in popular culture by the many movies, books, and artworks that contain references to elves and fairies.

Myths are both continuous and ever changing. Each generation updates the myths of the previous generations. Movies such as *Troy* and *King Arthur* are examples of traditional myths being reinvented. Movies such as *The Lord of the Rings* and the *Harry Potter* series represent traditional themes being used to create new stories and myths.

> **Magical Meaning**
>
> **Archetypes** are universal themes that are common within the human experience, such as mother, father, friend, lover, warrior, and magical being. They are inherited ideas that are created from the experience of the human and are present in the subconscious of every person.

As a child, everything is new and magical. As a result, children are more apt to believe that anything can happen and that magic is possible. Elves and fairies represent these magical aspects of life, and on a deeper level represent *archetypes* that provide a doorway into the human psyche. Psychologist Carl Jung, who wrote a great deal about the concept of archetypes, was responsible for weaving them into popular culture.

You'll find that the more you learn about elves and fairies, the more you learn about yourself. You'll find that not only has a doorway into your inner self opened, but also a doorway into an enchanting realm filled with magical creatures of every shape, size, and magical power is opened to you.

The Magical Realm of Elves

In Norse mythology, there were two kinds of elves: the light elves and the dark elves. The light elves lived above in the world of Alfheim and shone with celestial beauty and were helpful to mortals. The dark elves, also known as dwarves, lived in the underworld of Svartalfheim, and were generally ill-tempered and unfriendly to any mortals unfortunate enough to encounter them.

Popular culture has taken the concept of an elf and expanded it to mean many different kinds of magical beings other than light elves and dark elves. Over time, the portrayal of elves has become much more fairylike, to the point where they have become perceived as one of the many kinds of fairies.

Fairy tales such as "Snow White" have modified the popular image of dwarves to one that is a far cry from the nasty dark elves/dwarves. Like elves and fairies, dwarves have developed into beings that can at times be friendly and helpful to humans.

Light elves have a celestial beauty and are helpful to mortals.

Beginning with Santa's elves, which appear each year at Christmas, images and references to elves appear everywhere. If you walk into a store, you find images of elves everywhere, from the packaging of food products, cosmetics, and pet products to their images on figurines, note cards, and garden decorations. Elves have become part of everyday life to the point where there are elf hats, elf shoes, and costumes for people who want to look like elves.

Elves are as much a part of our modern world as they were a part of the world of the ancient Norse and Celtic peoples. Our art, literature, and popular culture suggest that even though the elven realm is normally invisible to humans, many people still seek to connect with that world and draw in the magic of elves.

Wizardly Wisdom

Brother of one of Iceland's most influential politicians, Magnus Skarphedinsson has the distinction of being head of The Icelandic Elf School. Complete with curriculum, classrooms, textbooks, and diplomas, elf school (*Álfaskólinn* in Icelandic) teaches its students the ways of elves, including field trips and ongoing research projects.

The Magic of Elves

There is a natural rhythm to elven energy that flows into everything they do. It is like an enchanting melody that draws you to them. Elves adore nature; everything about it fascinates them. Nature's energy flows to and from them, and joy and wonder fills their every thought and action. Elves seamlessly blend into the environment, becoming one with forest trees, riverbanks, or the tall meadow grasses.

Elves are insatiably curious, quest to learn and understand, and adore sophisticated and challenging games of skill and chance. They encourage beauty, imagination, creativity, and laughter, and always put their best effort forward, realizing that excellence is in itself enchanting.

Existing in a natural state, elves have extraordinary powers such as second sight and the ability to communicate directly from mind to mind. They do not age, but can be slain or die from other causes. They are playful, spontaneous, amusing, reserved, contemplative, and mysterious, and the depth of elven love both fascinates and arouses mortals. Elves do not sleep, but they rest their minds in lucid dreams.

Elves create enchanting music that you can hear at night in the woods or by a secluded lake. They dance in circles in green grass to the song of nature. You can see elves more readily in the forest woods at dusk. And when the moon rises, they come out and dance, sing, and party all night!

Different Kinds of Elves

The different kinds of elves depicted in popular culture range from Santa's helpers, portrayed as small doll-like elves, to the tall, exotic creatures with extraordinary powers in *The Lord of the Rings*. What all elves have in common is their pointed ears, and often they have catlike or owl-like eyes.

> **CAUTION**
> **On Guard!**
>
> Just as there are good elves and fairies, there are bad elves and fairies. The good ones will help you as long as you are kind, but stay away from bad elves and bad fairies, because they will cause you nothing but grief and harm. (For a complete explanation on how to distinguish a bad elf or fairy from a good one, please see Chapter 12.)

As I pointed out earlier, Norse mythology denotes two kinds of elves—light elves and dark elves. This designation of light and dark is not meant to represent "good" and "bad" so much as location. Light elves live out in the sunlight in the upper world, whereas dark elves or dwarves live underground where it is dark and they are hidden from the Sun.

The many kinds of elves include, but are not limited to, forest or tree elves, hill elves, woodlands elves, winged elves, high elves, lowland elves, meadow elves, mountain elves, blessed elves, fire elves, river elves, sea elves, lake elves, wind elves, moon elves, sylvan elves, eldar elves, gold elves, silver elves, gray elves, blue elves, and green elves.

The Magical Realm of Fairies

The traditional spelling of fairy is *faery* or *faerie*, stemming from the French word *fae*. In the time of Shakespeare, *fae* had three meanings:

♦ Enchantment

♦ A place where enchanting or magical beings dwell

♦ The inhabitants of a magical or enchanted place

The Latin root of the word *fae* means *fate*, a reference to the Greek goddesses known as the Fates, who influence past, present, and future. Also referred to as the "gentry," "little people," and "bright people," the current spelling of fairy comes from this idea that they are the fair people. *Fair* means something pure, bright, and just.

Another spelling for *fae* is *fay*, and a traditional English way of spelling *faire* is *fayre*, alluding to the origin of *fairs* as being a celebration of the fairy energy. This energy was traditionally celebrated at certain times of the year when the fairy energy was strong (see Chapter 11). Fairs are a way for mortals to acknowledge the influence that the fairy energy has on the many aspects of daily life, including love, health, and prosperity.

A flower fairy.

Through the Ages

Irish author James Joyce once remarked that parts of Connaught, a province in western Ireland, were more thickly populated with fairies than with mortals. This is not surprising, as Connaught is said to be the home of Medb, queen of the fairies.

Although fairies are often associated with places of the mortal world, such as forests, creeks, and even people's houses, ultimately all fairies reside in the fairy realm (which I'll tell you more about in Chapter 2). This is a magical realm that humans occasionally visit—sometimes by accident, sometimes by invitation, and sometimes by design.

The magical realm of fairies is all around you at all times. Sometimes while walking in the woods you might see a flicker of a shadow out of the corner of your eye that disappears the moment you turn to look at it. You might have the odd feeling that you're being watched or that someone is there with you, but when you turn to look, there is no one. It often sends a tingling sensation down your spine and makes your hairs stand on end. Anytime this happens, you know you are close to the fairy realm.

The Magic of Fairies

Sometimes referred to as fallen angels, and other times portrayed as an ancient race of people that predate our own origins, fairies and their magic come in mysterious and often far-reaching ways. One moment they can display human characteristics and emotions, and in the next moment they do something totally magical and unbelievable. They are continually testing and extending the bounds of human reality.

Tied to the power of nature and natural spirits, the magic of fairies comes in many forms. If approached with kindness and respect, they have been known to bless farmers with outrageously large fruits and vegetables, heal the sick, and bring good fortune. The fairy tale "The Legend of Knockgrafton" illustrates this point quite well. In this tale a happy-go-lucky humpbacked man named Lusmore hears the fairies singing, and when they stop, he beautifully carries on their song. In their delight, they transport him to the fairy realm, where he sings and dances with them, and they end by relieving him of his burdensome hump. When a second, not-so-nice, humpbacked person goes to the fairies to have his hump removed, he clumsily sings over the fairies' song and breaks the flow of the music. In doing this he shows his lack of respect for the fairies, and they retaliate by giving the man Lusmore's hump.

One of the common magical abilities attributed to fairies is the power to shape shift. *Shape shifting* is the ability to transform yourself or other things into different forms and shapes at will. Shape shifting is particularly handy when someone is trying to catch you, and is prominent in stories where a mortal must hold on to a fairy, such as a leprechaun, in order to gain the fairy's gold. While being held, the fairy turns into a variety of creatures in order to persuade the person to let go.

> **Fairy Tales and Legends**
>
> In the fairy tale "Jamie Freel and the Young Lady," a young man named Jamie rescues a well-to-do young lady from the fairies. As he carries her away, the fairies try to dissuade him by changing her into a barking and biting black dog, a glowing bar of iron that had no heat, and at last a sack of wool.

Different Kinds of Fairies

A great debate has continued through time as to what constitutes a fairy. One viewpoint claims that elves, dwarves, trolls, and such are all part of the world of fairies, whereas another, stricter view, maintains that elves, dwarves, trolls, and such are distinct from fairies and should not be included under that heading. This latter view is more traditional and based on mythology, and the other is a modern view derived from popular culture, which through time has lumped a variety of magical beings and creatures under the fairy banner.

This book combines both the traditional and modern viewpoints to fairies. Excluding elves and dwarves, which have been covered previously, fairies are all the magical beings that have humanlike characteristics. Dragons, unicorns, and phoenixes are covered in the following section on other magical creatures.

Coming within the context of fairies is a variety of magical beings that extend from sprites and nymphs to hobgoblins and dryads. Here's a sampling of fairies grouped according to their natural hangouts:

- ◆ Water fairies: alvens, gwradedd amnwn, nixie, nymphs, sirens, water sprites, selkies

- ◆ Household fairies: Billy Blin, brownies, hobgoblins, kobolds, pixies, redcaps

- ◆ Forest fairies: corrigans, dryads, oakman, sidhe draoi

Other Magical Creatures

Besides just elves and fairies, there are a multitude of other magical creatures that defy the bounds of convention. Stemming from the boundlessness of the human imagination, these magical creatures come in all kinds of different forms, from dragons and griffins to unicorns and phoenixes.

Of all other magical creatures, dragons continue to be one of the most popular. They come in all sizes. Some are good, some friendly, others are bad, and still others are shape-changers. Contemporary author Anne McCaffrey has written a series of fascinating books with dragons in them, called *Dragonriders of Pern*. McCaffrey's dragons are winged, magnificent, wise, and protective; communicate telepathically with their riders; have supernatural strength; and can time-shift between worlds.

A five-toed, winged dragon.

The two most familiar kinds of dragons are the winged, crested, barbed-tailed and barbed-tongued, fire-breathing heraldic dragon; and the worm, of Scandinavian origin, which is huge, wingless, and self-joining, with poisonous breath and a venomous sting, and often appears as a sea serpent. Both kinds of dragons are reptiles with ears and extremely rough hides covered with scales. They frequent lakes, pools, sulfurous springs, and wells, hunger for maidens and princesses, guard and hoard treasure, and are next to impossible to kill. Lakes, springs, pools, wells, caves, and caverns are believed to be guarded by dragons, and the killing, removing, or disturbing of these magical guardians can prove disastrous.

Wizardly Wisdom

The Anglo-Saxon word *drakan* is a Greek derivative from *draco* meaning dragon or large snake. It might also derive from the word *derkein*, meaning to see clearly; dragons have especially keen sight and can foretell the future.

Often, dragon stories are connected with the origin of ancient sites (or ley lines) of worship. The reason for this is the dragon represents raw elemental power, particularly earth energy. For example, seven thousand years ago in Sumeria, the ancient serpent dragon Zu (or Asag) stole from the Great god Enlil the Tablets of the Law, which regulated the universe and the earth's energy. Ninurta, the sun god, finally killed Zu and returned the tablets, thus keeping the universe from chaos.

In Europe, the dragon is synonymous with the Ouroboros Earth Serpent. The dragon in Celtic mythology is a symbol of sovereignty and supreme power, with *Pendragon* meaning *chief*. The red dragon of Cadwallader is the emblem of Wales. It represents the Great Red Serpent of the Welsh god Dewi and was the emblem on King Arthur's helmet in battle. The Saxons used the white dragon as the royal standard. The famous wizard Merlin (Myrddin) released two dragons, one red and one white, from a subterranean lake under Vortigern's tower at Dinas Emrys, located in a mountain region in Snowdonia, Gwynedd. These dragons represented the vitality of the land, which could only be harnessed by a true sovereign.

Fairy Tales and Legends

The Scandinavian Mester Stoorworm was father of all worms, the first and the largest, with its length stretching halfway across the world. His venomous breath could kill every creature and could wither up all growing things. It looked like a gargantuan mountain, with eyes that glowed and flamed like a ward fire, and a forked tongue thousands of miles long; he could sweep whole towns, trees, and hills into the sea. As he died, Mester Stoorworm spewed out his teeth and they became the Faroes, Orkneys, and Shetland Islands. His forked tongue entangled itself on the moon, and his body hardened into Iceland.

Besides dragons, other magical creatures also occupy a place within popular culture:

♦ Like the dragon, the *griffin* (also spelled griffon or gryphon) of Greek mythology guarded mines, treasure, riches, and gold. Also called a gryps or gryphus, the griffin dwelt in the high mountains in a country between the fabled Hyperboreans and the one-eyed Arimaspians. The griffin appears with an eagle's head, wings, and forefeet, a lion's body and ears, and a lion's or serpent's tail. Griffins line their nests with gold and pull the chariot of the sun as well as the chariots of the gods Jupiter and Nemesis. They are sometimes mentioned in Celtic fairy tales, and they have a prominent position in Welsh folklore. For instance, an image of a griffin is frequently seen on inn signs with names like "The Three Griffins."

♦ The deadly *basilisk* is a winged cross between a cock, snake, and toad, or the combination of a cockerel, snake, and winged lizard with feathers. The basilisk's back is covered by emeralds, and its gaze turns you into stone. Traditionally a mirror, lake, or pool surface is used to send its reflection back. Sometimes large, sometimes small, basilisks might be crested with a crown of flesh. Only rue, the herb of grace, is immune to the basilisk, and daylight drives it back to its lair.

♦ Similar to the basilisk is the *cockatrice*. It has the head of a cock, the wings and feet of a fowl, and a barbed serpent's tail. The cockatrice is a symbol of danger, death, violence, pain, and horror.

♦ The magical *karnabo* roams the woodlands and has a humanlike face with basilisk eyes and an elephant's trunk for a nose. Its nasal whistling breath paralyzes or kills those that come too close to its slate quarry lair.

♦ The deadly *codrille* will turn you into stone if it sees you before you have seen it. The salamander who has been served by the raven gives birth through her mouth to a codrille egg, which she places on a bed of stones, hidden under the yew. Whoever owns the land the yew is on will be obeyed by all the birds and snakes on land and in stagnant or salt waters. The best way to trap a codrille is when is it hatching.

♦ Unlike its deadly serpentlike counterparts, the *zaltys* is a helpful and auspicious serpent genie in Baltic countries. It is attracted by offerings of milk, honey, and cakes. When a zaltys favors a family, it brings happiness, joy, good harvest, prosperity, and healthy livestock.

♦ The magical *hippocampus* appears with the head and body of a horse and large fishlike sea serpent hindquarters. A hippocampus draws Poseidon's chariot, and hippocampus babies are called tadfoals.

- The *Margotine cats*, also called Foireaux or Courtaud cats, are the product of the union of fallen fairies and black alfs. The Margotine and Foireaux cats look like ordinary cats, well known in Brittany. The Courtaud cats, on the other hand, are taller than a human and have no tails. They have a single white hair under their black fur. If you pull this hair, your wishes will be granted by the black alfs and demons. When a magical cat goes hunting, its appearance alters; its legs, body, and teeth become longer, its fur flares out, ears prick up, and eyes glow like embers.

- *Pegasus* is a divine, white-winged horse from Greek mythology that was born from the slain Medusa's blood. It was tamed by Athena, given to the Muses, and kept at Corinth, and ridden only with a heavenly bridle. The fountain Hippocrene bubbled forth from the hoof strike of Pegasus.

- Another magical horse found in North America, India, Africa, China, and Southern France is the well-known *unicorn*. It is a larger-than-average, meek, gentle white horse with a single horn that measures 27 to 36 inches. The unicorn's horn has a white base, black middle, and red tip, and is listed as the possession of medieval kings, popes, and pontiffs, who used it to detect poisons.

A unicorn.

◆ The mythical *phoenix* lives in a secret garden and feeds on air. It represents the Empress, rebirth, resurrection, healing, and solar power. Appearing about the same size as an eagle or large red or golden swan, the phoenix weeps tears of incense and its blood is balsam. Phoenix is the Greek name for the fabled Egyptian Bennu bird or fire-bird that lived in Arabia, a heron sacred to Osiris, the Egyptian god of the underworld, resurrection, and agriculture, and Ra, the Egyptian sun god. When the phoenix ages a thousand years, it builds a funeral nest of cassia and frankincense in a palm tree. The nest is set ablaze by the sun, and in nine days, a new phoenix in the form of a worm rises from the ashes.

The Least You Need to Know

◆ Elves and fairies are magical beings that exist in a realm somewhere between the mortal and the divine.

◆ Popular culture continues to tap into the creative energy of elves and fairies as evidenced by the multitude of art, literature, and other products relating to them.

◆ Elves and fairies represent archetypes and aspects of the human psyche.

◆ Elves and fairies began as distinctly different magical beings, but through time elves have become more fairylike.

◆ Elves and fairies have a variety of extraordinary powers, including the ability to shape shift.

◆ Besides elves and fairies, there are a multitude of other magical creatures with extraordinary powers, including dragons, griffins, and basilisks.

Chapter 2

Fairy Tales: A Magical View of Life

In This Chapter

- ◆ The effect of fairy tales on how you view the world
- ◆ How fairy tales differ from folk tales and quest tales
- ◆ J. R. R. Tolkien's ideas on what makes a good fairy story
- ◆ Create your own fairy tale
- ◆ "Once upon a time …": the timeless quality of fairy tales
- ◆ A sampling of traditional fairy tales

Like the elves and fairies themselves, fairy tales offer a glimpse into a magical world whose scope defies the bounds of conventional reality. Their primary role is to entertain and teach, but beyond that, the goal is to introduce us to a world that makes each of us question the very standards that define modern life. We realize we're not alone, but instead are continually being influenced by a vast array of energies, including those that come from the fairy realm.

As children, we each have fond memories of listening to a bedtime story. We fell blissfully asleep to fairy tales such as Cinderella, Sleeping Beauty, and Snow White, stories that have been told for hundreds of years. At an early age, fairy tales begin to define our history, values, and constructs of the world, raising our awareness from the practical to the magical. Suddenly animals talk, the world becomes more than what it seemed before, and a halo of light permeates everything we do and everywhere we go.

The people who wrote down and collected fairy tales were not publishing their own creative works, but instead the creativity of humanity. As writing and books became more prevalent, books of fairy tales were meant to record the rich cultural heritage that had been flourishing since the time of bards and wandering minstrels. Many of the tales come in many variations, but there are common themes and ideas that they convey. Let's examine these themes and how they influence the way we view our world.

Growing Up with Mother Goose and the Brothers Grimm

The box office success of the movies *Shrek* and *Shrek II* point to the continued popularity of *fairy tales* in our culture. Revolving around the adventures of an ogre, a princess, and a talking donkey, the movies bring in characters from fairy tales, including the muffin man, Puss in Boots, Prince Charming, and a host of others. The movies use traditional fairy tales from *Mother Goose* and *Grimm's Fairy Tales* in order to create a modern fairy tale. In particular, the success of the movie *Shrek II* was so phenomenal that it is listed as one of the top ten movies of all time in the United States, based on box office receipts.

Magical Meaning

A **fairy tale** is a story involving fantastic forces and magical beings, such as elves, fairies, and wizards. These stories were originally sources of amusement and tools for teaching people moral lessons and about historical or extraordinary events.

Both *Mother Goose* and *Grimm's Fairy Tales* are collections of folk tales that were part of an oral tradition dating back to the time of bards and wandering minstrels. These were people who went from town to town, entertaining audiences with their stories and songs. Because they were part of an oral tradition that was forever evolving, these tales were continually being changed and new parts were always being added. Through time, these folk tales came to be known as fairy tales—whether they had fairies in them or not. Originally these tales were created for adults and the general population, and only later became known as children's stories.

Looking for Mother Goose

Frenchman Charles Perrault is credited with publishing an early volume of Mother Goose stories in 1697. Translated as *Histories and Tales of Long Ago, with Morals*, the book contained eight fairy tales, including the timeless classics "Sleeping Beauty," "Cinderella," "Puss in Boots," "Red Riding Hood," and "Jack and the Beanstalk." The cover of the book showed a picture of an old woman at a spinning wheel, telling stories to a group of children and a cat. Also on the cover was a placard with *Tales of my Mother the Goose* written on it.

Around 1765, John Newbery published a collection of Mother Goose rhymes, titled *Mother Goose's Melody*. This was the first popular book of children's rhymes, even though like the Mother Goose tales of Perrault, the rhymes were very old, and originally, for the most part, not created for children. The long list of rhymes in the book included the well-known "Jack and Jill," "Patty cake, patty cake," "This little piggy went to market," "Dickery, dickery, dock," and "High diddle diddle":

> "High diddle diddle
>
> The cat and the fiddle
>
> The cow jump'd over the moon;
>
> The little dog laugh'd
>
> To see such craft,
>
> And the dish ran away with the spoon."

Fairy Tales and Legends
Several women through history have been said to be the "real" Mother Goose. One of the more famous of these cases involves a woman named Elizabeth "Mother" Goose, who lived in Boston in the early 1700s. She is said to have sung the rhymes to her little grandson.

After Newbery published his collection of Mother Goose rhymes, there were a variety of other volumes that followed and included many of the original rhymes along with additional rhymes. One of the more renowned of these was titled *The Real Mother Goose*, published in 1916 by illustrator Blanche Fisher Wright. Included in this volume was the following rhyme about Mother Goose:

> "Old Mother Goose, when
>
> She wanted to wander,

Would ride through the air

On a very fine gander."

In these modern times, Mother Goose is still very much an integral part of our culture. There is a Mother Goose Society (www.librarysupport.net/mothergoosesociety/) whose purpose is to promote the folklore and rhymes. Additionally, Mother Goose Day has been designated as May 1 (May Day), one of the favorite days of the fairies.

The Brothers Grimm

Jakob and Wilhelm Grimm devoted their life to the preservation of folklore and the Germanic language. They published their first volume of folk tales in 1812 and the second in 1815. They were eventually translated into English in 1884, in a book titled *Household Tales* or, as it was popularly known, *Grimm's Fairy Tales*.

The Grimm Brothers were the founders of the scientific study of folklore. One of the main intentions of this study was to preserve and document the disappearing folklore, including the stories and practices. They wrote down Germanic tales that had been passed down verbally through the generations.

Along with their task of writing down and preserving folk tales, the Grimm Brothers were also interested in documenting the history of the German language. Their works were considered literary masterpieces because of their attempt to trace folklore and language back to its Indo-European roots. Their research and studies brought them to postulate two ideas that became basic to the study of folklore:

 ◆ Situations exist that are "so simple and natural that they reappear everywhere."

 ◆ Different cultures borrow folklore materials from one another.

The Effect of Fairy Tales

Because they have become mostly children's stories, fairy tales influence our social development and the archetypal images we form at an early age. As children we are quite willing to accept the idea that there is a magical quality to life. Talking animals along with elves and fairies are part of that magical quality. In this way, fairy tales set up our framework for magic.

As adults, we are taught that magic does not exist and that fairy tales are fantasy. We try hard to suspend our belief, but at the same time, the child inside us still wants to believe. Every time something extraordinary happens, our spirits elevate and we move back into that magical world of fairy tales, where everything is possible.

Through the Ages

In his book *The Uses of Enchantment: The Meaning and Importance of Fairy Tales* (1975), author and child psychologist Bruno Bettelheim wrote, "A child … who has learned from fairy stories to believe that what at first seemed a repulsive, threatening figure can magically change into a most helpful friend is ready to believe that a strange child whom he meets and fears may also be changed from a menace into a desirable companion."

Fairy tales teach us to be more understanding of other people and to allow for the possibility there are things that exist beyond our current perception of reality. What seems extraordinary today might be commonplace tomorrow. Two hundred years ago, the idea of talking with anyone in the world on a small handheld communication device was pure fantasy, and anyone who suggested such a thing was considered a lunatic. Today cell phones are very much a part of our normal reality.

The Elements of a Fairy Tale

The terms fairy tales, fairy stories, and folk tales are at times used interchangeably. In this book, fairy tales and fairy stories mean the same thing. All fairy tales are folk tales, but not all folk tales are fairy tales. This is because fairy tales have identifiable characteristics that make them a unique literary form.

Fairy tales share common elements with quest tales in that both have a hero or heroine who experiences a series of events, and as a result of these events, goes through some type of transformation. In quest tales, such as the search for the Holy Grail, the hero or heroine intentionally sets out on the quest, and through his or her actions, sets the course of events into play. The quest is what's important. In fairy tales, the importance is the human interaction with the magical world of the fairy. This interaction has a magical quality to it. Fairy tales have an accidental quality to them because the events are often not brought about by the intentions of the hero or heroine, but instead by the fairy realm, which you'll read about in the next section.

The purpose of fairy tales has been traditionally to entertain, impart moral lessons, explain the origin of magical things, and inform people about happenings in the fairy realm. These happenings can come in many forms, including contact with magical beings and creatures or a series of events that cannot be explained in logical and rational terms, and thus enter the realm of the magical.

When you enter the magical realm, you open the door to infinite possibilities. You push the envelope of conventional boundaries. You learn to expand your awareness so it includes realities other than your own. In particular, you enter the realm of the fairy, where events are enchanting and time seems eternal.

J. R. R. Tolkien's View of Fairy Stories

Tolkien had some very definite ideas as to what constituted a fairy story. He believed that fairy stories are not necessarily stories about fairies or elves, but are instead tales about the *fairy realm* (which he referred to as the "Faerie Realm" or "Perilous Realm"). As he explained, "Most good fairy-stories are about the adventures of people in the Perilous Realm or upon its shadowy marches."

Magical Meaning

According to Tolkien, the **fairy realm** is "the realm or state in which fairies have their being." Besides being home to elves and fairies, it refers to mortals experiencing the enchantment of the fairy realm. This is the basis of good fairy stories. In terms of *The Lord of the Rings*, Frodo enters the fairy realm the moment he comes into contact with the ring and leaves the Shire.

He defined a "fairy story" as being a tale that touches on or uses the fairy realm. The magic of the fairy realm comes from its operations, part of which satisfies certain primordial human desires. These desires are:

♦ To survey the depths of space and time

♦ To hold communion with other living things

Tolkien felt that magic played a great part in the fairy realm. He differentiated between the magic he was talking about and the magic of magicians by further defining the magic of the fairy realm as enchantment. His experiences with this enchantment came from encounters he had with fairies while in the trenches during World War I. He was not alone in these encounters. Many soldiers down in the trenches described similar encounters with the enchantment of fairy energy.

Creating Your Own Fairy Tale

Now that you have a basic background into fairy tales, including J. R. R. Tolkien's words of wisdom, would you like to create your own fairy tale? This section takes you through the steps to do just that!

To begin with you need to choose a main character, who in fairy-tale terms is referred to as the hero or heroine of the story. She or he can come in many forms, from beautiful young maidens and princesses to good-natured young men and charming princes. Preferably your main character should be likeable, but in no way perfect. The hero or heroine should always have room to grow and evolve as a person.

The next thing that needs to happen is, as Tolkien pointed out, the main character experiences the fairy realm in some fashion. This can happen in several ways, including …

- ◆ Encountering magical beings or creatures

- ◆ Experiencing a strange turn of events

- ◆ Entering the fairy realm itself

Wizardly Wisdom _____

Adventure, suspense, and mystery are all ways of adding excitement and depth to your fairy tale. The idea is to have your main character experience the enchantment of the fairy realm, where dreams and nightmares become real. Your character should then evolve from the experience.

Step three is the outcome, where the main character learns something or changes somehow as a result of her or his fairy experience. This change can be physical, mental, or spiritual. If physical, it is usually in the form of a healing; the mental change is a lesson learned, and the spiritual change involves a new understanding of and reverence toward the fairy realm.

Something to remember when designing step three of your fairy tale is that originally many fairy tales did not end happily. They were written for adults, and only later, when they moved into the realm of children's stories, did fairy tales become synonymous with happy endings. An example is "Red Riding Hood." In the original Charles Perrault version, the wolf eats both Grandma and Red Riding Hood, but in later versions, woodcutters save Red Riding Hood from the wolf, thus making for a happy ending.

The Eternal Nature of Fairy Tales

Fairy tales often begin with the line "once upon a time …" This is an allusion to their timeless nature. Stories in Mother Goose and Grimm's have been around for hundreds of years and are still very popular. Walt Disney made a career out of re-creating traditional fairy tales, and overall they were just as exciting as they were back in times when bards and storytellers captivated audiences with the same basic stories.

> **Fairy Tales and Legends**
>
> The fairy tale "The Well of the World's End" from *English Fairy Tales* (1889, collected by Joseph Jacobs), opens with the line "Once upon a time, and a very good time it was, though it wasn't in my time, nor in your time, nor any one else's time …" This variation on the traditional "Once upon a time" points out the timeless quality of fairy tales.

The reason fairy tales have an eternal nature is because they often address issues that are universal to the human condition. Overcoming people who mean you harm is an integral part of both fairy tales and "real" life. Learning from the experience is a sign of survival and evolvement. In the process we fulfill our need to go forth into the world and interact with other living things.

Fairy tales are as eternal as the fairy world they invoke. The fairy is said to have a timeless or eternal quality to it. Many a visitor has gone into the fairy realm for what they thought was a short time, but when they returned to the mortal world, a great deal of time had passed by. In one tale about two brothers, the first brother steps into the fairy realm to dance with the fairies. A year later, the second brother pulls the first brother back into this world, to which the first brother remarked that it seemed he had been dancing with the fairies for only a few minutes. In Rip Van Winkle's case, one night in the fairy realm turned into 20 years in the mortal world!

Because fairy tales deal with the interaction of humans with fairies, this timeless, eternal quality is inherent in the tales about this realm. This eternal quality is what takes it from the physical and mental into the spiritual. In human terms, eternal equates with the immortal and divine. When you place the experience in this context, it moves beyond the dimensions of time and space as we perceive them. Fairy experiences then take on a mystical or spiritual tone because of the way we as humans view them. Someone like Tolkien had no problem bringing the fairy experience into the spiritual realm because he was a devout Catholic and saw the fairy as sacred. When the experience moves into the sacred, this movement adds to the eternal quality of stories detailing this experience.

A Sampling of Fairy Tales

In the following sections, I give you an idea of the nature and universality of fairy tales. All of these examples involve magical beings and events that bring about a happy ending, usually in the form of marriage to their true love. I have tried to give you a flavor of the original fairy tale as well as some of the variations that came into being as the tale's popularity grew throughout the world.

"Cinderella"

Funk and Wagnalls Standard Dictionary of Folklore, Mythology and Legend calls this folk tale the best known in the world. Variations on the tale are found nearly everywhere in the world, with over 500 known versions in Europe alone. The version written down by Charles Perrault is the one we are most familiar with. This version includes the wicked stepmother and sisters, the godmother who is a fairy and changes everything into an enchanted form (the pumpkin into a coach, for example), the royal ball where Cinderella meets the prince, the hour of midnight when everything changes back into its original form, and the glass slipper that the prince uses to find Cinderella because only her foot will fit it. A notable difference in the Perrault version that was changed in later versions was at the end. In Perrault's version, the wicked stepsisters beg for Cinderella's pardon, and she forgives them for all their misdeeds to her. In later versions, the wicked stepsisters are punished.

"The Sleeping Beauty in the Woods"

This is a widespread European folk tale with the names "Little Briar Rose" and "The Sleeping Beauty," the latter being from Grimm's. The version contained in Perrault's early collection of Mother Goose fairy tales was titled *The Sleeping Beauty in the Woods*. More complex than the Grimm's version many of us are familiar with, in Perrault's version the king and queen have a daughter whose godmothers are seven fairies. At the celebration where the fairies give their gifts to the princess, an old, uninvited fairy comes in and says, "The princess will pierce her hand with a spindle and die of the wound." The fairy godmothers cannot undo this spell, but instead they amend it to a hundred-year sleep when pierced by the spindle.

The princess pierces her hand with the spindle, and then she, along with her court, sleeps for a hundred years. When she awakes she sees a prince kneeling before her. (Later versions of the tale have the prince awakening her with a kiss.) They marry, but because the prince's mother is an ogress, he leaves the princess in her palace in the woods and doesn't tell his mother. He tells her he is going hunting every day as he spends his time in the woods with the princess.

After the prince becomes king, he tells his mother of his marriage, moves the princess to his palace, and they have two children—Day and Night. The new king is then forced to go to war, and in his absence his mother, the ogress, asks the chief cook to cook up the children and the princess for her. The cook feeds the ogress animals instead, and when the king returns, the princess and children, who have been hidden, reappear, and the ogress kills herself.

"The Frog Prince"

"The Frog Prince" by the Brothers Grimm beautifully begins, "In the old time, when it was still of some use to wish for the thing one wanted …." This is the classic tale of the bewitched frog and the princess. In the Grimm version, the princess is throwing a golden ball into the air and it falls into the well. The frog agrees to retrieve it if she will love him and have him as her companion. She agrees, and when the frog shows up at her door later, her father, the king, insists she keep her promise to the frog. After eating, drinking, and having the frog up to her bed, she in frustration throws it against the wall and the frog turns into a prince because the spell is broken. With her father's consent, they become bride and groom.

The English fairy tale "The Well of the World's End" is basically the same story with a few variations. In this version collected by Joseph Jacobs, the girl has a wicked stepmother, who hands the girl a sieve and says, "Go, fill it at the Well of the World's End and bring it home to me full, or woe betide you." With the help of a frog she completes her task, but not before promising to do whatever the frog bids for one night. When the frog knocks at the door, the stepmother insists the girl honor her bargain with the frog as a punishment. After sharing her food, drink, and bed with the frog, the creature then orders her to cut off his head. She reluctantly obliges him and out comes a prince, who then makes her his princess.

> **CAUTION**
>
> **On Guard!**
>
> Be sure to keep your intentions good when dealing with fairies. Fairy tales consistently point out that humans with a good nature and intentions are often helped by fairies, whereas the greedy and ill-tempered are treated with scorn.

"The Lazy Beauty and Her Aunts"

This tale, from W. B. Yeats's *Fairy Tales of Ireland*, has similarities to the Grimms' story "Rumpel-Stilts-Kin" (or "Rumpelstiltskin," as it was later spelled), but with some beautiful differences. In "Rumpel-Stilts-Kin," a young girl is touted as having the ability to spin straw into gold. A king takes up the boast, and the young girl must prove her worth. Not capable of the task, her crying brings a little man, who spins the straw into gold, each time demanding something in return. On the third exchange, the little man demands the girl's firstborn child. When the child is born, she takes up the challenge to guess the little man's name. After two wrong tries, she is advised by one her messengers that his name was Rumpel-Stilts-Kin, and so the third try she guesses his name and the little man's plans are thwarted. The girl goes on to become the queen.

In "The Lazy Beauty and Her Aunts," a beautiful but lazy girl is touted by her mother as having the ability to in one day, turn flax into thread, the next day, turn the thread into fabric, and on the third day, turn the fabric into clothes. A passing prince hears this and takes her home to meet his mother, who then sets about testing the boast. Having no ability to complete the task, the girl accepts the help of three fairies who perform the task on three successive nights. In return, each asks to be invited to her wedding to the prince. When they arrive in turn at the wedding, they tell the queen how spinning has caused them to have big feet, be large around the middle, and to have a long, red nose. The prince, upon hearing this, decrees that the princess shall never have to work a day at the spinning wheel.

The Least You Need to Know

- Fairy tales affect our view of the world, giving us a framework for magic.

- All fairy tales have certain characteristics that make them unique.

- The three steps to creating a fairy tale are choosing a hero or heroine, having your hero or heroine encounter the fairy realm in some way, and having your hero or heroine evolve from the experience.

- Like quest tales, fairy tales involve a transformation of the main character.

- Fairy tales have to do in some way with the fairy realm.

- Fairy tales have a timeless or eternal quality to them, which is why they continue to enjoy popularity with each new generation.

Chapter 3

Folklore and Mythology

In This Chapter

- ◆ A closer look at folklore and myths
- ◆ The origin of elves and dwarves according to Norse mythology
- ◆ The ancient Celts and how they helped originate fairies
- ◆ How Shakespeare, Spenser, and other early writers helped make fairies legendary

Now that we have talked about fairy tales and how they affect our view of elves and fairies, let's take the discussion back even further to their source in folklore and mythology. The basic roots of fairy tales stem from mythology and folklore. In the case of elves, their creation is well documented in Norse mythology, and the creation of fairies along with why and how they moved into the fairy realm is told in the myths and legends of the Celts.

This chapter explores these mythological origins, and how some early literary writers, such as William Shakespeare and Edmund Spenser, added to this folklore and mythology.

What Are Folklore and Mythology?

In 1846, English antiquarian William John Thoms introduced the term *folklore* as a way of replacing the term in use at the time, *popular antiquities*. Folklore has come to mean a culture's traditions as preserved in their myths, legends, folk stories, proverbs, and other oral forms of folk art. Folklore has also come to mean the study of folk cultures through their myths, beliefs, and customs.

Magical Meaning

Folklore is the traditions, beliefs, and customs of a culture, saved within their myths, legends, folk stories, proverbs, and other oral forms of folk art. It is also the study of folk cultures. **Mythology** is basically the collective myths and legends of a particular people, displaying their perception of the power of order in the world.

Coming from the Greek word *muthos*—meaning mouth, to speak, or to tell a story—"myth" is a traditional story that usually focuses on the deeds of gods and goddesses or heroes and heroines. These stories often explain some natural phenomenon such as the origin of elves and fairies.

Myths tell us how the world works and how our lives work while at the same time showing us the hidden structure of the world. The insights contained within myths move beyond the spoken word into experiences that must be innately understood.

The Greek word *logo* is a philosophical concept that refers to "the power of order in the world, a unifying force." As the second half of the word *mythology*, this concept acknowledges that myths are part of a cosmology that gives order to the chaos while also acknowledging the connection between mythology and the divine. As such, mythology is the collective myths and legends of a particular culture, displaying its collective vision of world, particularly with respect to divine order.

Through the Ages

Author D. H. Lawrence had this insightful observation: "Myth is an attempt to narrate a whole human experience, of which the purpose is too deep, going too deep in the blood and soul, for mental explanation or description."

Anthropologist Adolph Bastian discovered that myths from all over the world seem to be built on the same "elementary ideas." As you'll recall from Chapter 1, psychologist Carl Jung called these elementary ideas archetypes, the building block of not only the unconscious mind, but also the collective unconscious. The collective unconscious is to the individual unconscious mind as mythology is to myth. Both the collective unconscious and mythology are collective databases of personal and cultural information.

In 1949, Joseph Campbell took the whole notion a step further with the publication of his book *The Hero with a Thousand Faces*. In it he proclaimed that all stories and myths are basically the same story, which he calls the "hero's journey." Campbell opened the door to the idea that all religions are really containers for the same essential truth. No matter what spiritual path you seek and take, ultimately you end up in the same overall place—the divine.

The Origin of Elves and Dwarves in Norse Mythology

The Norse were a combination of Germanic tribes who moved northward and settled in the area now known as Scandinavia—Sweden, Denmark, and Norway. In the Middle Ages, the Norse were known as Vikings, fierce warriors who invaded all their neighboring lands from Ireland, England, and France to Iceland, Finland, and Russia. Through these invasions, the customs and mythology of the Norse were spread throughout parts of Europe. In most places, Norse mythology became integrated into the mythology of the people who were there before the Norse. In the case of Iceland, the Norse were the first inhabitants. As a result, the Norse who originally settled there preserved their Nordic culture.

The Norse preserved their mythology in a series of narrative poems called *eddas*. As with Mother Goose and Grimm's, the only reason the eddas exist today is because Icelander Snorri Sturluson, in the twelfth and thirteenth centuries, collected and published them. These eddas tell the stories of the Norse gods and goddesses, along with the origin of the world and everything in it, including elves and dwarves.

Magical Meaning

Eddas are a series of narrative poems that tell the stories of Norse mythology, including all about the origin and world of elves and dwarves.

According to Norse mythology, "In the beginning, before the world was created, the only thing that existed was Ginnungapap," a primordial soup that is similar to a yeasty rime. In terms of making bread, it is the "starter," and in terms of making beer, it is the "wort." As the world began moving from the unmanifested to the manifested, a gigantic cow known as Audhumla came forth and began licking the rime until it freed the first of the rime giants, Ymir, a troll, whose name means "the roarer" signifying the primal note or vibration.

From Ymir came the giants who fought with the gods back before the time of humankind. These gargantuan, ancient, and wise magical beings were called the frost-giants, rime-thurses, or thursars, and signify the primal elemental forces in nature. The hoarfrost were the giants from Nifelheim, which was the cold land. The fire-giants were from Muspelheim, the fire land. The combination of cold and hot accelerated the growing process within the yeasty rime.

Audhumla's warm breath created a man called Bor, who then mated with Bestla, the daughter of a giant. Their union produced the great Norse god Odin along with his two brothers Vili and Ve. Together the three brothers slew the giant Ymir, put his body in the hub of Ginnungapap, and used the various parts to create the cosmos. Ymir's blood made the seas and lakes, his flesh the earth, his hair the trees, his bones the mountains, and his teeth and jaw the pebbles and rocks. Also created was Midgard (Middle Earth), and the eight worlds that surround it, including the worlds of the elves and dwarves.

The Norse eddas describe that when creatures came to feed on Ymir's brain, they, like everything else, were transformed into a part of creation. In this case, they transformed into elves and dwarves, who inhabit the worlds of Alfheim (elf home) and Svartalfheim (dark-elf home). The elves and dwarves were given a place somewhere between the worlds of the gods and goddesses and the human world.

From the hub of Ginnungapap, or the center of creation, sprang the world tree, Yggdrasil, whose branches held the nine worlds. In the middle is Midgard, home of humans. From there the World Tree looks like this:

Upper worlds:

♦ Asgard—Home of the Norse gods

♦ Alfheim—Home of the elves

Middle worlds:

♦ Midgard—Middle Earth, the human world

♦ Nifelheim—Home of the frost giants or hoarfrost

♦ Jotunheim—Home of the giants who came into creation with Ymir

♦ Muspelheim—Home of the fire-giants

♦ Vanaheim—Home of the Vanir, the nature gods and goddesses

Lower worlds:

◆ Svartalfheim—Home of the dwarves

◆ Hel—Home of all who died from natural causes, ruled by the goddess Hela

Bulfinch's Mythology gives this description of elves: "The Edda mentions another class of beings, inferior to the gods, but still possessed of great power; these were called elves. The white spirits, or Elves of Light, were exceedingly fair, more brilliant than the sun, and clad in garments of a delicate and transparent texture." They loved light and were favorites of the Norse sun god Freyr, who ruled over Alfheim. Overall, they were said to be friendly to humans, and in the early days of the world, had many an adventure with them.

Dwarves were referred to as dark elves or night elves because they lived underground and avoided the sun because its light would turn them into a stone. Called the "Dvergar" in Norse mythology, dwarves were known to have extensive knowledge in the mysterious powers of nature. The dwarves' home, Swartalfheim, is a realm of sensation, where the dark elves transmute base minerals into higher forms. Dwarves have dark skin, long beards, green eyes, and a short, stocky build. They also have caps and cloaks that made them invisible.

The Origin of Fairies in Celtic Mythology

The Celts were a group of Germanic tribes that gradually migrated west and up north through Scandinavia. They eventually settled in present-day Ireland, Scotland, Wales, England, and the western coast of France. Like the Norse, the Celts spoke several different languages and were known to be fierce warriors.

Because the Celts were driven into hiding by the Romans and later by the Christians, much of their mythology was never written down except in a few texts, such as *The Mabinogi*. Otherwise, Celtic mythology was an oral tradition that was passed down for generations in folk tales and myths. Academic authors, such as Thomas Bulfinch and Charles Squire, have collected and documented these myths.

Wizardly Wisdom

Recent surveys report that over one third of the people in the United States have Celtic ancestry. This high percentage is a result of the Celtic migration throughout the Western world. Everywhere the Celts went, they spread their ideas and influence—an influence that is still evident today.

Irish mythology, a central branch of Celtic mythology, combines history and folklore. Irish mythology talks about five invasions of Ireland. The last invasion is when the Milesians, also known as the sons of Mil, invaded Ireland and defeated the Tuatha De Danann, setting up the creation of the fairy.

Some researchers argue that the origin of fairies reaches back to the remotest antiquity. Some say they are the surviving members of an ancient race of beings that inhabited the British Isles during the Neolithic period (6000–1800 B.C.E.). The fairy came into popularity at the time when humans moved from being nomadic hunters into agrarian farmers and herders. When this happened people began staying in one place, and over generations they became spiritually linked to it. In the same way, the strength of the fairy stems from the land, a land made sacred through the generations of ancestors buried in it.

Although difficult to pinpoint, the origin of the fairy is credited by many writers to be the ancestors of the people of Ireland. These ancestors are known as the *sidhe* (pronounced "shee"), the Irish word for fairy. The first use of the term *sidhe* was as a means of identifying the Tuatha De Danann after their defeat by the Milesians, who were the first Gaels.

Fairy Tales and Legends

Legend has it that the Milesians first came to Ireland in a fog on May Day, one of the great days of celebration for the fairies.

When the Milesians, or sons of Mil, arrived in Ireland, they found the area inhabited by the Tuatha De Danann, whose name means "the people of the Goddess Dana." In the ensuing battle, the Milesians defeated the Tuatha De Danann, whose people became part of the land, where it is said they remain to this day in the hollow hills or *sidhe* mounds. These first occupants of the fairy underworld became the *Daoine Sidhe*, the very cream of the heroic fairies.

As the Tuatha De Danann divided the hills and mounds of Ireland into kingdoms among themselves, they simultaneously wove a permanent veil of invisibility for themselves, thus dividing Ireland into two kingdoms: the seen and the unseen. In terms of modern physics, they created a new morphogenic field of resonance or vibration just beyond the spectrum of normal human perception. In simpler terms, they became energy forms that could shift their shape at will, and as such, control whether humans could see them or not. They were normally invisible but could become visible if they so desired.

Fairies are the sacred spirit or presence that animates and enlivens all of nature. Regarded as earth spirits, the sidhe-dwellers are the land fairies and are called the *dei terreni*, meaning deities of the earth. The water fairies, called merrows, are thought to bring bad weather; they come out of the sea in the shape of hornless cows or humans with fish tails.

Often the fairies are also thought to be the ancient ancestors made up of distinct tribes. Each tribe's fairies have personal names that are not necessarily the Tuatha names, and they rule over specific areas. Each area or territory has a fairy queen and king; for instance, Ailill is king and Medb is queen of the fairies of Connaught. In this way, the basic social order of the sidhe reflects the old aristocracy of ancient Ireland.

Belief in fairies with extraordinary powers beyond those of mortals once played a huge part in the lives of people living in rural Ireland, Scotland, and Wales. People considered the fairies to be the spirits of the old agricultural goddesses and gods of the earth. These fairies or sidhe of the subterranean mounds were thought to control the ripening of the crops and the milk yields. Because of this belief, offerings were given to the fairies regularly to ensure their help rather than hindrance.

Although often associated with places in our world, such as forests, creeks, and even people's houses, all fairies ultimately reside in the fairy realm. This is a magical place that humans occasionally visit—sometimes by accident and sometimes by design. Both fairies and the fairy realm have provided inspiration for countless myths, fairy tales, and the stories from early literature.

Elves and Fairies in Early Literature

Early writers—such as Geoffrey of Monmouth, author of the Arthurian tales, and William Shakespeare—moved mythology and fairy tales to the mythical and legendary level. These writers eloquently preserved these tales not only for their own generation, but for succeeding generations as well.

Human events, particularly with regard to heroic actions, have a tendency to move through a progression:

- History

- Folk tales, fairy tales, and myths

- Mythical legend

Events generally began as history: People experienced the event firsthand or were told about it by someone who experienced it firsthand. After several generations, when everyone associated with the events has passed away, the event begins to be incorporated in folk tales, fairy tales, and myths. The people associated with the event also begin to take on extraordinary characteristics. Eventually, when writers commit the story to paper, complete with all the literary prose afforded them, the stories begin to move into the area of mythical legend, and the people associated with them begin taking on a divine quality.

Fairies in Shakespeare

William Shakespeare (1564–1616) is probably the best-known author who brought history and folklore into the realm of mythical legend. His play *Hamlet* is a historical Danish folk tale that he elevated to legendary proportions. Another of his plays, *Taming of the Shrew*, is based on the fairy tale "The Haughty Princess," in which the princess is humbled by her husband into not complaining about everything so much.

If, when you think of fairies, you see an image in your mind of fairies dancing on the fairy rings and residing in the flowers and woods, then you are thinking of Shakespeare's addition to the mythical image of fairies. Fairies play important roles in several of his plays, including *A Midsummer Night's Dream*, *The Tempest*, and *The Merry Wives of Windsor*. In particular, *A Midsummer Night's Dream* contains one of the most creative representations of the fairy realm.

The folklore of a small valley in Wales is said to be Shakespeare's inspiration for much of the fairy material in *A Midsummer Night's Dream*. The fairy aspect of the play revolves around a boy named Puck who is raised by his mother. She never once mentions his fairy origins, much like Harry Potter's aunt and uncle never tell him about his magical origins. When he is six years old, Puck runs away from home. Alone in the woods, he falls asleep and has a dream of the fairies. When he awakes, Puck finds a scroll from the king of the fairies, Oberon, conferring on Puck the magical powers to grant wishes and shape shift. Oberon places a condition on the powers in that they are to only be used to help the good and thwart the bad. If Puck succeeds in following this condition, he will be allowed into the fairy realm. In the story, Puck displays the characteristics of a true hobgoblin, and plays out a variety pranks, often meant to be a lesson for the mortals he encounters.

> **Through the Ages**
>
> In *The Tempest*, Shakespeare uses the term "played the Jack with us." This expression refers to a Jack o' Lantern or Will o' the Wisp, which like Puck were considered mischievous.

While at times preserving English folklore regarding fairies, Shakespeare at other times takes literary license in elevating the fairies to legendary status. In *Romeo and Juliet*, he addresses the queen of fairies under her traditional name, Queen Mab, but in *A Midsummer Night's Dream*, he calls her Titania, a name of his own invention. Through time, most people familiar with Shakespeare are more likely to remember the queen of the fairies as being Titania.

As for Oberon, he has origins in the German elf king Alberich. Shakespeare learned of the reference through the romantic French story, *Huon of Bordeaux*. Once again, Shakespeare was a master at weaving myth and story into legend.

Other Early Literary References

Besides Shakespeare, two other early authors helped give elves, fairies, and other magical creatures their legendary status in our culture: Edmund Spenser and Geoffrey of Monmouth. Although there are other authors of stories on the fairy realm during the Elizabethan period in England, they are not nearly up to the caliber of Shakespeare and Edmund Spenser.

Edmund Spenser (1552–1599) first wrote and published his classic narrative poem *The Faerie Queene* in the late 1500s. The original story was in six separate books that were dedicated to Elizabeth I. *The Faerie Queene* tells the story of a knight's journey into the fairy realm in search of the queen of the fairies, known for her remarkable beauty. *The Faerie Queene* contains references to dwarves, elven knights, and "legions of sprights," a type of fairy that can at times be bothersome. Edmund Spenser goes to great literary lengths to boost all of these magical creatures to legendary status.

Geoffrey of Monmouth (1100–1154) is credited with elevating King Arthur from an historical English king to the mythical figure that he is today. He also moved Merlin the wizard into legendary status as the archetype of a classical magical wizard, complete with wands, and shape shifting and astral-traveling abilities. Geoffrey also wrote down old English legends and fairy tales, such as *Jack the Giant Killer*. He wrote his literary tales in the twelfth century. After almost 900 years, the legend and magic of Camelot continues to grow larger with each generation, as evidenced by the 2004 summer release of the movie *King Arthur*.

Other authors who later helped elevate the legendary status of elves, fairies, and other magical creatures include the following …

- **Hans Christian Andersen** (1805–1875) wrote a series of fairy tales, including the classic "The Little Sea-Maid," which in the hands of Disney became the popular movie *The Little Mermaid*.

- ◆ **Sir James Matthew Barrie** (1860–1937) wrote the *Peter Pan* that features the fairy Tinkerbell. Like *The Wizard of Oz*, this story has become a timeless fairy story in a short period of time.

- ◆ **L. Frank Baum** (1856–1919) is author of such stories as *The Wizard of Oz* and *The Sea Fairies*. Within less than one hundred years, *The Wizard of Oz* has become a classic, largely due to the movie starring young Judy Garland.

- ◆ **Hermann Hesse** (1877–1962) is author of such classics as *Siddhartha* and *Steppenwolf*. He was also given to writing German fairy tales that are still read today.

- ◆ **Oscar Wilde** (1854–1900) grew up with parents who were both renowned collectors of traditional fairy tales. It's not surprising that their son sat down and wrote a series of his own fairy tales.

The Least You Need to Know

- ◆ The beliefs of a culture are reflected in its folklore and mythology.

- ◆ Norse mythology explains the origin of the cosmic order, including elves and dwarves.

- ◆ Celtic mythology illustrates how fairy energy was created.

- ◆ Through time, human events move from the historical to the legendary; authors such as Shakespeare and Spenser have helped elves, fairies, and other magical creatures achieve legendary status.

Chapter 4

Spiritual History

In This Chapter

- ◆ A spiritual view of mythology and folklore
- ◆ Traditional perceptions of elves and dwarves
- ◆ The mystery of the runes
- ◆ Celtic and early European perceptions of fairies

Because the fairy realm is somewhere between this world and the divine, it follows that when you experience it, you move that much closer to the divine. In terms of mortal reality, both experiences have a similar quality to them. The experiences are extraordinary because they take you beyond your physical bounds into worlds that are both abstract and eternal. Normal human senses of seeing, hearing, tasting, touching, and smelling give way to a mystical sense of connection to the whole of creation with every part of your being. When this happens you begin moving beyond the physical to a place where the mythical joins with the spiritual.

This chapter takes you deeper into the magical world of elves and fairies and shows you how to unlock the mysteries of your own being, as well as exploring how you fit in and connect spiritually with your world.

The Spiritual Side of Mythology

Myths speak in terms of symbols, which communicate to the part of our consciousness that extends beyond the physical world into the mythical and spiritual. In this case, a symbol moves past its literal meaning to a place that is one with the consciousness of the beholder. The communication is innate, and on the spiritual level transcends logical knowledge and thought. Symbols could include the individual (main character), the quest, and divine help or guidance. In a personal sense, we each have a different concept as to who we are (the individual), what we are doing (the quest), and how we perceive the divine. But at the same time, in a universal sense we all know symbolically what the individual is, what the quest is, and how the divine influences our life. Essentially, symbols are akin to archetypes.

Through the Ages

In an interview, Joseph Campbell said, "By getting to know your own impulse system and its images and the things you really are living for, and then to get support for universalizing and grounding this personal mythology, you can find support in the other mythologies of humankind."

Through symbols, myths convey teachings or truths about the universal problems that we all face in life. Rather than something that can be conceptualized, these truths are understood within terms of the human condition from which they come. What we understand through these universal truths is our own role in the universe, including how we spiritually connect to the whole of creation.

Mythologist and author Joseph Campbell's work showed the universal quality of myths. Akin to Carl Jung's "collective unconsciousness" and Edgar Cayce's Akashic records (an energetic database containing the history of every soul), Campbell's universal quality of myths traverses a higher level, where all spiritualities converge together in their attempt to explain the basic spiritual questions confronting us all in this lifetime, including questions about other lifetimes. As with the collective unconsciousness and Akashic records, this dominion where spiritualities converge as one is somewhere we can tap into to gain personal insights into our own spirituality.

The elves and fairies are a way of moving into this universal spirituality. They open up the mystery of your own being. Magic is all about believing in yourself and achieving your full potential.

Traditional Norse Elves and Dwarves

In the twelfth-century Icelandic poem *Alvismal*, also called *The Lay of Alviss*, the dwarf Alviss explains what motivates various creatures: mortals have literal names for everything; the gods are interested in how things function; the giants are interested in how they can use things; and dwarves and elves view things in poetic, multidimensional terms. This provides the perfect introduction to the traditional Norse perception of elves and dwarves.

As discussed in Chapter 3, in Norse mythology the world of elves and dwarves is distinct from our own world, but within the world tree, called Yggdrasil by the Norse, there are connecting points between the worlds, where mortals, elves, and dwarves can interact. The world of elves and dwarves is akin to the magical realm of the *wyrrd*, a force in Norse spiritual traditions that basically means the magical interconnectedness and synchronicity of all things.

Magical Meaning

In Norse spiritual traditions, **wyrrd** refers to a magical energy where everything is interconnected. Rune masters use this energy when they use the runes to look into the future.

The Norse had an old saying that translated as "beautiful as an elven woman." This saying later became the Middle English expression that translated as "She was so fair as if an elf-maid from another world." What they alluded to was two things:

- Elves were perceived as having beautiful, fine features.

- The elves of Norse mythology were often female.

Norse tales tell of the lvor, stunningly beautiful girls who lived in the forest with an elven king. Said to be long-lived and lighthearted, they were often seen at night dancing over meadows. In the morning, people would find circles, called lvdanser (elf dances) or lvringar (elf circles). Humans who watched their dance would discover that even though only a few hours

On Guard!

Always remember that time in the elven world is much different and often slower than in the mortal world. As with the speed of light, time is often relative to where you are. When you are in the magical realms, time has a tendency to slow down, and when you return to the ordinary world, more time has elapsed than you realized.

seemed to have passed, in fact many years had passed in the mortal world, much like with the fairy tales about humans who visit the fairy realm. This was also the case with the fellowship in Tolkien's *The Lord of the Rings*. When the main characters visit the elven land of Lothlorien, time moves relatively much slower.

In the traditional Norse view, elves have the following qualities:

- They are as tall as humans.

- They are beautiful and fine-featured.

- They are strong, fierce warriors.

- They excel in the arts, especially music, possess the gift of foresight, and can bestow this gift upon mortals.

- They live in a world removed from mortals.

- They have their own language.

- They sometimes mate with mortals.

In addition, elves were originally a race of lesser gods that were associated with the forces of nature and fertility. Norse tradition decrees that famous humans can be elevated to elf status after death. It was common for nobles to claim elven ancestry. Again it is one step removed from the divine.

The Norse name for magic is *Seiour*. It is synonymous with the word *alfatofrar*, meaning elf magic, referring to any enchanting effect. This shows how the Norse viewed elves as an essential power within the realm of magic.

Elves and Dwarves, Sun and Earth

As described in *The Lord of the Rings*, elves and dwarves are in many ways polar opposites of one another. Even so, there is a kinship between the two because they originated from the same source. Outwardly they appear quite different, but inwardly, in a magical sense, elves and dwarves share many similarities.

Dwarves live in the lower world of Svartalfheim. Included in their basic characteristics are …

- Dark skin, long beards, and green eyes.

- A short, stocky build.

- Excellence as craftspersons, specializing in metallurgy, masonry, and mining.

- Caps and cloaks that make them invisible.

- Turning to stone in the sunlight.

Fairy Tales and Legends

In Norse mythology, head dwarf Alviss seeks the hand of the Norse god Thor's daughter. Thor makes Alviss answer a series of questions including saying the names of the world, sky, moon, sun, clouds, wind, calm, fire, sea trees, night, wheat, and beer in all the worlds of creation. Being very wise, Alviss knew the answers to all the questions, but answering them took so long that as he was finishing, the sun came in the room and nearly turned him to stone.

Elves and dwarves are symbolic of the divine relationship between the sun and the earth. The elves represent the sun and everything associated with it, including light, the creative fire of life, and the upper world. The dwarves represent the earth and everything associated with it, including the darkness of the underworld, minerals, stones, and the lower world. The elves are airy, sensual, free-flowing spirits; the dwarves are much more grounded and practical.

Divine Elves and Dwarves

In Norse mythology, the term Alfar (light elves) is synonymous with Vanir, the name of the earliest gods and goddesses. The Goddess Freyja and her brother Frey, "the lady" and "the lord," are the main goddess and god of the Vanir along with their mother Nerthus, goddess of the earth, and father Njord, god of the wind and sea. The Vanir were once fertility gods and goddesses, but over time they became known as nature deities, controlling the natural energies of weather, crops, and commerce. The gods and goddesses of the Vanir lived in the world of Vanaheim, located west of Middle Earth.

The idea that the Vanir eventually became the gods and goddesses who embody the forces of nature is what makes them synonymous with the Alfar or light elves. Elves are also closely associated with the various aspects of nature. Another thing that tightens the synonymous relationship between the Vanir and light elves is that the Norse sun god, Frey, is also the ruler of the elven world of Alfheim.

Besides being the sun god, Frey also controls the natural forces of fertility, male sexuality, prosperity, marriage, and sacred kingship. Considered the god of growth and the fruitful rain, in Sweden Frey is called "Veraldar Gudh," which means "God of the World."

Wizardly Wisdom

Norse mythology can be confusing at times because the myths seem to contradict one another. For example, Frey and Freyja are originally part of the Vanir, but in the myths they become part of the Aesir, the main body of Norse gods and goddesses that includes Odin and Thor. On a related note, in Scandinavia, Frey is associated with law and justice. Legal oaths are sworn with the words, "So help me, Frey, Njord, and the almighty god (Thor)."

Along with the light elves, the dark elves or dwarves also have a close association with the gods and goddesses of the Vanir, namely Frey and Freyja. Being master craftspersons, the dwarves are credited with making Thor's hammer "Miolnir" and the magical ship "Skidbladnir," a present to Frey. Skidbladnir was so large that it could hold all the Norse deities along with their personal possessions. So skillfully was it made that the ship could be folded together and inserted into a pocket.

Along with Frey, the dwarves were known to have an intimate relationship with the goddess Freyja. In one tale, Freyja finds the stone threshold of the subterranean world of the dwarves open. She enters and finds the dwarves of the four directions called Alfrig, Dvalin, Berlingr, and Grer, forging the magnificent gold and amber necklace called the Brisingamen. Freyja tries every means to get the dwarves to part with their treasure, but with no success. Only after agreeing to spend a night with each of the dwarves is she then given the necklace. This story is symbolic of Freyja's shamanic journey. In this journey she joins with the four directions and their elemental correspondences, and by doing so, perpetuates the seasonal cycles of nature.

The goddess Freyja rules over plant life, the trees and animals of the forest, natural love, female sexuality, and magic. As the goddess of love between men and women, she is often called upon for help in matters of the heart. She is described as traveling through the nine worlds of the Yggdrasil wearing a cloak of falcon feathers in a chariot pulled by mighty cats or bears. Freyja also teaches Odin all about shamanism and love magic, making him the first male with access to this traditionally feminine wisdom.

The Magic of Runes

Besides being the first male to learn love magic, the Norse god Odin is also the first to learn the mysteries of the *runes*. He does this by metaphorically hanging himself from the branches of Yggdrasil, between the nine worlds of creation. Again, it is representative of a shamanic journey, in particular, the rite of initiation. This is where the "old self" symbolically dies and is replaced by the new initiated self. It is much like being spiritually reborn. This image ties in with the Hanged Man card in Tarot, a card that generally signifies change and transformation.

After Odin learns the runes, he teaches them to the gods and goddesses, elves, and mortals. Dain was the elf who was taught the runes, Dvalin was the dwarf, and Asvid was the giant. As mentioned earlier, Dvalin was one of the dwarves of the four directions. Dain, the first elf to learn the runes, could shape shift into a mystical stag, who was one of the four winds who roam the world tree, Yggdrasil.

Like the rings of power in *The Lord of the Rings*, the knowledge of the runes was sent out among the various groups—gods and goddesses, elves, and humans. The runes represent an integral part of the Norse spiritual tradition because they are a magical form of writing that offers the seeker a doorway into the magical realm of the wyrrd—a place where the past, present, and future merge together as one.

Because of this timeless and magical quality, runes are often used to foretell the future. Each rune stands for or symbolizes a cosmic force in nature. An example is the "F" rune, Fehu, which symbolizes the primal forces of prosperity. As with Tarot, runes can be used in layouts that can answer questions you have about your past, present, and future.

Magical Meaning

Runes are an ancient form of writing and divination. Each rune stands for both a letter in the alphabet and a primal force in the universe. Runes were originally carved on wood and used straight lines that went across the grain of the wood. Their primal or magical aspects are what give them their ability to predict future events. "Elder Futhark" is the name given to the original runes. "Futhark" is the name of the first six runes.

Through the Ages

In *The Runes of Elfland*, authors Brian Froud and Ari Berk write, "If we truly wish to understand the transformational power of the runes, we must travel the paths of tradition into Elfland, the stronghold of myth, magic, and imagination. The key to that land resides—as it always has—in the act of storytelling."

Each of the 24 runes in the Elder Futhark provides a doorway into the otherworld of elves, dwarves, and fairies. Runes preserve in symbol the mythology and teachings of a spiritual path that dates back several thousand years. And like the realm of elves and fairies, the symbols of the runes are eternal.

Each rune is a magical symbol that represents cosmic energies at work in the universe as well as a letter in the alphabet. In addition, each rune is embedded in Norse mythology, and is representative of the stories of the gods and goddesses, and how they relate to the creation of everything—both in this world and the fairy realm.

Traditional Celtic Fairies

When the Tuatha De Danann moved into the hills of Ireland, they wove a veil of invisibility around themselves. This divided this world into two realms—the seen and the unseen. These hills or mounds represent the fairy realm, a dimension of awareness that exists in a different tense that is one step beyond our "ordinary" perception. In these hollow hills or subterranean sidhe mounds, the fairies still dwell, occasionally interacting with mortals.

Within the fairy lore of Scotland and Ireland are the remnants of the old Celtic religion, with gods and goddesses acting as the guardian ancestors of the clans. Every clan claims descent from a particular goddess or god, who appear in local tales, and through time are transformed into fairy kings and queens. They reside in the fairy realm while at the same time acting as guardians of forests, lakes, rivers, villages, and cities.

As the people of the Tuatha De Danann moved into the hills and other natural settings, they became nature spirits. Much like the elves and dwarves of the Norse tradition, they became associated with energies and places in nature. Through time, most of the members of Tuatha De Danann took on divine status, thus becoming the Celtic gods and goddesses.

Fairy Queens

The fairy realm is populated in great numbers and ruled over by a queen and king, with the queen generally being the primary leader. Called *bean righean na brugh*, which means *fairy queen of the palace*, these queens are the goddesses of local tribes. To this day, many of these fairy queens are said to be still guarding the Irish clans.

Medb begins as a heroine of Irish myths, and through time becomes transformed into queen of the fairies. The legendary queen of Connacht is said to have lived with nine kings. This symbolizes her role as the source of creation. Queen Medb and King Ailill had a daughter named Findabair, who is akin to the Arthurian Queen Gwenivere.

The hill of Aine, near the parish of Knockainey, is thought to be one of the strongholds of the popular fairy queen of Munster who is honored throughout Ireland. Daughter of the druid Owel, Aine was a mortal woman who was taken by the fairies. Every year on Midsummer's Eve, people go in a procession around the hill of Aine, and then carry flaming torches through the crop fields to insure abundant harvest. Some say Aine herself was seen on many occasions leading the procession. She is still associated with the fertility observances on Cnoc Aine on Midsummer's Eve.

Cliodna of the Fair Hair is one of the three great fairy queens of Munster and a master shape shifter. She was once an Irish princess, then a Munster Goddess, and now a fairy queen. She is known to take mortal lovers, and is reputed to be a sensuous and powerful seducer of young-spirited men, especially at fairs on May Day. Cliodna's name means "shapely one," and she becomes the most beautiful of all women when she takes human form. Eldest daughter of Gebann, Chief Druid to Manannan, Cliodna is loved and cherished by the people of County Cork, where a number of places are associated with her. She is the guardian goddess of the O'Keefes and also believed to be the special banshee of families in the south of Munster.

Grainne of the Bright Cheeks is the popular fairy queen in the northeast of Leinster and has her home on Cnoc Greine. In the Finn cycle of Irish heroic story and romance, she is the strong-willed daughter of Cormac mac Art, who fell in love with Diarmuid after being promised by her father to the hero Finn MacCool. On Diarmuid's forehead was a magical love spot, and when Grainne saw it, she fell helplessly in love with him. In the Irish sagas, Grainne persuaded Diarmaid to run away and elope with her. Across Ireland, where the lovers traveled and slept in rocky alcoves, there are cairns and cromlechs still known as the beds of Diarmuid and Grainne.

Folk Beliefs About Elves and Fairies

The Welsh name for fairies is *y Tylwyth Teg*, which means "the fair folk or family." The longer version, *y Tylwyth Teg yn y Coed*, translates as "the fair family in the wood." Both of these names describe a family that is both light-filled and drawn to nature in a spiritual way. The association with nature is ever-present with all elves and fairies. Although they don't reside in the mortal world, they have very close ties with the natural aspects of our world.

Within the Welsh tradition, there are five different types of elves and fairies:

- The Ellyllon or elves
- The Coblynau or mine fairies
- The Bwbachod or household fairies
- The Gwragedd Annwn or fairies of the lakes and streams
- The Gwyllion or mountain fairies

By contrast, the Scandinavian tradition lists four different types of magical beings and creatures:

- The elves
- The dwarves or trolls
- The nissies
- The necks, mermen, and mermaids

Two examples of folk beliefs and practices are the idea of giving a gift to beings of the fairy realm, and the idea of not building on fairy trods (fairy pathways). Sacrificing a gift to the fairies is a concept that goes back to Norse times, when people put out gifts of milk and beer for the elves. Akin to the myth of Santa Claus, in which the children put out gifts of cookies and milk, the idea of a gift given and a gift received is one of those primary energies of the cosmos. Within the runes, Gebo, the "X" rune, embodies this concept of the exchanging of gifts.

Fairy Tales and Legends

The fairies chose the location of the church at Knowle (in Warwickshire, England). Work was originally begun on the hill above St. Anne's Well. The problem was that the fairies did not want it there, and so each night they removed the stones and placed them at another site. After this kept happening night after night, the workers finally relented, and built the house on the site the fairies preferred.

The Least You Need to Know

- ◆ Symbols take mythology to a higher, more spiritual, level.
- ◆ Traditionally, elves and dwarves were linked with nature deities.
- ◆ Runes are gateways into the fairy realm.
- ◆ Different regions of Ireland have their own fairy queens.
- ◆ Folk beliefs about elves and fairies have grown from their traditional roots.

Part 2

Modern Elves and Fairies

Although elves and fairies have their origins in ancient mythology and fairy tales, they continue to be an integral part of our modern world. Every Christmas, images of Santa and his elves grace store windows, books, and movie screens across the land. During the rest of the year, books and movies such as *The Lord of the Rings* and *Harry Potter* add to our modern perceptions of elves and fairies. These perceptions are in one way handed down in the traditional fairy tales that we grow up knowing, and in another way in the modern fairy tales that are constantly changing our view of these magical beings.

This part deals with the role of elves and fairies in modern culture. This modern role is examined in terms of modern fairy tales, metaphysical references, fairy traditions, and fairy magic. So let's begin our magical adventure into the modern world of elves and fairies.

Chapter 5

Modern Fairy Tales

In This Chapter

- ◆ How modern mythology influences our lives
- ◆ The impact of J. R. R. Tolkien's *The Lord of the Rings*
- ◆ How J. K. Rowling's *Harry Potter* books have made magic popular again
- ◆ A selection of modern movies and books that feature elves, fairies, and other magical creatures

When growing up, traditional fairy tales help form the basis for who we are and how we view the world, particularly in terms of our beliefs. Upon reaching adulthood, modern fairy tales continue to influence our beliefs and perceptions.

In particular, modern fairy tales that reveal the existence of elves, fairies, and other magical creatures challenge us to push the proverbial envelope as to what's possible. Suddenly the idea of fulfilling our potential doesn't seem out of bounds, but instead is completely within our grasp. What it does is open up a whole other world that is waiting to be explored. In this chapter, we'll take a closer look at some of the modern fairy tales that continue to capture our imagination and shape our world.

Creating Modern Mythology

One of the defining moments in J. R. R. Tolkien's *The Lord of the Rings* comes when Frodo tries to give Galadriel, the elven queen of Lothlorien, the ring of power. For a moment, she must decide whether to take the ring and the dark power it brings, or to help Frodo in his quest to destroy the ring. She shape shifts into an all-powerful, albeit horrible, dark queen, showing Frodo and herself what would happen if she accepted the ring. Afterward the elven queen helps Frodo by letting him see into the future and on what path his journey would lead him. It is at this point he discovers he can trust no one, and that the task and burden of ring bearer is his alone to carry.

Through the Ages

During an interview, "In the footsteps of the Hobbits," with Keith Brace, J. R. R. Tolkien said, "Myth can convey the sort of profound truth that was intransigent to description or analysis in terms of facts and figures, and is therefore a more powerful weapon for cultural renewal than is modern rationalist science and technology."

This sequence in the story between the elven queen Galadriel ("lady of light") and Frodo is important because it brings to mind many archetypes that exist on several different levels. The primary level deals with the battle between light and dark, and how on a personal level we all have to make a choice in life as to which path to follow. On another level, it shows how power has the potential to corrupt all who embrace it. This is why Frodo must abandon the fellowship, because ultimately he can trust no one with the power of the ring but himself.

As with all mythology, modern mythology concerns itself with illuminating certain universal rites of passage, or as J. R. R. Tolkien called them, "transcendental truths." These truths are what every creative artist taps into, either consciously or unconsciously, when he or she creates a work of art that communicates to people on a level that transcends into the spiritual. Great paintings, poetry, and stories send shivers of delight that vibrate an inner chord and communicate something beyond mere images and words. Some great works such as *The Lord of the Rings* and *Harry Potter* seem to take on a mythical quality from the moment they are published. These are the works of true magic!

One of the defining moments in J. K. Rowling's *Harry Potter and the Sorcerer's Stone* comes when Harry is under the sorting hat, waiting to find out which of the four houses will be his home at Hogwarts. The hat tries to persuade him to choose the dark house of Slytherin, by telling Harry that he would do very well there. But Harry resists the temptation, and the hat chooses Gryffindor as Harry's house. As was the case with Frodo and Galadriel in *Lord of the Rings*, Harry's choice of the light pits him against the forces of darkness that seek to destroy him.

This is the beauty of myths—their ability to deal with situations in life that essentially happen to everyone. Early on in life, we are all forced to choose between the light or dark path. The first time someone dares you to do something you know is wrong, such as stealing, you are forced to choose between the light and dark, just like Frodo and Harry. These situations are ageless, which is why they keep popping up in both life and mythology.

Each generation creates its own modern fairy tales and updates the mythological cycle. Our world is much different than it was two thousand years ago in that we have electric lights, cars, computers, airplanes, and countless other technological devices. But although the world around us has dramatically changed, the basic psychological and spiritual issues that face us as human beings have remained the same. We still must choose between light and dark and seek to understand the many questions surrounding birth, life, and death.

As our world becomes more high-tech and the stress of day-to-day life increases, we have an increasing need to find ways of escaping these modern pressures. Fantasies like *The Lord of the Rings* and *Harry Potter* offer a perfect vehicle for this escape because they give us a place to go where our minds don't have toworry about everything for a while. This is another reason why they are so popular.

The Lord of the Rings

Originally published in the mid-1950s, J. R. R. Tolkien's *The Lord of the Rings* has already experienced several popular revivals, to the point where many people already consider it a classic. It has inspired more creativity and commentary, and gained more of a following, than any other modern-day work of literature. The idea that it was designed as a classic fairy tale, complete with elves, dwarves, wizards, and a hero who must complete a given task in order to stop darkness and restore the light, shows the immense impact that fairy tales still have on modern popular culture.

The Lord of the Rings trilogy actually begins with *The Hobbit*, a book that centers on the adventures of Frodo's uncle, Bilbo Baggins. *The Hobbit* sets up the events in *The Lord of the Rings* by introducing readers to the world of Middle Earth as well as the characters of Gandalf the Wizard, Gollum, and the hobbit, Bilbo, who finds the ring of power. This is the same ring that becomes the essential element of *The Lord of the Rings*.

On Guard!

Don't listen to the critics! Literary critics originally panned Tolkien's *The Lord of the Rings* as being "too long, too mythical, and too boring." Fortunately the critics were wrong; over the last fifty years the books and movies have had phenomenal sales. Peter Jackson's 2003 movie release of *The Return of the King* is second on the list of all-time most popular movies worldwide in terms of box office receipts.

In classic fairy-tale style, Tolkien divides *The Lord of the Rings* into three parts. The first part, *The Fellowship of the Ring*, introduces the main characters and sets up Frodo's quest to destroy the ring. The fellowship was made up of four hobbits, an elf, a dwarf, and two humans. One of the humans is the mysterious and extraordinary Aragorn. Other events that take place in the first part include:

1. Gandalf battles his teacher Saruman the White, who has allied with the dark lord Sauron.

2. Frodo and his comrades (the fellowship) set out to destroy the ring in the fires of Mordor.

3. The members of the fellowship become divided—Frodo and Sam go it alone to Mordor and the others go to fight the battle for Middle Earth.

The second part of the trilogy, *The Two Towers*, is about how the two dark forces of Saruman's Isengard and Sauron's Mordor combine in their efforts to enslave Middle Earth. In particular, Saruman amasses a huge army of monstrous creatures, such as Orcs and Uruk-hai, in order to capture the human kingdom of Rohan. All the while, Frodo, Sam, and their new companion, Gollum, continue their journey to the dark land of Mordor. The sequence of events for part two is as follows:

1. Gandalf is victorious in his battle with the Balrog, and as a consequence becomes Gandalf the White, whose power now equals that of his former teacher, Saruman.

2. Gandalf frees the king of Rohan from Saruman's spell, and a huge battle ensues as the forces of Isengard attack Rohan.

3. Rohan is saved and Isengard falls with the help of the Ents, who are ancient trees that talk and move.

An Ent is half tree, half human.

Part three, *The Return of the King*, is, as its name implies, about Aragorn taking his own power and becoming king of Gondor. Of course before this can happen, he must depose the current caretaker king and overcome the dark armies of Mordor, and Frodo must destroy the ring of power. In the tradition of classic fairy tales, everything eventually ends happily ever after. The events unfold as follows:

1. Gandalf goes to Gondor in order to mobilize their forces against the impending attack by Mordor.

2. Aragorn, with the help of the ancient sword forged by the elves, is able to unite the old alliances, defeat the forces of Mordor, and fulfill his heritage to be king of Gondor.

3. Frodo overcomes several obstacles, such as a giant spider and Gollum's treacherous directions; and with the help of Sam, Frodo destroys the ring, thus ending Sauron's power.

The Lord of the Rings is essentially three quests interwoven into one story. The first quest is that of Gandalf, who evolves into a different person when he becomes Gandalf the White. His battle with the Balrog is reminiscent of a traditional shaman's initiation to the next level of magic. The second quest is Aragorn's realization and final acceptance of his true potential—in this case, his ability to lead his people to victory over the forces of darkness. The third quest is that of Frodo and the ring. He begins as a simple hobbit living in the Shire, and then within the course of the story, he meets all the challenges that are presented to him during his quest and saves Middle Earth. For his efforts, he is invited on the ship leaving for the elven realm of eternal life.

Fairy Tales and Legends

At age 18, Peter Jackson read J. R. R. Tolkien's *The Lord of the Rings* and thought it would make a great movie. Later, while directing another film, he realized, "Anything you can imagine is possible to put on film." The first studio wanted him to condense the trilogy into one film. On an all-or-nothing bet, his last stop was New Line, who agreed to make three films. At the time, everyone said it would be the downfall of New Line. It went on to become New Line and Peter Jackson's greatest success!

When interwoven, all of the quests in *The Lord of the Rings* make for a modern mythological fairy tale that has a great deal of depth in terms of what it conveys as both entertainment and as a part of the modern mythology and perceptions of elves, fairies, and other magical creatures.

Harry Potter

Another author who has greatly influenced how elves, fairies, and other magical creatures are perceived is J. K. Rowling. Her *Harry Potter* books (and now movies) have had an immense effect on how popular culture views magic. Whereas Tolkien sets his story in the mythical world of Middle Earth, Rowling uses the modern world, living side-by-side with the usually unseen magical world, much like the traditional view of the fairy realm.

Harry Potter and Frodo Baggins have several major similarities:

- They both are in humble surroundings when they receive a calling for a quest to fight the forces of darkness. Gandalf gives Frodo care of the ring on Bilbo's one hundred eleventh birthday, and Hagrid brings Harry the news that he is a wizard on Harry's eleventh birthday.

- Both Harry and Frodo essentially inherit their calling from their family—Frodo because his uncle found and had possession of the ring, and Harry because his parents perished at the hands of Voldemort, thus setting up Harry's legacy.

◆ Both Harry and Frodo must ultimately face the personification of darkness alone. Rather than running away in fear, they both rise to the occasion, and in the end both are successful in thwarting the plans of the dark lord in their respective stories.

J. K. Rowling uses mythological beings and creatures, such as centaurs, unicorns, elves, basilisks, and phoenixes, in a modern setting. Nonmagical people are called "Muggles," and the task of making sure the Muggles remain ignorant of the magical world going on all around them is left to the Ministry of Magic. Rowling has taken mythology and magic and brought them into the twenty-first century. Suddenly wizards and witches are as up to date as the Jedi Knights of Star Wars.

Wizardly Wisdom

Life sometimes mirrors fairy tales: During the writing of her first *Harry Potter* book, *Harry Potter and the Sorcerer's Stone*, J. K. Rowling says she reached the lowest point in her life with the dissolution of her marriage, raising her daughter alone, and being on public assistance. After publication of the book, her life began mirroring the fairy tale she was writing. Since the first book, the popularity of *Harry Potter* has continued to grow at a phenomenal rate worldwide.

The battle between Harry Potter and the Dark Lord Voldemort begins when Voldemort kills Harry's parents; but when he tries to kill Harry, his magic backfires, and he loses his body and most of his power. So far, Rowling has written five books, with two more planned in the future. The books center on Voldemort's attempts to regain his power, and Harry's successful attempts at upsetting the dark lord's plans, usually with the help of his friends Ron and Hermione.

Here's an overview of the first five *Harry Potter* books, with an emphasis on magical beings and creatures.

Harry Potter and the Sorcerer's Stone (1997) plays host to a variety of mythological themes beginning with the similarities between the sorcerer's stone and the "philosopher's stone." (In England and elsewhere in the world, the book is titled *Harry Potter and the Philosopher's Stone*.) In mythology, the philosopher's stone had the power to turn other metals into gold as well as the power of immortality. In the story, Voldemort attempts to gain control of the sorcerer's stone so that he can regain his physical body. In the classic style of all the great myths and fairy tales, Harry, as the hero, must overcome certain tasks or tests in order to gain entrance into the final battle with Voldemort. In the end, it is the love of Harry's mother that gives him the power to defeat the dark lord and his henchman.

Some of the magical beings and creatures introduced in this book include wizards, witches, three-headed dogs, trolls, unicorns, centaurs, ghosts, and dragons. The centaur alerts Harry to what Voldemort is up to in terms of trying to find a new body.

Harry Potter and the Chamber of Secrets (1999) centers around a diary that Voldemort had when he was a student at Hogwarts School of Witchcraft and Wizardry. Even after his defeat the previous year, Voldemort is back with Harry at Hogwarts, using the diary to ensnare a girl to do his bidding. The girl is the sister of Harry's best friend Ron. In conjunction, a secret chamber has been reopened, and an ancient curse once again comes to the forefront. The curse has to do with a hidden horror in the chamber of secrets, and how it will end in the death of someone who isn't pure-blood. Harry once again disrupts Voldemort's plans by slaying the basilisk (a giant serpent), overcoming Voldemort, and saving Ron's sister. One of the most moving moments comes at the end when Harry is mortally wounded by the fang of the basilisk, but is saved by the mythical phoenix, whose tears heal Harry's wound.

Some of the magical beings and creatures introduced in this book include house elves, basilisks, acromantula, flying cars (like a flying carpet), pixies (a type of fairy), and of course, the phoenix.

A young wizard.

Harry Potter and the Prisoner of Azkaban (1999) begins with Harry inflating Aunt Marge into a balloon for insulting his dead parents. Harry escapes in the confusion of everyone trying to catch her as she slowly floats up toward the sky. Afterward, Harry learns of the escape of Sirius Black—his godfather—from Azkaban prison. He supposedly betrayed Harry's parents to Voldemort, and is now seeking to destroy Harry. In the end, Harry learns that his godfather is an Animagus (a wizard who can shape shift) who takes the form of a black dog. The Defense Against the Dark Arts teacher—Remus Lupin, childhood friend of Harry's parents—is a werewolf, and Ron's rat is a person—named Peter Pettigrew, or Wormtail—who was thought to be dead. Wormtail is the person who really betrayed Harry's parents, instead of Sirius Black, though no one but the kids and Lupin are present for this revelation. The story ends with a time-traveling episode in which Harry and Hermione go back in time to save Harry's godfather as well as a hippogriff.

Some of the magical beings and creatures introduced in this book include werewolves, shape shifters (Animagi), hippogriffs (half eagle, half horse), and boggarts (mischief-causing fairies).

Harry Potter and the Goblet of Fire (2000) has the overtones of a classic fairy tale in that Harry is mysteriously chosen as one of the participants in the Triwizard Tournament, and then must complete three tasks in order to win. The first task is to get past a dragon and collect the golden egg with a clue to the second task. The second task is to recover from the merpeople what was taken from each participant. The third task has to do with a maze filled with deadly traps and monstrous creatures. Harry completes the challenge of the three tasks, and thus wins the tournament. Harry then meets Voldemort, who is resurrected by Wormtail. In the end, Voldemort is unable to destroy Harry because he has essentially become Voldemort's equal or counterpart of light. This symbolizes the mythological theme of the light and dark being energetically connected and balanced by one another.

Some of the magical beings and creatures included in this book are house elves (they do much of the work around Hogwarts), dragons, sphinxes, scarabs (beetles), Blast-Ended Skrewts, and merpeople.

Harry Potter and the Order of the Phoenix (2003) escalates the battle between Harry and Voldemort as Voldemort becomes stronger and more intense in his attempts to destroy Harry. In the beginning of the story, no one believes Harry when he explains that Voldemort is back. In the course of the story, the Order of the Phoenix (a group of wizards assembled to stop Voldemort) and a small band of students battle with Voldemort's Death Eaters. Sirius Black is killed, but Headmaster Dumbledore saves

Harry from the killing curse. Everyone witnesses Voldemort's return, and Harry understands that eventually either he or Voldemort must die in the ultimate clash of light and dark.

Some of the magical beings and creatures included in this book are goblins, doxies, puffskeins, boggarts, giants, thestrals, and centaurs.

Other Movies and Books About Elves and Fairies

Besides *The Lord of the Rings* and *Harry Potter*, a number of other movies and books have been made and written that enhance the modern mythology of elves and fairies. The following are a selection of enchanting movies and books that fit this bill. Each of these movies has influenced the public's view of magical beings such as elves and fairies, and in that sense, has contributed to modern mythology in creating modern fairy tales.

Elf and *The Santa Clause*

Through the years a lot of movies have been made depicting Santa Claus and his elves, some better than others. Three recent movies that had fun with the whole concept while staying fairly traditional in their depictions are *Elf* (2003), *The Santa Clause* (1994), and its sequel, *The Santa Clause 2* (2002). The beauty of these movies is that they reaffirm a spirit of Christmas that heralds back to the Yuletide celebrations of ancient Europe. The Christmas spirit embodies the themes of giving, goodwill to all, and peace on Earth. These are eternal and universal themes.

Elf is about a baby who is mistakenly taken by Santa Claus to the North Pole where he grows up among the elves. When older and much taller, the young man is told of his heritage. Never being that good at doing elf things such as making toys, the young man goes to find his real family in the big city. His real family, a father and a brother, are both greedy and self-absorbed, and do not want an elf as a family member. After some hilarious sequences where Elf tries to adapt to New York City, he begins to think all is lost until Santa crashes into Central Park, and needs Elf's help in making Christmas Eve happen. Everything ends happily, and belief in the Christmas spirit is restored.

The Santa Clause and *The Santa Clause 2* both center on the theme that a man named Scott Calvin is having a lousy Christmas Eve with his young son when they hear a crash on the roof. Going out to investigate, they find that Santa has fallen off the roof. Scott puts on the Santa suit, and through a legal clause becomes the new Santa Claus. Both movies have fun with the folklore about Santa and elves. In particular, there's a sequence in the first movie where the police have Santa locked up in jail and the elves come to rescue him. They fly into the police station and inform the sergeant that they are "elves with attitude." Both movies are about affirming the idea that Christmas is a magical time whose spirit lives on in all of us no matter how old we grow.

Fairytale—A True Story

Some fairy stories are based on events that reportedly really happened. Two stories that exemplify this genre are *Fairytale—A True Story* (1997) and *The Secret of Roan Inish* (1994).

Fairytale—A True Story is a lovely tribute to the power of belief. It opens with a couple who lose their son. Their remaining daughter and her friend then begin seeing fairies in the garden, and are soon taking pictures of them and alerting the world. The story contains two historical personalities—Sir Arthur Conan Doyle and Harry Houdini, who play a believer and a skeptic, respectively, of the extraordinary. In the end, it is belief that is the inspiration of the movie.

The Secret of Roan Inish, in the tradition of many ancient fairy tales, is also a movie based on reportedly true events. The story is about a man who catches and marries a selkie, who is a woman and also a seal. If a man can take a selkie's skin, then she will stay with him, but when she finds her skin, she returns to the world of seals. What happens in this story is that the selkie takes the family's first-born son, and through a series of events involving his sister, the family returns to the island of Roan Inish and their son comes home to live with them. It's very much a modern Irish fairy tale based on traditional Irish mythology.

Ferngully and Other Animated Tales

Animation has been a great way of making movies out of fairy tales. The two animated features that represent modern fairy tales are *Ferngully: The Last Rainforest* (1992) and *Faeries* (1999).

Ferngully: The Last Rainforest is about the efforts of a young fairy to save the last rainforest. The ultimate bulldozing machine is moving through destroying everything in its path in the name of technology. One of the loggers on the machine accidentally becomes small and enters the world of fairies. Through his encounter, he changes his perception of nature and helps the fairies in their effort to save the last rainforest.

Faeries revolves around a sister and brother who enter the forest world of the fairies. The movie follows their adventures in the fairy realm, and the main characters discover it's not always so easy to leave. They eventually escape their fairy world and evolve from their experience.

Other popular animated fairy tales include *A Troll in Central Park*, *Kiki's Delivery Service*, *Beauty and the Beast*, *The Sword and the Stone*, *Snow White*, *The Swan Princess*, and *Thumbelina*.

Literary Interpretations

The world of literary fiction featuring elves and fairies is ripe with a multitude of great authors who have written magical fantasies of many varieties. The following is a brief listing of these authors and books. Please see Appendix A for a more complete listing.

- John Crowley—*Little, Big* and others
- Elaine Cunningham—*Forgotten Realms* series of books
- Philip José Farmer—*World of Tiers* and *Riverworld* series
- Ursula Le Guin—*The Farthest Shore* series and others
- Ursula Le Guin—*A Wizard of EarthSea (EarthSea Trilogy, Book 1)*
- Janet Taylor Lisle—*Afternoon of the Elves* and others
- Anne McCaffrey—*Dragonriders of Pern* series
- R. A. Salavatore—*The Dark Elf Trilogy* and others
- Robert Stanek—*The Kingdoms and the Elves of the Reaches* series

In addition, *Dungeons and Dragons* has inspired many books and thousands of websites on the Internet. It is a role-playing game that involves mythology and creating dungeons with magical beings and creatures that are then traversed by anyone willing to take on the challenge. Elves, fairies, and other magical creatures have always played an intricate part of the game.

The Least You Need to Know

♦ Modern mythology has certain "transcendental truths."

♦ Each generation creates and updates the mythological cycle.

♦ *The Lord of the Rings* is made up of the combined quests of Frodo, Aragorn, and Gandalf.

♦ *The Lord of the Rings* and *Harry Potter* deal with battles between the light and dark.

♦ Many popular movies feature elves, fairies, and other magical creatures, and there are volumes of literary interpretations of elves and fairies to read.

6

The New Age of Elves and Fairies

In This Chapter

- ◆ Coming face to face with fairies

- ◆ Understanding the basics of fairy magic

- ◆ How elves and fairies mirror us—and how we mirror them

- ◆ Working with the energy of elves and fairies

- ◆ Connecting with the magic of nature

- ◆ Creating your own fairy rings

Author J. R. R. Tolkien's fairy encounters began in the trenches of World War I, where he experienced unusual nature energies that opened the doorway into the world of the fairy. In 1692, Robert Kirk (no relationship to Captain James T. Kirk of the *Starship Enterprise*), the minister of Aberfoyle, Scotland, encountered fairies while he was walking on their hill, a short distance from the parsonage. This experience had a profound effect on his life. Nobel laureate author W. B. Yeats, who had several fairy encounters of his own, said "Only we who have neither simplicity nor wisdom have denied them (the fairies), and the simple of all times, and the wise ones of ancient times have seen them and even spoken to them."

Each of these people had fairy experiences that had a profound effect on their lives. In the following sections, you will learn how to increase the chances of having your own fairy encounter—and how the experience will benefit your life.

Modern Fairy Encounters

In 1976 Brian Froud's life changed forever when he moved to the small country village of Chagford in Devon, England. Up until that time he had lived in London and worked as a graphic artist. London is a huge city with lots of buildings and people, and being a graphic artist was about drawing and painting what other people pay you to draw or paint. These assignments often took him outside. As Brian walked through the forests of oak and ivy across the wild expanses of Dartmoor, he began to hear words and stories whispered by the land with its wealth of folklore and myth. These encounters with nature began opening him up to the realm of the fairy. He began to draw the images of the magical beings he encountered, producing the fascinating books *Faeries* and *Good Faeries, Bad Faeries* (see Appendix A).

"They were all around me, tangible pulses of energy, spirit, emotion, and light. They took on form as they stepped into my art, cloaked in shapes of nature and myth," reflects Froud. These fairy creatures guided, disrupted, enchanted, and plagued his daily life while visibly inspiring his pictures in every way. Nothing is made up in his fairy art; the images come from direct fairy communications.

Since it was first published in 1978, *Faeries* has gone on to sell five million copies and become one of the definitive books on fairies. The year 2003 saw the publication of a twenty-fifth anniversary edition that sold over 100,000 copies soon after its release. In addition, Brian Froud went on to have some of his fairy images used in the popular movies *Labyrinth* and *The Dark Crystal*.

Brian Froud's experience is similar to other modern fairy encounters. These encounters occur more often in a natural setting, where the land is wild and undeveloped. In addition, folklore says that the fairies only bestow their magic on those who are sincere, good at heart, kind and gentle, truthful, open-minded and relaxed, and most of all respectful.

Fairy encounters happen at places and times when two points or elements come together. Examples include between the sea and the land, where mountains meet the flatlands, where woodlands blend into meadowlands, where a tree trunk meets the earth, and where a river winds through its stone and earthen riverbed. Magical encounters also frequently occur during times when light and dark converge such as at dawn and dusk. Optimum sites for encounters include fairy circles and mounds (see "Creating Fairy Rings" later in this chapter), wondrous caves, and bubbling creeks that speak to your inner spirit.

When you encounter fairies, elves, and other magical creatures it feels like no other experience. It can either bring an immense amount of magic or mischief, depending on you, your attitude, and the fairies themselves. When it brings magic, the encounter takes on divine proportions, and at that point, anything is possible. What qualifies as a miracle or act of magic is a matter of who induced the event. When God or Goddess creates a rainstorm in a drought it is called a miracle, but if a fairy or elf creates the same rainstorm, it would be called magic. The difference is in how you perceive it. Miracles have divine implications, whereas magic is viewed as sleight of hand or something that is not as it seems because it attempts to deceive onlookers. In terms of this book, miracles and magic are basically the same thing. They are extraordinary events that are very much real.

The journey to fairyland and the magic of the fairies can have a profound effect on your life. Fairy encounters open the doorway to other kinds of experiences that can have a creative and healing influence.

What Is Fairy Magic?

Sitting serenely on the shoreline, you watch as the setting sun slowly sinks into the watery depths of the horizon. As the last vestiges of sunlight glisten on the top of the water, your mind becomes aware of the sound of the waves as they splash upon the bank of tree roots, rocks, and sand. Delving deeper, you hear and feel the breeze as it whispers through the trees. Your senses seem to be more acute as you begin noticing everything from the fragrance of the pine trees to the feel of the earth beneath your feet.

Suddenly your awareness shifts to a fluttering out of the corner of your left eye. As you turn to look, you gain a momentary glimpse of something that moves quickly out of your vision. You experience an eerie sensation that tingles your spine and unsettles your stomach. You find your mind racing as if on a roller coaster, with your perceptions and boundaries constantly changing. As your awareness moves into the fairy realm, you see a sign that says, "Leave your meanness, greediness, and contemptuousness at the door. You have entered the Land of the Fairy. Mortal rules don't apply, no matter how hard you try."

Fairy magic is what you find when you leave the ordinary world behind and enter the extraordinary realm of the fairy. When you enter this realm, you open yourself up to all kinds of different experiences that can give you perspective on your life and help you on your personal path. When you enter the fairy realm, you unleash your magical self. Your magical self is that part of your inner self that still believes in the existence of magic. In terms of Christmas, those people who deny the expression of their magical self are called "Scrooges," named after the miserly Ebenezer Scrooge in the classic book and film *A Christmas Carol* by Charles Dickens. This is because those who cut off their magical self have a tendency to develop an embittered and curmudgeonly attitude toward life.

> **Magical Meaning**
>
> **Fairy magic** refers to when you leave the ordinary world and enter magical realm of the fairy. Fairy magic is about developing and getting in touch with your magical side. Elves and fairies, and the world they live in, represent this magical side of life.

In *A Christmas Carol*, Scrooge goes through a transformative night in which all of his miserly ways are shown to him by spirits. By looking at his past, present, and future, Scrooge is given a choice between the proverbial "light" and "dark." His experiences of that night move him to choose the light. Once he is shown the magic of Christmas, he becomes a joyful, giving person.

A Renewed Interest in the Magical

The belief in fairy magic remains intact in places like the Scottish Lowlands, and it is gaining popularity worldwide. Besides movies, music, and books, the revival of elves and fairies becomes evident by the increased number of festivals, artworks, fairy shops, and websites. Elf and fairy things for sale include cards, calendars, T-shirts, ornaments, costumes, and statues for the home and garden.

In June 2004, the fourth annual Fairy Congress was held in the natural beauty of the Hood River Valley in Oregon. Presenters included David Spangler and Dorothy Maclean from the Findhorn New Age Community in Scotland, and one of the modern kings of fairy magic, R. J. Stewart, author of such books as *The Living World of Faery*. Included in the event were fairy meditations, prayers, and workshops on communing with nature spirits (fairies) for guidance and help.

The 2004 Faerieworlds Festival was held at Hornings Hideout in North Plains, Oregon. Speakers included Brian and Wendy Froud (creatrix of *Star Wars*' Yoda), and artist Amy Brown, who, like Brian Froud, paints beautiful depictions of fairies. Activities included music, multimedia shows, live interactive performances, and a variety of artwork relating to fairies. Participants in past festivals include a 12-foot tall dancing satyr, pixies, gnomes, a dragon, and just about every other magical creature imaginable.

Brian Froud explains the recent renewed interest in fairies as coming from the fairy realm itself. He says, "Fairyland is like the sea. Like the tide, sometimes it is out a long way and fairyland is very difficult to reach." By the same token, sometimes it's very easy to reach, and more people come into contact with the Otherworld. This seems to be one of those times when the tide is in and the fairy realm is flowing into us and a lot of people are experiencing contact.

Another point of view regarding the magic of fairies comes from Ari Berk, professor of Folklore at Central Michigan University. He says, "They're about the expression of things in everyday life that we can't express openly. Fairies have always spoken to the human desire to have some kind of conversation with the environment around them." The reason this rings true is because fairies have become a symbol of nature and our relationship with nature.

As I mentioned, fairies are expressions of our magical selves. So if fairies are symbolic of us conversing with our environment, they are also representative of us speaking to the magic in the world around us as well as within ourselves. Encountering and tapping into this fairy energy is a matter of expanding our senses so that we become aware of the magic that is continuously happening around us and within us. We become aware of the ebb and flow of the tide of magical energy washing through us from the fairy realm.

> **Through the Ages**
>
> According to J. M. Barrie, author of *Peter Pan*, "A fairy dies every time someone says they do not believe in them." On the other hand, every time someone says they *do* believe in fairies, a fairy is reborn to spread its magic throughout the world.

Magical Powers

Whether a brownie, an ellyllon (Welsh elf), a shellycoat (Scottish bogey), or a dryad (wood nymph), all fairies have certain magical skills that make them extraordinary.

Different elves and fairies have their own magical powers, but all elves and fairies are thought to have the power …

- ◆ To fly or move from place to place instantly

- ◆ To change shape (shape shift)

- ◆ To appear and disappear

- ◆ To transform the shape of other things

- ◆ To appear eternal and forever young

The purpose of fairy magic is to connect with the fairy energy and to bring this magic into your life. There are several ways to connect with this energy, from communing with nature to acting out empowering rituals with the intention of bringing the magic of the fairies into your life. Ritual is the physical acting out of myths, a re-creation of sorts, that symbolically opens the doorway between this world and the realm of elves and fairies. Every time you do a ritual, it opens the doorway and connects you with magical energy. Fairy magic happens when all the energies come together as one, creating a power with infinite potential. This is a power that lies dormant within you, waiting to be released and realized.

The Mirror of Elves and Fairies

Watching my young niece as she opened her presents last Christmas, I noticed how elven she looked and acted. Within the context of her small frame, I marveled as her face came alive in fits of joy each time she opened a present. The fine lines and diminutive features reminded me of all the good things that elves and fairies bring into our lives, not only at Christmas, but every day of the year.

My experience at Christmas began to make me aware of how much the people around us look like elves, fairies, and other magical creatures. Sitting on the beach at Santa Cruz, California, I observed the people around me. The woman tanning herself next to me had delicate, fairylike features, and her movement made her seem to glide over the air like she was flying. The man lying on the towel next to her had thick hair, was short and stocky, and reminded me of a dwarf. His features were coarse and his toes and fingers were stubby. A short distance away, there was a man well over six feet tall, whose body was gigantic in every way. His cheekbones and features on his face were large, well defined, and reminded me of the literary depictions of a giant.

As a simple fairy awareness exercise, go to a crowded place and sit someplace where you can observe people and the way they move through the world. Ask yourself, "What magical being or creature does the person's appearance and actions suggest?" Do they remind you of an elf, dwarf, pixie, giant, troll, or unicorn? The more you observe, the more people become a mirror of elves, fairies, and other magical creatures.

This exercise points out the fact that elves and fairies do indeed mirror us mortals, just as we mirror them. On a larger level it shows the energetic connection that exists between mortals and magical beings, a connection that tells us something about ourselves as well as the elves and fairies. Besides exhibiting characteristics of particular magical beings, we also all have a little elf and fairy in us that usually remains hidden, but sometimes peeks its head out in a moment of magical joy and happiness.

The Elf and Fairy in Everyone

While at the Santa Cruz Beach during an Eddie Money concert, I watched as a crowd of adults and children began hitting giant beach balls into the air to one another. People of all ages seemed to be getting into the act. I watched as older people seemed to lighten up, laugh, and become almost childlike as they hit the ball into the air. It was as if I could see the elf and fairy energy in each of them spring to life as they laughed and played with the ball.

Elf and fairy energy is playful. It's comparable to kittens whose main interest is exploring and playing whenever they aren't sleeping. Kittens move so fast and are so agile that sometimes you could swear they were flying. They are curious about everything and as a consequence get into everything, often causing mischief. They change from little terrors to soft, purring pussycats in the blink of an eye. Overall, a kitten's main goal in life is to enjoy everything in its environment. All of this behavior is especially reminiscent of elves and fairies.

The elf and fairy in all of us shines through in the practical jokes we play on one another. We love to do it so much that we designated a special day each year for playing practical jokes on one another. On April 1, better known as April Fools Day, we all get to let the elf and fairy out of the closet for the day, and go around making joyful mischief, such as switching the sugar and the

Wizardly Wisdom

Linguistically the word *yourself* refers to *yours elf.* In this way, the word *self* is connected to elf, showing the inherent connection of *ourselves* (*ours elves*) and elves. This means there is an "elf" in every "self."

salt in the shakers. We call it harmless fun, but really it is the innate expression of our elven and fairy self that we usually keep locked up inside.

Besides a love of practical jokes and little bits of mischief, the other major example of the elf and fairy in everyone is our undying belief in magic and the good of the world, particularly during the winter holidays. Once again it brings out our inner child, and belief that anything is possible as long as you believe in the spirit of Christmas. It is a time when we are more open to accepting the extraordinary, such as magic and miracles, which are the stock and trade of elves and fairies.

Stepping Through the Looking Glass

In *Alice in Wonderland,* as Alice slips through the looking glass, everything starts moving in reverse. Light and dark become reflections of the same image, with the world in between being the integration of both into a synthesis of one. Like Harry Potter and Voldemort, they are always mirrored images of one another. A choice made is as a consequence—a life lived. Make the right choices and you make it possible to have most anything you want. Make the wrong choices and you might struggle in everything you do. The choice is yours to make.

The hole that Alice crawls down is very much like a *wormhole*—a path that can take you through time and space at a very fast rate. Wormholes basically enable you to fold space, allowing you to move through great spaces in a short amount of time.

Magical Meaning

Wormholes are basically highways through space that enable you to move across galaxies in shorter periods of time. The plot of the movie *Contact* centers around some of the implications of wormholes. The main character, played by Jodie Foster, moves from this world to a world clear across the galaxy. In terms of Albert Einstein, wormholes are an indication that space and time are "relative." In a larger perception, wormholes are also avenues to the Otherworld—to the realm of fairies and elves.

When you look into a mirror, you see a reflection of yourself in reverse. The looking glass offers a window into the inner world that you usually keep closed off from the world. It is a reflection of who you are beyond the appearances that you allow others to see in everyday life. In this case, the reflection is that of the elf and fairy energy that exists within you.

Overall, the elf and fairy energy represents the antithesis of the conditioned mind that we have to develop as adults. Society basically conditions our mind into a perceived state of "grown up." In order to be viewed as grown up, we must act in a particular way. One of the aspects of the grown-up or conditioned mind is to deny the existence of elves and fairies, even if they are dancing jigs right in front of us. The conditioned mind tells us we are not to play anymore and that there is no such thing as magic.

In psychological terms, elves and fairies are expressions of our inner child that we continually submerge further as we grow older. Childhood is that time before our mind was conditioned into being adults. Mirroring the story line in *Peter Pan*, we become adults and as we do so we lose our belief in elves, fairies, and all the magic in the world. After this happens, we laugh less and have a whole lot less fun because everything goes from being play to being work. We no longer have time to play and stop looking at our world in new and interesting ways. This takes the magic out of the world.

Working with Elves and Fairies

Although as adults we become less aware of elves and fairies, they still exist in the world around and within us. Rather than ignoring or irritating the elf and fairy energy, it is wiser to learn to work with this energy. This will make it so the energy does not cause you unwanted hardships, and might even help you in your endeavors in life. The idea is to work with rather than against these magical energies.

The best way to work with elves and fairies is to go out and experience nature firsthand. Go to power spots where the natural environment exudes the magical energy of elves and fairies. Lay your hands on the bark of a tree, and feel the power of the land as it surges in waves through all levels of your being. Stop to smell the roses—literally!—and marvel at their innate beauty. You sense different layers of yourself coming to life as you remember to express and work with the elven and fairy energy.

The idea is to make an effort to express your magical self wherever you go. Where you live, where you work, and out in nature, the intent is

> **On Guard!**
>
> When working with the fairies, never carry or wear iron or steel (these metals are harmful to them). Be sure to check your jewelry, shoe and belt buckles, pocket contents, and the buttons on your clothes. Always be gracious and completely honest with elves and fairies. If not, they won't help you or grant you favors and gifts, and will hinder you at every opportunity.

the same—to connect with the energy of the elves and fairies. As Brian Froud says, "You don't use your eyes. You see a fairy through your heart."

The Magic of Nature

As symbols of nature, elves and fairies represent the magic of nature coming alive. Whether a park, garden, or terrace, the idea is to connect with the natural energies in your environment. These energies represent the magic of elves and fairies as they move through your life. The more you connect with nature, the more you become in rapport with the magic of the elves and fairies.

Every spring, as life begins anew, the elf and fairy energy seems at its highest. The abundance of new life is spreading its light throughout the world until everything seems a little brighter. You can plant a seed, add a little water, sunlight, nutrients, and love and from it comes life renewed again. The creation of life is the key to the magic of nature.

Different elves and fairies embody the many aspects of nature. If nature were a queen, then each elf and fairy would be one of her attendants that manages or influences one small area. In some traditions, nature is equated to a goddess, and sometimes the fairies were called goddesses. In several folk ballads the fairy queen is addressed as "queen of heaven." Welsh fairies were known as "the Mother's Blessing," a reference to the Mother Goddess. Breton peasants called the fairies "godmothers," again referring to their association with the divine mother of nature.

The magic of nature is played out in the annual cycle of life, death, and rebirth. Within this framework, nothing is linear, but instead is circular and cyclical. Each stage brings about a change in the magical quality of life. Death in this cycle is not so much the cessation of life as the mythical transition to the next level of life. The energy of elves and fairies can help you make it through these transitions of life, death, and rebirth.

Creating Fairy Rings

Through fairy rings you can connect and work with the energy of elves and fairies. Also called fairy circles, dancing elves, and lightning strike, a traditional fairy ring appears as a circle of tall grass within a ring of toadstools, surrounded by a ring of darker earth or dark stones. These favorite dancing places of the fairies, where music and merry revelry lure mortals into fairyland on full moons, can bring good or bad luck, healing or illness, pleasant dreams or nightmares. It all depends on your intention.

The reason for making your own fairy ring is to attract helpful elves and fairies, and other divine energies such as the Goddess and God. These beings will bring you good fortune in the form of fairy gifts and favors.

When you craft your own fairy ring for ritual, meditation, or prayers, you create a vortex of light. You have complete control over this sacred space so it's safe, unlike fairy rings in nature which are often extremely dangerous. This personally crafted fairy ring is one in which you stand, sit, relax, or even sleep. It is akin to a stargate, a portal to the Otherworld of fairyland. You don't take your body with you, but you experience the magic of fairyland through your senses and your intuition.

The ideal place to make your fairy ring is outdoors in nature—in your garden, back-yard, forest, meadow, park, or near a body of water such as a lake or the ocean. It needs to be a spot where you will not be disturbed. Quite simply, it is easiest to gain rapport with friendly fairies and elves outdoors in a natural setting. If it's not possible to create your fairy ring outdoors due to bad weather or other practicalities, you can make one indoors by adapting some of the instructions to fit your space. For example, instead of anchoring the string in the ground, use something heavy to anchor it in the center of your space. Do not use a nail or tack. Instead of dragging your heel to mark the circle, use a tiny trail of white flour to mark it, or use small twigs or tiny white stones.

To make a fairy ring, follow these steps:

1. Obtain a nine-foot piece of cord, string, or ribbon. (Nine, as a multiple of three times three, is the power number of the divine feminine.) Fasten one end of the cord to a stick and put it in the ground at the center of your ring. Stretch the cord out, and walk around in a clockwise circle, dragging your heel to mark the circumference of the fairy ring.

2. Slowly walk clockwise around the ring, and put herbs and flowers such as rose-mary sprigs, lavender blossoms, and rose petals on top of the ring's outline. Ask the helpful fairies to accompany you into the ring. Step into the ring and medi-tate, create works of art, write in your journal, dance with your loved ones, sing, read, sit, or daydream.

3. When you are done enjoying your fairy ring, scatter the herbs and flowers in the ring here and there. Blend the ring mark into the ground with your shoe or foot in a counterclockwise circle. Thank the fairies.

Having a fairy ring next to your house is most fortunate. You can make this flower fairy ring yourself to bring you good fortune and the best of luck! It is a fairy flower ring that magically reappears in your yard each year to bless you with abundance and good luck. You will need 33, 66, or 99 naturalizing daffodil bulbs, depending upon the size of your ground; some bone meal; and potting soil. (The numbers 33, 66, and 99 are particularly powerful and magical.) You can naturalize early-blooming daffodils into a wild part of your yard or into your lawn. If you plant the bulbs in your lawn, delay mowing until the daffodil foliage turns yellow. If you prefer, you can use your favorite kind of flower bulbs instead of daffodils. Feel free to experiment with the color scheme and types of bulbs to make your flower fairy ring truly your own.

Follow these steps to create a fairy flower ring:

1. Mark out the fairy flower ring in an area that gets full sun. The ring can be any size you like, depending on the number of bulbs you plant. Plant the bulbs in autumn. Use a bulb-planting trowel to dig small holes at the proper depth around the edge of the ring. Plant a daffodil bulb in each hole, following the directions provided on the package, add a bit of bone meal, and fill the planted holes with potting soil. Water as needed.

2. Walk three times clockwise or sunwise around the planted fairy flower ring, and sing a happy song or hum a favorite uplifting tune aloud. Dedicate your fairy flower ring to the helpful fairies, including the flower fairies and woodland elves.

3. In early spring, the bulbs will transform into beautiful yellow and white blooms in a perfectly natural fairy ring. You can lay, sit, stand, sing, dance, paint, sculpt, make wishes, dream, or meditate in your golden fairy flower ring. Every year the bulbs will multiply and your fairy flower ring will be larger, thicker, and slightly different.

The Least You Need to Know

- Fairy encounters are magical experiences that can be informative.

- Fairy magic happens when you enter the fairy realm.

- Elves and fairies offer a mirror into our inner being.

- The magic of nature is an expression of our magical self.

- You can easily create your own fairy rings to bring you good fortune, beautify your garden, and attract friendly elves and fairies.

Chapter 7

Fairy Traditions Today

In This Chapter

- ◆ The enduring legacy of fairy traditions
- ◆ The connection between elves and fairies and the four elements
- ◆ How fairy rituals help open the garden gate into the fairy realm
- ◆ Bridging the gap between the past and the future
- ◆ Technology meets tradition

The foundation of fairy traditions is aligned with the magical energy of elves and fairies. Like these whimsical spirits of nature, fairy traditions stem from roots deeply embedded in the womblike recesses of the divine Earth. These traditions have evolved over the course of thousands of years, with each generation adding to and passing on knowledge and teachings. These ranged from the practical (knowing when to plant and harvest) to the spiritual (connecting to the divine).

Hang on as we begin our adventure into the magical world of modern fairy traditions, soaring with the wings of the fairy queens and kings into a world where the past and the future merge into one.

What Are Fairy Traditions?

In the Swedish fairy tale "The Boy and the Water Sprites," three brothers divide their inheritance by the eldest getting the family cottage, the second, everything inside the cottage, and the youngest son, a coil of rope. Being resourceful, the youngest makes a snare from the rope, and then proceeds to catch a squirrel and a hare. While fashioning a larger snare to catch a bear, the boy is approached by a young water sprite. When asked, the boy tells the sprite that he is going to catch the water in the lake with it. After three challenges in which the sprite unwittingly loses to the squirrel in a race to the top of a tree, to the rabbit in a foot race, and to the bear in a test of strength, the sprite agrees to fill the boy's hat with gold coins. The youngest son digs a hole, where he puts his hat with the top ripped open so that the sprite has to give up a barrel full of coins in order to fill it.

Returning to the cottage, the other two brothers are amazed at the younger brother's sudden wealth, and when they ask him about it, he tells them that he had used the rope to catch animals and that is how he became rich. The two brothers then demand that he trade them the rope for the cottage and everything in it. He obliges them, and as a consequence, winds up with his inheritance, and a great deal of wealth.

This fairy tale provides a nice introduction into the idea of fairy traditions for three reasons:

◆ It is about the magic of fairies, in this case water sprites.

◆ It demonstrates how fairy magic is tied to nature, in this case a lake and animals.

◆ It shows the importance of inheritance (heritage), and how it relates to tradition.

A tradition is the handing over of inherited information, beliefs, and customs by word of mouth or example from one generation to another, creating continuity within a group of people and within the culture. This handing over of tradition is done through mythology (stories), social customs, and spiritual practices. Tradition is all about heritage, and how this heritage is passed from generation to generation, while continually evolving and reinventing itself, much like the cycle of mythology.

Elves and fairies are part of our mythology, and as a result, our heritage. In this sense, the magic flows through our veins and circulates within. Modern movies, books, music, and art are current expressions of this flowing heritage, just as fairy tales and myths represent our ancient bond with this energy. Elves and fairies have become an innate way for mortals to express their spiritual bonds with the earth and nature. This bond and relationship has remained constant. At the same time, it has evolved through the generations.

Fairy traditions encompass a diverse variety of spiritual and magical traditions that work with the energy of elves and fairies. Many of the fairy traditions have Celtic roots that again relate back to the mystical Tuatha De Danann. Danu, or Anu, the mother goddess of the Tuatha, is in many fairy traditions viewed as the primary or "mother" fairy goddess. Within Western cultures, the Celtic influence is widespread and significant.

The primary philosophy underlying fairy traditions is that everything in this and in all other realms is alive and imbued with its own soul or spirit. The belief that all matter, living or nonliving, is imbued with spirit is called *animism*. This means there are tree, plant, and flower spirits, rock, water, lightning, and air spirits, and many others.

Magical Meaning

Derived from the Latin word "anima" meaning "soul," **animism** is a belief that everything, whether animate or inanimate, has a soul or spirit. This spirit has life beyond the physical form, and as such, connects the physical world with the spiritual realm.

Elves and fairies are essentially manifestations of spirit energy. Early in history, elves and fairies were tied to nature spirits, but later came to inhabit other places such as people's houses. These days, it can be said they inhabit everything from our cars and computers to our cell phones and remote controls. As the world changes, so do elves and fairies. They adapt to the times, shifting from being mostly nature spirits to spirits that inhabit all of our electronic devices. How many times have you given a car or some other device a nickname? What you are doing is acknowledging, and in a basic way identifying, the elf and fairy spirit that resides within it.

We'll further explore the implications of fairy traditions on modern society in the technological age in the section "When Technology and Tradition Meet," later on in this chapter. For now, let's look at the roots of fairy traditions, beginning with their connection to the divine Earth.

The Divine Earth

The belief in elves and fairies is closely tied to nature and the idea that everything is alive and has spirit, including the planet Earth herself. In terms of the earth, this spirit has been depicted in mythological tales as being divine. Also because of its connection to creation as the bearer of seed and giver of food, the divine Earth becomes mother to mortals, elves, fairies, and other magical creatures.

Understanding the relationship between early people and the divine Earth or Earth Mother is helpful when looking at the spiritual connection that fairies have with both the earth and mortals: the earth, because elves and fairies are often tied to natural settings, such as lakes and forests; and mortals, because when people began viewing the earth as divine and mother of creation, they began ascribing magical and spiritual qualities to her many aspects. Elves, fairies, and other magical creatures became the embodiment of these qualities and aspects.

Within terms of human history, the origin of the Earth Mother seems to come from a time when people were changing their eating habits. Instead of primarily hunting for animals, they began raising and herding animals, and instead of foraging and gathering fruits, grains, nuts, and vegetables, people began to farm the land. It's at this point that people became more acutely aware of the natural cycles of the earth. For example, when you gather food, you need to know when it's ripe and ready to eat. When you raise your own food, you need to know the best time to plant seeds, the best environment for the plant, how to nurture and care for the needs of the plant, and the best way to harvest and gather the seeds for next year. Each crop holds the potential, the seed, for the rebirth of the next crop. Suddenly the eating process becomes much more complex and connected to the cycles of the earth. In this way, the earth takes on definite divine and feminine aspects.

Although procuring food became more complex, the rewards were astronomical because:

◆ There was more food available as more seed was planted.

◆ It was available at predictable times of the year—harvest time.

◆ Because it was plentiful and predictable, food could be stored.

Wizardly Wisdom

When people began to live in accordance with the cycles of the Earth Mother, they began to honor and celebrate different times of the year. These are the same times of the year that people have traditionally celebrated the magical energy of elves and fairies, including the planting and harvesting festivities of La Baal Tinne and Lughnasadh.

As their connection with the earth became stronger, ancient cultures increasingly viewed the earth as alive and mother of all things. They watched her yearly cycles and saw on one hand how they seemed to coincide with birth, fertility, and the harvest, and on the other hand, the cycles seemed to be eternal in that they happened every year. This added to the divine aspects of Earth, mother of all things, until eventually she was called the great Mother Goddess.

Besides the Celtic Danu (Anu), other mother goddesses include the Sumerian goddess Inanna (also known as Ishtar), the Greek goddess Gaia, the

Mediterranean goddess Cybele, and the Egyptian goddess Isis. Earth Mother and mother goddess are not entirely the same in that some mother goddesses are not necessarily the embodiment of the earth, but instead are the mother of the divine. In the Greek pantheon, Rhea is called a mother goddess because she is mother to Zeus and all the other gods and goddesses. The Greek goddess Gaia is the primordial mother from whom all things come and ultimately is the embodiment of the earth, making her an Earth Mother as well as mother goddess.

The mother goddess was often viewed as a sole deity from whom all growing things come. The other deities were then perceived as being aspects of the mother goddess rather than separate divine entities. Different gods and goddesses become the divine spirit of each of the mother goddess's aspects. In the Greek context, Demeter (which means *barley mother*) represents the seasonal cycles and harvest, Poseidon represents the oceans, and Persephone represents the fertility of spring—all divine aspects of the mother goddess Gaia.

This compares favorably with the idea of elves and fairies being embodiments of the living spirit that resides in all aspects of the earth and nature. In both instances, they are individual parts of a whole. With elves and fairies, they are part of the fairy realm, which is part of the divine Earth—mother to all creatures—magical or otherwise.

Queen of the Fairies

Fairy queens have long inspired the imaginations of artists involved in a wide range of creative endeavors—from painters and musicians to poets and storytellers. From Edmund Spenser's Elizabethan musings in *The Faerie Queene* to J. R. R. Tolkien's depiction of the elven queen in *The Lord of the Rings*, fairy queens have through the ages touched not only creative artists but also people in fairy traditions who are trying to connect and work with the energy of the fairy realm.

Fairy queens are analogous to the Celtic concept of the "sleeper kings," who were basically ancestral kings whose energy and knowledge waits to be summoned by future generations. Two of the more famous sleeper kings include King Arthur and the Irish hero Fionn MacCumal. The similarities between fairy queens and sleeper kings are:

◆ Both are connected to the land and the divine sovereignty of the earth.

◆ Both reference and work with ancestral energy.

◆ Both are keepers of ancient knowledge and wisdom.

Fairy queens have long inspired storytellers and other artists.

Traditionally, a divine connection to the land and ancestry were basically the same thing. Families lived on estates or in areas for generations, to the point where each landmark often had an ancestral tie. When walking through the woods, these folks could feel the energies of their ancestors walking with them, often offering knowledge as well as energetic protection against harmful spirits.

Fairy Tales and Legends

Aeval, fairy queen of the "Midnight Court" in Munster, Ireland, was called upon to settle an argument between mortal women and men. The women said that the men were not meeting their sexual needs. After listening all night to both sides of the argument, the fairy queen ruled that men were indeed being entirely too prudish. She then instructed the men to comply with the desires of the women.

Through time the fairy queens gradually became fairy goddesses. The fairy queens Danu, Medb, Bridgit, Morrigan, Aine, and Boann all became goddesses in their own right. Like the sleeper kings, these powerful feminine forces await our call so that they might once again awaken and let their magic fill the world in new and wondrous ways.

Basic Ideas Behind Fairy Traditions

The television series *Star Trek* features a race of creatures known as the Borg, who have individual bodies but are connected through their minds to the whole of the Borg. In one of the episodes, Mr. Spock does a "Vulcan mind-meld" with one Borg, and by doing so, he is able to tap into the collective mind of the Borg. By doing this, Spock ascertains the problem, and as a consequence, resolves the dispute.

The basic idea behind fairy traditions is a lot like the Borg. By tapping into an individual elf or fairy energy, you ultimately connect with the whole of fairy energy. This energy can be used to answer questions you have or help you move magical energy toward the things you want to have happen. The only limitations are those within your own imagination. When you give your imagination free rein, it can take you anywhere you want to go, even fairyland. You can be whoever you want to be, and in the process, become a shape shifter in your own right.

Because elves and fairies are living aspects of the divine Earth, the best way to commune with the magical energy of elves and fairies is to go out and experience nature. When you are in a flower garden and everything is in bloom, and all around are butterflies and dragonflies, it's much easier to see and commune with elves and fairies. They seem to pop out everywhere, spreading their joy and merriment wherever they go.

An Overview of the Four Elements

One prominent way of connecting to elf and fairy energy is through the magic of fairy rituals. Ritual is a way to actualize the mythical relationship between mortals and fairies. It once again forges those ancient ties between us that have endured for centuries. The other way of connecting to the magical energy of elves and fairies is by working with the elements. Everything in nature is tied to the four basic elements of *earth, air, fire,* and *water.*

Elves and fairies are elemental beings, and as such connect with the four elements of nature. For example, dryads and dwarves represent the earth element, flying and winged fairies the air element, salamanders the fire element, and water sprites and nymphs the water element. The elements are essentially the component parts or energies of nature. The close tie between elf and fairy energy and nature is the reason their energy resonates with the various elements.

Each of the four elements has certain physical and abstract qualities. Knowing these qualities can help you better understand the energy of a particular type of elf or fairy. The following is a listing of each element along with its physical and abstract qualities.

- **Earth.** Physically the element of earth is solid and provides a fertile environment for seeds. The elemental earth elves and fairies originally came from the Earth, such as dwarves, gnomes, and the sidhe. These are the elves and fairies that work with the earth element, such as the way dwarves have become master crafters of metals, stones, and other treasures of the earth. Magically, the earth element has a grounding effect that is stable, like the roots of a tree spreading deep into the soil. It provides for strong foundations both physically and energetically.

- **Air.** Physically the element of air is elusive to us except when it blows against us like a wind or when we take a breath. The elemental air elves and fairies are the nymph-like sylphs and the flying sprites, who usually appear in pictures with butterfly- or dragonfly-like wings. Magically, the powers of air allow you to move through your world in new and innovative ways. Energetically it refers to the creative breath of life.

- **Fire.** Physically the element of fire is hot and light-filled. The elemental fire elves and fairies are the salamanders and fire sprites, who are spirits that adore gifts of nuts, acorns, and sweet words of flattery. Magically, fire is the element of heat and light. Energetically it has to do with your desire in life—whether in the area of love, ambition, or spiritual pursuits.

- **Water.** Physically the element of water is fluid. Every time you try to grab it, it flows through your fingers. The elemental water elves and fairies are alvens, mermaids, nixies, selkies, and undines, who all live in watery environments. Magically, the water element helps you flow from one place to another. Energetically it is the element of emotion, feeling, and compassion.

Spirit is the energy that connects all the elements. As noted earlier, everything in this and other worlds has a spirit that makes it magical. As a result, spirit is often considered the fifth element or the union of all the other elements. This union forms the divine quintessence. Within fairy ritual, spirit is a key component and dwells in the center of the circle, symbolizing its role as the connector of all things.

The Magic of Fairy Rituals

Within the experience of life, many things can be termed rituals. Getting together with your family every Sunday and taking a walk through the park can be a ritual. Giving thanks before eating a meal can be a ritual. Driving in your car to work every day can be a ritual.

The reason all of these activities qualify as rituals is because they each have basic procedures that are followed in order to achieve a desired result. In terms of driving your car, you must first turn on the ignition, put the transmission into drive, and then let up on the brake before the car will go anywhere.

Rituals are systematic and repetitive ways of doing things that work. Within spiritual traditions, such as those of the fairy, the procedures being followed have evolved over a number of years. When you perform these traditional rituals, you bring the past into the present, and in the process, connect with your ancestral roots.

Within fairy traditions, the rituals are prescribed ways of interacting and working with the energy of elves and fairies. Fairy rituals often are done at particular times when the energy of elves and fairies is more prevalent (Chapter 11 will discuss this in depth). This makes the ritual even more effective as a means of connecting to the magic of elves and fairies.

Through the Ages

Author and mythologist Joseph Campbell believed that participation in ritual generates a direct experience of mythic reality. In his words, "A ritual is the enactment of a myth, enactment referring to the life act you are engaged in. People ask me, what rituals can we have today? My answer, what you are doing, including having dinner with your friends."

Fairy rituals usually involve drawing a fairy ring and a magical fairy circle. Then you bring the elements into the fairy circle. The dwarves of the four directions guard these elemental gates by allowing the helpful elf and fairy energy into your fairy circle, while at the same time protecting the gates to the circle from other unwanted energies. Each direction has a corresponding element:

- North—Earth
- East—Air
- South—Fire
- West—Water

Living Traditions

Within the context of ritual, modern fairy traditions often work with the energy of fairy queens as well as fairy gods and goddesses. These deities come in many forms. The modern fairy tradition called the Feri honors a deity called the Star Goddess. As with the concept of the mother goddess, all other deities are aspects of the Star Goddess.

Bringing the energy of particular fairy goddesses and gods into your magical circle is a way of opening the doorway between this world and the realm of elves and fairies. After the door is open, your circle becomes your portal into the Otherworld. You can then become better acquainted with the magic of elves and fairies.

By the fact that they are traditions, modern fairy concepts and rituals are often consistent with traditional beliefs and practices. Examples are the magical or fairy ring and fairy circle, a concept that goes back thousands of years. Working with the elemental energies is also an ancient, traditional concept still used in modern fairy traditions. These traditions are called *living traditions*.

Magical Meaning

Fairy traditions are **living traditions** because they see everything as being alive, and they are like a living being, who is forever changing and evolving in order to meet present-day tasks and future challenges.

Besides using traditional techniques to achieve their results, modern fairy traditions also incorporate modern techniques to make the ancient techniques even more effective. They are constantly faced with adapting to an ever-changing world. The true mark of a great philosophy is its ability to stay viable even when the world has very little resemblance to what it looked like before. The ideas, especially spiritual ones, need to adapt to the behavior of mortals rather than expecting that behavior to remain trapped by ideas that have lost their viability in a modern world. This is the true test of modern spirituality.

Merging the Past with the Future

In the years since fairy traditions first began, the physical world has dramatically changed. Food production, travel, and communications have made enormous leaps in the last several thousand years. Machines have begun filling every part of our daily life to the point where we feel lost without them.

Even though the world around us has gone through a complete metamorphosis, we as people have remained amazingly the same. We still live, die, love, hate, worry about tomorrow, and wonder why we are here. We still go to war, clear-cut forests, and succumb to greed. We still sacrifice ourselves to save others and have dreams of a brighter future.

Modern fairy traditions are about blending the past with the future. In doing this, it helps us as people to evolve so that we can be on an equal footing with our technology. We must learn to apply wisdom in using technology so that it helps us rather than destroys us. Elves and fairies, by nature, are just the beings to teach us how to build a bridge between nature and technology, so that they can live side by side, nourishing each other and providing for each other's well-being.

Modern fairy traditions teach us about the world of mystery and magic, as it exists in the realm of elves and fairies. It teaches us to believe in ourselves and in our abilities, to expand beyond the boundaries that right now seem to limit us. The fairy energy is all about moving beyond the normal bounds of reality into a place where you fulfill your true potential.

When Technology and Tradition Meet

In traditional Irish and Scottish folk culture, illness was believed to be caused by the fairies and could only be cured by a "fairy doctor," someone who was knowledgeable in herbal medicines. In accordance with fairy traditions, the herbs had to be gathered in a special manner to ensure their optimum healing power. Fairy rituals were performed to give strength to the healing process.

Modern technology and medicine has shown that many of the herbs used by traditional fairy doctors do indeed have healing properties. Herbs such as yarrow, vervain, and eyebright, once the mainstay of fairy doctors, are now being used in herbal medicine. Some of their healing powers are next to impossible to duplicate synthetically, so the natural herbs themselves are once again gaining popularity among health practitioners and patients.

The previous example shows how fairy tradition influences modern technology. Another way they come together is when technology moves into fairy tradition. Examples abound from demagnetizers and Q-links that break up energy fields to electronic fairy wands with crystals that act as amplifiers that enhance energy fields. Technologists are continually trying to find better ways of doing things, whether communicating with someone across the globe or trying to tap into the magical energy of elves and fairies. Continual change is the basic nature of technology. The main problem is making sure that these innovations are actually better ways of doing things.

Elves and fairies began as nature spirits because that's how people viewed these powers. People spent most of the time outdoors, and they usually made their livelihood in ways relating to the earth and nature. These early peoples also perceived everything as being alive with spirit, and the elves and fairies offered the people a way of communicating with these living nature spirits.

Now that our world has become more technological, some of the elves and fairies have begun inhabiting mechanical devices. This move has created a host of new technical terms, such as "a ghost in the machine," "the gremlins did it," or "there doesn't seem to be anything we can see causing the malfunction in either the software or hardware." Although no one wants to admit it, the only thing left is to blame it on the mischievous pranks of elves and fairies, particularly when the next time you turn on the machine, it works just fine!

The Least You Need to Know

- Everything is alive with spirit.
- The earth is the divine mother of everything, including elves and fairies.
- Fairy queens and sleeping kings represent fairy energy waiting to be awakened.
- Ritual is a prescribed way of doing something that works.
- Fairy traditions blend the past with the future.
- As our world becomes more technological, elves and fairies reflect this change.

Chapter 8

Fairy Magic in the Twenty-First Century

In This Chapter

◆ The inherent connection between fairies and nature

◆ Exploring different approaches to working with fairies

◆ Practicing fairy magic alone or in groups

◆ Fairies and visions of prophecy

In the Turkish fairy tale "The Crow Peri," a young man catches a crow, who is secretly a fairy. She promises him that if he will let her go, in return she will give him a better prize. He agrees, and in a short while, a beautiful colored bird flies into his net. The crow tells him to take the bird to the Sultan, who in return gives him great rewards. Next comes a series of events in which the young man is threatened by the Sultan to perform a series of tasks or else face death. Each time, the crow helps the young man by advising him on the best course of action to achieve success and gain even more rewards from the Sultan. The tasks include building an ivory tower for the bird, fetching the fairy queen so the bird will sing, and finally securing a potion to heal the fairy queen. In the end, the Sultan and the fairy queen are married as well as the young man and the crow peri, who has been changed back into a beautiful fairy maiden by the fairy queen.

This tale is basically metaphor for how fairy magic works. The crow is a peri, a Turkish word that means "fairy" or "beautiful girl." In this context, the crow represents the fairy energy. The young man, every time he is in need, seeks the help of the crow (the energy of the fairy) in order to bring about the desired results. These are the basics of fairy magic—to have an intention and then to work with the energy of the fairy in order to help make it happen. This means metaphysically bringing the forces of heaven and Earth together for an intended purpose.

Fairy Magic All Around Us

Ted Andrews, author of *Animal Speak* and other books, tells the story of being a trail guide with a nature center and taking a group of about 15 preschoolers, along with their teacher and a few parents, out in nature. As they were walking along, they came upon a mound of earth rising up from the forest floor. Ted told the group about the lore behind "fairy mounds," including the idea that communities of fairies and spirits often live in the mounds. The teacher responded to this information by reminding the group that no one any longer believed in elves and fairies. A hush fell over everyone, particularly the children.

Finally a small boy broke the silence by asking how to get into the mound. Ted answered by describing how small openings at the base of nearby trees act as doorways into the realm of the fairy mound. A small girl who had been listening immediately disagreed by telling everyone that the elves and fairies used flowers as the doorway to the mound, and then she proceeded to point to some of the flowers around her.

Continuing their walk through nature, the group came to a pond. Ted began telling the group how if they tickled the water just right, fairies would come out riding on dragonflies. Ted and the 15 preschoolers excitedly began tickling the water, along with the reluctant help of their parents and teacher. Suddenly, to everyone's delight, hundreds of dragonflies started flitting everywhere around them. The moment seemed alive with the magic of elves and fairies.

This is one of the best introductions into what's happening now in the world of fairy magic. No matter how old we get or how many times our rational minds tell us elves and fairies don't exist, something happens that makes us stop and wonder, questioning this rigid view of reality. Nature particularly likes to be that something that helps us see the world in a new light.

More than anything else, people going out and experiencing nature and having these fairy and spirit encounters keeps fairy magic ever current. These encounters are multisensory experiences that are as much felt, heard, smelled, and tasted as they are seen. It's like the spirits of nature coming alive and inviting us to experience their wondrous and magical world on every level of our being.

The experience has been known to have a profound spiritual effect on people. This accounts for the continual draw that both natural magic and fairy magic continue to have on people. As we progress into the twenty-first century, the spiritual nature of elves and fairies still attracts many mortals to the doorways of the fairy realm. This innate spiritual attraction is what fuels the revival that elves and fairies are presently undergoing within popular culture.

As elves and fairies gain popularity, an interest in angels is growing. This is interesting because of the close association that elves, fairies, and angels have enjoyed throughout mythology. In particular, Christian mythology tells stories of how fairies and elves are fallen angels, who because of temptation were banished from heaven to live in a realm between heaven and Earth. Tales tell of how elves and fairies fell from the sky, and wherever they landed became the region associated with them, such as forests, waterways, and so forth.

Angels are said to be the spiritual beings who attend to the deity. This is very much akin to the idea of fairies and their queen, as well as being a metaphor for the relationship that elves and fairies have as a connecting point between the human and the divine. As such, elves and fairies offer a means of moving from this world into the Otherworld, and from there into the domain of god and goddess. This is the essence of spirituality and the motivation for fairy magic.

Working with the energy of elves and fairies is a means of entering the divine experience. In this sense it is a means to an end in that when you experience fairies, it puts you that much closer to the divine. This connection to the divine is what spirituality is all about. When we connect to the divine, we gain perception of our human face, fairy face, and divine face. These three faces integrate into the totality of who we are.

> **Fairy Tales and Legends**
>
> Angels are said to be the heavenly guardians, ministering spirits, and messengers, who, like fairies, act as intermediaries between the divine and the mortal.

You show this trinity, these three faces, at different times in different situations. You show your human face when out in the world dealing with other people, and all the aspects of living in the twenty-first century. Your fairy face is often hidden (especially when you become an adult). It's a magical face, one of whimsy, mystery, and filled with wonder. Your divine face reflects god and goddess, oneness, the greater good, or by the name with which you address the divine.

Different Approaches to Working with Fairies

You can approach the idea of working with fairies in several different ways. One approach involves integrating fairy magic into a pre-existing spiritual base, such as Christian or Celtic Druidism. Another approach is to make fairy magic the spiritual base, and from there incorporate other ideas into this fairy base. An example of this approach would be someone who mainly works with the fairies, but at the same time likes to bring in angel energy.

Author J. R. R. Tolkien's experiences with the fairy realm began when he was in the trenches in World War I. A devout Catholic, Tolkien had no problem bringing this spiritual experience of the fairy into his Catholic beliefs; if anything, his Christian spiritual base gave him a reference point for understanding and integrating the fairy. This is interesting, because many of the most vivid written accounts of elves, fairies, and other magical creatures is by Catholic priests, who saw these nature spirits as part of the larger divine order that included—among other things—archangels and holy spirits.

When you follow the ways of a particular spiritual path, it gives you a framework for acting out in the world and a perception of what the divine is. When you have an experience with something like the fairy, you then take the experience and put it within this framework and perception. Within the Christian context, elves and fairies are often viewed as being extensions of God. Because of this, the fairy experience can help you become closer to God.

Spiritual traditions other than Christianity integrate fairy magic into their framework. One such spirituality is druidism of the Celtic tradition. The connection between the Celtic and the fairy is natural because they are both similarly rooted in the mythology of the Celtic countries: Ireland, Scotland, and Wales. Many of the Celtic goddesses and gods are the same as the fairies, particularly when it comes to the deities related to the Tuatha De Danann.

Various Celtic spiritual practices have similarities with those of fairy traditions, including …

- Setting up a circle of light.

- Working with the elements.

- Bringing in the energy of the Goddess as well as God.

- Influencing the energies of magic so that they help rather than hinder you.

- Bridging the gap between heaven and Earth.

The two basic approaches to working with the fairy realm as a spiritual base are the traditional approach and the New Age approach. Within these two basic approaches are a multitude of paths that often differentiate themselves in terms of degree. In other words, some traditional paths insist that everything be consistent with the tradition of fairies that has been handed down for thousands of years, while other paths are willing to incorporate modern techniques with traditional practices.

Wizardly Wisdom

Y Tylwyth Teg is one of the oldest Welsh-based fairy traditions. It maintains its deep Celtic roots, while at the same time spreading out through the world. In the United States it is called the Welsh Traditionalist Church. It has members nationwide, and is one of the fastest-growing fairy traditions.

A New Age approach to fairies involves viewing fairies as part of other Earth energies, such as nature devas, and working with these energies. This is integrated into New Age practices that include things such as channeling, organic gardening, and working with herbs, oils, crystals, and gemstones. An example of this approach is the Findhorn community in Northern Scotland, where fairy magic and organic gardening have worked together to produce some extraordinary results. I'll tell you more about Findhorn in Chapter 18.

No matter which approach you choose to working with fairies, you can do it either solitarily or with a group. Both ways have their advantages and disadvantages. Solitary practice enables you to choose your own speed and direction, but it can be limiting when you need help sorting out what is happening to you physically, mentally, and spiritually. Sometimes it's nice to have a little help. Group practice enables the participants to generate a great amount of energy because everyone is giving to the whole, but can be frustrating when you want to move in a particular direction, and the group decides against it. In this way, it can sometimes limit your forward movement. Let's take a closer look at both ways of working with elves and fairies.

Solitary

Traditionally, people practicing fairy magic did so in groups because they lived in close-knit communities, where the members of the community got together and practiced their spirituality as a group. Because people have become more mobile, the group structure has gradually broken down. I've heard many stories of groups breaking up because the members move to other locations, and other stories of people moving to new areas, and trying to find new groups to join. What this has done is to make for a lot more people practicing fairy magic on a solitary level.

The solitary path can help you get in touch with who you are and your perceptions of the world. The relationship between the human and the divine is one-on-one; at some point it is just between you and the creator. With the vast number of books, videos, and workshops on elves and fairies, it has become easier than ever to access information that enables you to keep moving forward on your spiritual path. Please refer to Appendix A for a selection of books.

Many people become initiated into the fairy tradition in a group setting, but at some point in their development need to become solitary. Groups often have a built-in hierarchy, with leaders making decisions for the group. This can sometimes be constraining. Also, with groups usually comes conflict because anytime you get an assortment of people together, there are basic disagreements. People might decide to become solitary because they feel the hierarchy and conflict get in the way of spiritual growth.

Try the following solitary exercise for going out in nature and experiencing the magic of elves and fairies all around you. Begin by finding a special spot in nature where the elements run wild. I always like the seashore on a sunny day because one is surrounded by the four elements: the sand represents the earth element, the breeze represents the air element, the sun represents the fire element, and the ocean represents the water element. These are places where the elf and fairy magic is especially high.

Get in a comfortable position, and take three deep breaths while imagining a green cord moving from your navel into the surrounding earth.

Take nine breaths, each time becoming more aware of the elemental energy around you. With each breath, call out, "I am the earth, I am the wind, I am the sunlight, and I am the water."

Now sense the Oneness that connects them all together. As you do this, imagine your senses expanding and becoming more acute. Become aware of every feeling, sound, and aroma as they fill your senses. Expand even further and imagine all of nature around you as being alive—from the flowers and the trees to the rocks and the land. Expand your senses until they include the fairy realm. After you expand to that point, then move into the fairy realm, letting your senses experience magical sensations coming from nature. Sit for a while and enjoy the elves and fairies as they dance all around you.

With Groups

My first experience of working with a group was something that I will always remember. We were all holding hands and moving around in a circle while chanting the name of the fairy queen. I could sense the energy moving higher and higher with each turn of the circle. We were doing a healing for the earth, and with each turn of the circle I could sense the energy crescendo as the fairy energy engulfed the room, I felt my whole body vibrate as everyone released the energy out into the world. For the rest of the night, the room and everyone in it, including myself, seemed to glow.

Working with groups can be rewarding because it involves the focused energy of several individuals rather than just one. Simple physics tells us that the more energy you have, the greater the effect this energy will have. The important thing is to focus this energy on a particular intention.

Working with groups in fairy magic also offers a forum for discussing ideas and experiences. Because spiritual ideas and experiences are usually abstract—they are felt rather than seen—it's nice to share them with other people as a means of getting outside input. Often you will find other people who have had similar experiences, and as a consequence, they often have suggestions on how to assimilate the information or work through the experience.

CAUTION

On Guard!

Beware of groups that attempt to control your thoughts and actions, sometimes by alienating you from your family and friends. Always question any group that tries to restrict your freedom or brainwash you.

As I noted earlier, the constant movement of people from one living location to another is the main reason there are more people choosing the solitary route. When you move to a new location, especially when it's a long distance away from your previous residence, it's often hard to meet people with your same spiritual beliefs. Fortunately, technological innovations such as the Internet have made it easier for people to connect. The Internet can be used as a way to network with people in your area, as well as anywhere in the world.

General Coming Trends

One of the main trends in spirituality is that people have been blending spiritualities together to produce a synthesis of ideas and practices. One of the results of this trend has been to create personal spiritualities that are tailored more toward the individual rather than organized religion. People have been individualizing personal spiritualities because everyone's needs are different, and it's hard to develop an all-purpose set of spiritual rules that work for everybody.

Through the Ages

In his book *Earth Light*, R. J. Stewart states, "The Underworld (fairy) tradition affirms that universal wisdom and regeneration are not found exclusively in heavenly or ethereal dimensions, but also in the heart of the sacred land, the planet, within Mother Earth."

As author and mythologist Joseph Campbell insightfully pointed out, all religions and spiritual paths are essentially the same in that they all ultimately offer a path to the divine. Perceptions and methods for getting there can be different, but the outcome of connecting to deity is the same. Like the knight searching for the Holy Grail, we are on a spiritual adventure that can lead us to many places, but eventually our path leads us to the grail, where we drink from the divine waters and become one with our creator.

Fairy magic continues to be a spiritual trend as more people tap into the fairy as a means of bridging the gap between the divine and the mundane. Fairy concepts increasingly become integrated into the whole of a person's personalized spirituality. The fairy then becomes spiritually blended with the concepts of traditions, such as Christianity, Buddhism, and Shamanism. Together they forge a way for the individual to move through his or her world, eventually progressing to the level of the divine.

People without previous spiritual bases who have fairy encounters and experiences often find themselves on a spiritual path as a result of the experience. Their fairy encounter awakens something within them that begins moving them toward divine enlightenment, a state where a person comes to terms with their spiritual place in the universe. This usually involves becoming one with the divine mind, and in the process being filled with the divine light that makes a person whole again.

The Future for Fairies

As long as there is nature and human beings, there will be elves and fairies. The agreement was made many years ago by the gods and has since been sealed by ages of experience. Problems arise when we begin to forget this agreement. This agreement was forged at the inception of creation, when everything moved from the unmanifested to the manifested.

We continue to move at dazzling speeds into the future, where technology flourishes and makes our lives more comfortable. At the same time, our human roots connect us to the earth and the source of creation. As we attempt to reconcile these two polarities, we are drawn to the energy of elves and fairies that represent our past, present, and future connection to nature and this planet.

No matter how much we might think we've outgrown the concept of elves and fairies, they continue to occupy a space within our consciousness. The realm of the fairy moves beyond the constraints of time and space, and as such is not limited by them. This is why elves and fairies always seem relevant no matter where we go or how much time passes.

Through the ages, elves and fairies have become an intricate part of who we are as human beings. They represent aspects of ourselves that exist somewhere between the mortal and the divine. As with Frodo's boat trip with the elves at the end of *The Lord of the Rings*, the fairies offer us transportation to the immortal world of the divine, a place where we all can fulfill our desires to be one with both Goddess and God.

Fairy Prophecies

The world of the fairy has always been ripe with visions of *prophecy*. Offspring of elves and fairies, both King Arthur and Merlin the Wizard were the products of fairy parentage. Merlin forecasted events that led to the creation of Camelot. This included Arthur's pulling the sword from the stone, an essential part of the later mythology.

Magical Meaning

Prophecy is the ability to predict events before they actually occur. The word itself means to "speak," as prophecy frequently blends elements of prediction, forecasting, and divination. Also thought to be of a psychic and spiritual nature, many prophecies are considered messages from the divine.

In Geoffrey of Monmouth's book *The History of the Kings of Britain*, the "Prophecies of Merlin" contains a considerable amount of Celtic lore. It describes Merlin's prophecies made when he was a youth. These prophecies were uttered all at once and covered King Vortigern's reign, King Arthur's rise to power, and also the future of Britain, well into the twenty-first century. In his book *The Elements of Prophecy*, Scottish fairy expert R. J. Stewart explains that when Merlin uttered these prophecies, he burst into tears.

In his book *Merlin, Priest of Nature*, Jean Markale describes how Merlin obtains his powers in the castle of glass. They include: "The gifts of clairvoyance (prophecy), metamorphoses, and invisibility; influence over the elements; comprehension of the language of animals and power to command them are given him, as well as the gift of medicine and resurrection of the dead. All of these powers are those attributed to the druids by Irish and Welsh literary traditions."

This story illustrates that the only difference between prophecy and mythology is that in time, prophecy, if it comes to be true on some level of perception, then enters quickly into the fabric of modern mythology. This is analogous to the baseball hero Babe Ruth standing at home plate and waving his bat toward a place in the outfield. After he hits the ball in that general direction, the whole experience becomes mythology on the grandest of scales.

After you enter the fairy realm, far beyond the boundaries of time and space, then prophecy becomes a regular event in your life. Essentially, prophecy is the ability to perceive entities and events and how in time they will fulfill their destinies. Sometimes it's exciting to look into the future to see how events will turn out, and other times you wish you didn't know. Although you might not like knowing how things are going to turn out, in the end it's better to know because at least then you have the option of doing something about it. It doesn't mean you can change what is going to happen, but at least you have the option. Without prophecy and the ability to see into the future, you helplessly await your fate by swimming blindly. Without vision, you will aimlessly swim in circles until you drown from exhaustion.

Fairy prophecy is about looking into the fairy realm for insights into what will happen in the future. Being the place where time and space merge together, the fairy realm offers the perfect place for prophecies. It's like going to a sneak preview, and then when the movie comes out, knowing everything that is going to happen before it happens. This is the essence of fairy prophecy. It's a look into the future that you can either live with or attempt to change. The choice is yours to make. If you see it coming and you don't do anything to prevent it, it at least partially becomes your fault although you didn't cause it. This is one of the paradoxes of being.

The Least You Need to Know

- ◆ The primal power of the fairy comes from the spirit of nature.
- ◆ People with other spiritual bases often have no problem accepting the idea of fairies.
- ◆ You can practice fairy magic alone or in groups.
- ◆ Like angels, elves and fairies are intermediaries between heaven and Earth.
- ◆ Prophecy is an inherent part of fairies and their magic.

Part  3

Habits and Habitats of Elves and Fairies

Here we take a closer look into the world of elves and fairies—their habits, what they look like, and what you can expect if you meet one. I'll tell you about the habitats and places that elves and fairies frequent, along with the best times for meeting or avoiding them, depending on your preference.

This part of the book also discusses the magical days of celebration—the times when elves and fairies come together to celebrate the seasonal cycles and all of nature. I'll describe methods of attraction and protection, and explain which elves and fairies are good and which are bad, as well as share techniques for attracting good elves and fairies—and for protecting yourself from the bad ones.

Elf and Fairy Behavior

In This Chapter

◆ What do elves and fairies look like?

◆ A look at their characteristics and habits

◆ What to do when meeting an elf or fairy

◆ The connection between mortals and fairies

◆ Exploring the nature of elves and fairies

In the world under the waters—under a lake in the West of Ireland in this case—I saw a blue and orange coloured king seated on a throne; and there seemed to be some fountain of mystical fire rising from under his throne, and he breathed this fire into himself as though it were his life. As I looked, I saw groups of pale beings, almost grey in colour coming down one side of the throne by the fire-fountain. They placed their head and lips near the heart of the elemental king, and then, as they touched him, they shot upwards, plumed and radiant, and passed on the other side as though they had received a new life from this chief of their world.

This vivid account of a water fairy is included in the book *The Fairy Faith in Celtic Countries* (Citadel Press, 1990) by W. Y. Evans-Wentz. Although there are many different accounts and tales recounting the appearance and habits of elves and fairies, these accounts have similar qualities to them. This chapter continues your fairy adventure into the personal habits of elves and fairies. This includes their appearance, behavior, and interaction with mortals. So mount your coomlaen (elven steed), and ride your wishes like horses into the fairy realm.

What Elves and Fairies Look Like

Because elves and fairies are shape shifters, they can appear in any form they choose. In this sense, they are spirit taking material form, and as such, that form is relative to the image they project, as well as the image you are more likely to perceive. Sometimes elves and fairies appear as shining beings of light whose form is not distinctly defined in a physical shape.

Through the Ages

In a documented account in the early 1900s, an old schoolmaster in West Ireland described the fairies he encountered as beings who were tall, beautiful, and shone with every color of the rainbow.

Different kinds of elves and fairies have their own unique appearances. Many times the way they appear reflects the place in which they reside. Woodland elves and fairies have a tendency to be forest green and brown, whereas water elves and fairies come in the colors of aqua green and blue. Examples include wood elves who are fair skinned beings with darker brown hair and wear green and brown apparel; and the Selkies, who are described as having large, round black eyes, long bluish-black hair, and slender bodies that are slightly silvery.

The idea that elves and fairies are small is relatively recent in terms of their history. Part of the reason this diminutive appearance has become prominent in popular culture is because small is less threatening and more childlike, and it explains why they're less likely to be seen.

The Basic Elven Look

From their mythological origins, our perception of how elves look has changed. Traditionally they were perceived as tall, thin, and elegant, with fine, graceful features and pointed ears with no lobes. Through time, they have become much smaller and more animated or childlike in both their features and actions, like Santa's elves. This transition is one that has gradually happened over the years, although

J. R. R. Tolkien's *The Lord of the Rings* trilogy takes a more scholarly and traditional view of elves.

Tolkien describes tall, graceful, stately elves who walk in a light that is radiant like moon- and starlight. This light glimmers on their hair, eyes, skin, silken clothes, and jeweled hands. Their hair is like spun gold, woven silver, or polished jet. Because they were the first race to speak, elves have mellifluous voices that are as beautiful and subtle as water.

Within the Elizabethan era of the 1600s, both Edmund Spenser in *The Faerie Queene* and Lord Dunsany in *The King of Elfland's Daughter* portrayed elves as being the same size as humans. At the same time, William Shakespeare in *Henry IV* (night-tripping fairy), *Romeo and Juliet* (Queen Mab), and *A Midsummer Night's Dream* (Oberon and Titania and their fairy court) makes the idea of elves and fairies synonymous while at the same time describing them as little people, who are often the size of insects. Other authors such as Michael Drayton aided in this effort to make the perception of the stature of elves small rather than tall.

By the time Victorian literature became the rage, elves were portrayed as tiny men with pointy ears and stocking caps. That set the tone for what was to come—elves as small fairylike beings, who are skilled craftspeople along the line of Santa's elves. They make the toys for all the children at Christmas. This cute, albeit erroneous, image of elves has persisted up to modern times.

Within modern culture, one of the things that have begun to define the appearance of elves is the advent of games such as *Dungeons and Dragons*. Within the game, worlds are created and races of elves are seeded from mythology and literature. Modern literature, with its multitude of books about elves and mythology, continues to contribute to the evolution of the appearance of elves.

The Basic Fairy Look

As with elves, the basic fairy look began in mythology and evolved from there. The fae, descended from the Tuatha De Danann, were larger than humans or at the very least, the same size as them. In Irish folklore, and contrary to popular perceptions, fairies (or the Sidhe) are referred to as being tall rather than small. In one account written by Evans-Wentz, the fairies are described as opalescent beings that are about 14 feet tall! Most accounts do not describe fairies as being quite so tall, but there is a general consensus historically, as with Irish seers, that the fairies are as tall as or taller than mortals.

People who have had fairy encounters often speak of the opalescent, light-filled quality of fairies. Their luminescent aspect gives rise to the name "the Shining Ones." Fairies are described many times as being luminous to the point where they light up the space around them. Evans-Wentz writes about Ben Bulbin country in County Sligo, which is a rare place in Ireland where fairies are thought to be visible. People there refer to fairies as "the gentry," and it is said the gentry live inside the mountains in beautiful castles. The following is one of these accounts from County Sligo in the early 1900s, where the person saw a whole troop of shining fairies:

> There was at first a dazzle of light, and then I saw that this came from the heart of a tall figure with a body apparently shaped out of half-transparent or opalescent air, and throughout the body ran a radiant, electrical fire, to which the heart seemed the center. Around the head of this being and through its waving luminous hair, which was blown all about the body like living strands of gold, there appeared flaming wing-like auras. From the being itself light seemed to stream outwards in every direction; and the effect left on me after the vision was one of extraordinary lightness, joyousness, or ecstasy.

Here's a basic guide to the appearance of Irish fairies:

- Gnomes—Large, round heads, stocky bodies, 2 to 3 feet tall
- Leprechauns—Often bearded, small stature, wizened
- Little people—Slender with fair features, smaller size
- Sidhe—Refined features, as tall as or taller than humans, shining appearance

Through folklore and literature, fairies have come to represent a variety of different energetic beings who have many names and just as many types of appearances. These include bad fairies such as barquests, who have horns, large teeth, and claws, and like to shape shift into shaggy black dogs; undines, who appear beautiful and humanlike with skin that shimmers blue-green like the water; sylphs, who come in a variety of sizes and are winged, transparent, and surrounded by a glowing radiance; and brownies, who are smaller in stature than humans and have brown-colored skin, a wizened face, and hair all over their body.

By all accounts, fairies come in hundreds of different forms. Also, as shape shifters, many types of fairies, such as barquests, change their form at will, making it impossible to ascribe a specific appearance to them.

Through the Ages

Some fairies have several different names, but at the same time many similarities, especially in appearance. An example of this are leprechauns, clurichauns, and far darrigs. In *Fairy and Folk Tales of Ireland*, W. B. Yeats writes, "The Leprachaun, Cluricaun, and Far Darrig. Are these one spirit in different moods and shapes? Hardly two Irish writers are agreed. In many things these three fairies, if three, resemble each other. They are withered, old, solitary and dress with 'unfairy' homeliness. Unlike the sociable spirits, they are the great practical jokers among the good people."

Characteristics and Habits

As with their appearances, elves and fairies have personal habits that are both similar and contrasting to those of mortals. Their habits often reflect their country of origin, the surrounding environment, and personal characteristics. Those who live in groups with others of their own kind have a tendency to be more social, whereas the solitary elves and fairies generally do not like to be bothered, especially by mortals.

Even though elves and fairies display different characteristics and habits, here are some of the more general characteristics exhibited by a large percentage of them:

- They appear in different forms and are often truly larger than they appear.
- They can make the old look young, the small look big, and the big look small.
- They play beautiful music.
- They have magical, silvery voices that are quick, melodic, and sweet.
- They have magical powers that include seeing through the earth.
- They either live in troops or as solitary individuals. Trooping fairies travel together in groups. Sometimes the group is very large, while other times it is comprised of a handful of members.
- They favor the good-hearted with fortune, and despise and heap misfortune on the greedy.
- They like to dance and play games, particularly trooping fairies.
- They like to create mischief and play practical jokes on mortals.
- They are fond of good food and drink.

Now that you have a basic idea as to the general characteristics and habits of elves and fairies, it's time to explore what to expect when you meet an elf or fairy. As with anyone new you meet, it's best to know the proper protocol so as to make the best impression.

How to Behave When Meeting a Magical Being

Imagine yourself walking down a forest path, where the greenery overwhelms everything around it. On the wind, you hear the voice of someone singing a song more beautiful than any you have ever heard before. Taking in a deep breath, you smell the flowers and trees of the forest as they linger on your senses. Totally caught up in the natural beauty, you don't see the being on the path in front of you until suddenly you are face-to-face with an elf. What do you do? What do you say?

Having been created before the race of humans and living in a world between the mortal and the spirit, elves have an aristocratic quality to them. When meeting an elf, it is best to give deference to their origins and place in the world. Elves generally like humans, but are put off by mortals who are unduly loud, boisterous, coarse, or egotistical. These characteristics are contrary to the habits of elves, and thus they find them offensive and will have nothing to do with you if you choose to behave in these ways when you encounter them.

Wizardly Wisdom

When meeting an elf, remember to defer to him or her and mirror their own behavior patterns—soft voice, flowing actions. Let the good intentions in your heart shine like a beacon of light. Elves avoid mortals who are loud, boisterous, coarse, or egotistical.

Elves usually live in groups and can be very sociable to both their own kind as well as mortals. Relations between mortals and elves have been better in the past and have been a little strained in modern times. This does not mean that elves are not friendly to mortals, provided the mortal acts with good intentions and has a respect for the ways of nature. Many of the problems between elves and mortals have arisen because people have been disregarding, abusing, and destroying nature and Mother Earth.

When you are outdoors in nature, be aware of all the layers of reality that are simultaneously happening around you. Sometimes, simply moving a rock or breaking off the stem of a plant can cause problems to the ecosystem. This has a direct connection to the elven world. Though you can't always see them, elves are most likely watching you when you're out in nature, especially in the forests and wooded areas. If you respect and are aware of nature in all its beauty, then the elves are more likely to want to befriend you and include you in their good fortune.

In *The Fairy Faith in Celtic Countries* by W. Y. Evans-Wentz, a mother recounts her first fairy encounter. She was out gathering wild berries one morning when she saw something in a hole under a stone. Upon further investigation, she discovered it was a leprechaun, whom she described as being not much larger than a doll with a perfectly formed mouth and eyes. Later on, when she told people about the encounter, they excitedly exclaimed that if she had caught him, she would have gained access to his treasure.

In another encounter, a man describes the sensation of hearing and feeling the "good people" as he called them, coming on the wind. He describes some of the fairies as the spirits of our ancestors, who rejoice when good fortune happens to us. He recounts the day when his mother won a court case, the fairies rejoiced in the family's fields, celebrating the victory.

People talk about hearing music before encountering fairies. Often described as being the grandest of music, it is said to play through the night, but once the sun dawns, it comes to an end. Often the music dances on the breeze as it glides through the trees. It's a music that sings to the soul while awakening the spirit. To this music, the fairies dance the night away in processions that extend across the land.

> **CAUTION**
>
> **On Guard!**
>
> When encountering fairies, remember to never eat or drink anything they offer you unless you want to join them in fairyland for eternity. If you eat or drink in fairyland, you never are able to eat human food again and you must live in fairyland forever, never to return home.

The Connection with Humans

Humans have long maintained close connections with fairies. Folklore and literature explain that people who can see the fairies have what is called *second sight*. Also called clairvoyance, second sight is the ability to perceive things beyond the range of ordinary perception. It involves sensing psychically with your intuitive mind beings and objects that are in the fairy realm. Moving beyond ordinary perception, second sight is extraordinary awareness.

Magical Meaning

Also called clairvoyance or extraordinary perception, **second sight** is the ability to psychically perceive with the mind things that are beyond ordinary perception, such as beings and objects from the fairy realm.

Some people inherit the ability of second sight from their ancestors; others develop the ability. Some of the ways of developing the ability is through lucid dreaming, by experiencing a blow to the head, by stepping on a strong electromagnetic spot on the earth, or by holding the hand or coming in contact with a person with second sight.

Fairies, as I've mentioned, have a tendency to mirror the mortals they encounter, meaning that they give back the energy that they receive. They are good to the people who are good to them and bad to the people who are bad to them. This is consistent with fairy tales, where the fairies reward those mortals who are honest and good-hearted, while smiting those who cheat and lie or are abusive and mean-spirited.

Fairies are extremely sensitive to moods, thoughts, feelings, and emotions. They are easily offended to the point where some people think that you should not speak of fairies except to call them the gentry or daoine maithe, a term that means "good people." Just as the fairies are quickly offended, they are also easily pleased by human gifts of kindness. If you leave a little dish of milk on the windowsill at night, they will bring you luck and keep misfortune from your home.

Fairy Tales and Legends

Many a mortal has been captivated by the exquisitely beautiful sound of the music coming from the fairy realm. The legendary Celtic bard Carolan is said to have slept on a fairy "rath," where he heard the music of the fairies. From that time on, he wandered the countryside playing these magnificent fairy tunes for the pleasure of all who heard them.

How Fairies Act Around Humans

Fairy behavior can at times be humanlike, only with a lot more capricious energy. This unpredictable impulsiveness, this magical spontaneity, is what makes them appear childlike.

When around humans, elves and fairies love feasting, fighting, making love, dancing, singing, and playing the most beautiful music you have ever heard. Fairies are generally interested in one thing: having a lot of fun! The only fairy that is in the least bit industrious is the leprechaun, who is often portrayed in folklore as being a shoemaker. Their name in Irish is *leith brog*, meaning the "one shoemaker," because they are often seen working on one shoe at a time.

Making Mischief with Mortals

Immortalized by Shakespeare, Puck exemplifies the way that mischievous fairies interact with mortals. Usually done in fun without malicious intent, the mischief is often meant as a way to teach humans the error of their ways. If someone has put too much importance on material things, the fairies might come and borrow an item for a while, causing the human untold aggravation searching for it. Then after a period of time, the item miraculously turns up as if it had been there all along.

Fairies in particular love to mess with people who are grouchy and uptight. They delight in dirtying these people's clothes, blowing important papers away on the wind, and burning out the light and sending them into complete darkness at the most inopportune times, such as when showering or bathing. The merriment of fairies only increases when the person reacts with frustration and anger. The fairies then know that their mischief has had its intended effect.

You can sometimes hear the laughter of the fairies when you are looking for a missing sock, when trying to untangle string or a necklace chain, or when a mechanical device suddenly goes on the blink. Most often, if you sit back and look at the inherent humor in the situation and chuckle a little, things begin to turn around, because you are beginning to understand the mischievous nature of fairies. Again, their intention is usually not to harm, but to have fun and to aid in the teaching of nature's lessons. So remember not to take life so seriously, and make every effort to go with the flow, rather than struggling with your world.

Pixies in particular enjoy messing with travelers, causing them to become lost. This includes misplacing the map, becoming disoriented even in places you're familiar with, winding up miles from where you want to be, and losing the keys to the car. When you are on a trip away from home and everything you can imagine goes wrong, and it seems as though your inner strength and resolve is being tested, you can be sure that the fairies are nearby.

Understanding Their Nature

Fairies have a carefree and fun-loving nature. They appeal to the side of you that is given to actions that are spontaneously impulsive and unpredictable, and often seemingly illogical. Fairies emulate the characteristics of the child you once were and still hold inside of yourself. They bring out the part of you that still loves to run

Through the Ages

In *Good Faeries, Bad Faeries*, renowned fairy artist and author Brian Froud writes, "By experience I have found faeries to be irrational, poetic, absurd, paradoxical, and very, very wise. They bestow the gifts of inspiration, self-healing, and self-transformation ... but also create the mischief in our lives, wild disruptions, times of havoc, mad abandon, and dramatic change."

on dew-wet grass, roll down the hillside, dance and sing in meadows of wildflowers, and play with every aspect of your world.

In mythology, fairies are not good enough to be part of the divine, but not bad enough to be part of evil. They fell out of grace but were not lost because their evil was entirely without malice. This mirrors the basic human condition. This is why there is such a kinship between elves, fairies, and humans.

Now that we have an idea as to the characteristics and habits of elves and fairies, it's time to explore their habitats and places they frequent. The next chapter gives you clues as to magical sweet spots where elves and fairies hang out.

The Least You Need to Know

- Elves and fairies come in many sizes and shapes.
- Fairies are made of spirit, and thus are often luminescent in appearance.
- Always show your positive nature when encountering an elf or fairy.
- Some fairies like to mess with humans for fun and mischief.
- Many similarities exist in the nature of elves, fairies, and mortals.

10

Where to Find Elves and Fairies

In This Chapter

- ◆ Where do elves and fairies like to hang out?

- ◆ Earth fairies and where to find them

- ◆ Exploring the world of water fairies

- ◆ Looking for dragons and other fire fairies

- ◆ Discover where the winged fairies fly

- ◆ An exercise to help you connect to the fairies of the four elements

All elves and fairies ultimately live in the fairy realm or Otherworld, but at the same time, particular fairies are often associated with specific environments within the mortal world. These habitats offer them an ideal element for their magic and extraordinary powers.

Gnomes are a good example of this idea. Like dwarves, Gnomes live in the earth under oak trees located in dense forests, which is great for them because they move through the earth as easily as fish swim through water. These habitats are also where you can go to find elves and fairies, as well as doorways into the Otherworld.

Basic Habitats

Within mythology, the people of the Tuatha De Danann moved into the hills or "Sidhe" and became the original fairies, known as the "daoine Sidhe" or "people of the hills." The word *Sidhe* shows the early fairy connection with the hills because the word means both hills and fairy, inferring they are one and the same. This connection between the Tuatha De Danann and the fairy realm will be further explored in Chapter 14.

In the case of elves, their mythological origins are from worlds that they still call home. The light elves' home is an upper world and the dark elves' home a lower world. This gives rise to their basic habitats:

- Light elves are naturally drawn to upper world environments such as forests and lakes.

- Dark elves are naturally drawn to lower world environments such as underground caves and caverns.

From these beginnings, elves and fairies now inhabit a variety of environments and locales. Wherever you experience nature, from the ocean to the mountains, they are there, embodying the spirit of nature. Sometimes you have to go out to where the pavement ends and the dirt path begins in order to find them.

CAUTION

On Guard!

When you are looking for elves and fairies, be sure to be respectful of their habitats. Remember that they do not like their habitats disturbed. Be careful where you step because you might be stepping on one of their homes. Also be aware of what you touch and how you move because you might disturb them and find yourself the focus of their mischief. When you leave, make sure things are as you found them.

As elves and fairies branched out into different habitats, they began to take on the characteristics of their environments. Through time, these environmental influences created all the different varieties of elves and fairies that now occupy the multitude of books, movies, and pictures about them. Besides all the traditional kinds of elves and fairies, new ones are continually being discovered as more people venture out in nature and encounter these energies.

The following sections give you an idea of where you can go to meet particular elves and fairies while at the same time letting you know what kinds of elves and fairies to expect when you go to a specific locale. Next time you're picnicking by your favorite river or lake, you might hear the golden harp of the nixies playing among the splashing sound of the water.

Where the Elves Are

In *The Lord of the Rings*, the elves inhabit a place known as Rivendell. It is a refuge located in a steep hidden valley on a piece of land angled between two great rivers. In among the trees, the house and valley were guarded by elven enchantments that caused the rivers on either side to rise up and repel invaders, as they did when death riders attempted to pursue Frodo and the ring into the elven realm of Rivendell.

Within folklore and literature, several different kinds of fairies are related to the race of elves. The first of these are leprechauns and all of their close relations. The second are house fairies, who have been popularized in *Harry Potter* books and movies as "house elves." These related kinds of fairies are included in this section on the habitat of elves.

- ◆ Elves like to settle in dense forests or on the wooded banks of rivers and lakes. Dark elves or dwarfs live underground in hills or caves as well as in the deep, dark recesses of forests. Elves generally shy away from human contact, but still welcome and provide refuge for those humans who show signs of wisdom and kindness.

- ◆ Leprechauns can generally be found around clear springs, among the tall reeds in wetlands, and under the rows of hedges that surround or separate fields. They like to make their homes in abandoned burrows, hollow trees, or caves with openings hidden by bushes and trees. Leprechauns like to inhabit places that take very little magic or *glamour* to make them blend into the landscape, and keep them from being discovered by humans. Other names for and relatives of

Magical Meaning

Glamour in this context is the magical ability to make things appear in a certain way to those who look at it. It is a shape-shifting technique that elves and fairies use to hide their homes and to make themselves invisible to the eyes of mortals not possessing second sight.

leprechauns include luricaunes, clurichauns, lurigadaunes, luriceen, logherymen, luchrymen, leith bhrogan, pixies, spriggins, ganconer, red caps, and the far darrig.

♦ Brownies are a kind of house elf or fairy that occupy people's homes, do unfinished jobs, tend to household pets, and bring good fortune to a household. If offended, they can wreak havoc. Related fairies include urisks, bwca, and kobolds.

Although elves and leprechauns are said to have different origins than fairies, they all have since become intermingled with the fairies. Part of this is due to art and literature, and part is because they are all nature spirits who have a commonality in the way people perceive them. As a result, elves and leprechauns are now described as types of fairies.

The Fluidity of Fairies

In the fairy tale "All Change," included in Joseph Jacobs's *European Folk and Fairy Tales*, a man starts with a single pea, but by taking advantage of circumstances, changes it into a series of other things. When a chicken eats the pea, he takes the chicken. When a sow eats the chicken, he takes the sow. When a horse kicks the sow, he takes the horse. When a young girl loses the horse, he takes the girl, but is tricked by the girl's aunt into taking a black dog, which is a symbol of the fairies.

A tale of metamorphosis and change, "All Change" is a retelling of the Celtic myth of Gwion Bach and the ensuing magical chase. The goddess Kerridwen and her son Gwion change into a series of forms before he returns to her womb and is born again as the renown sixth-century bard Taliesin.

Fairy tales and myths are about how everything shifts shape as it progresses through the stages of life. The idea of shape shifting is an integral part of fairies because they can become anything they want and change into most any form. For example, in "All Change" and the myth of Gwion Bach, the main characters are continually changing their form. As aspects of nature, these forms reflect their many habitats. As form changes, so does habitat, and as habitat changes, so, too, does form. It's a bit of both. This shows the integral relationship between the two.

Fairies are fluid and transmutable; they flow from one element to another. By shape shifting, they become the physical manifestation of the four elements: earth, water, fire, and air. Each element brings out certain characteristics that translate into their magic and glamour. In addition, fairy forms often have natural bonds with a specific elemental energy more than other elemental energies. For example, mermaids have a natural connection with the element of water.

The following sections give descriptions of the four elemental habitats and the fairy forms that frequent these places. Rather than being separate, these elements connect together and at certain points overlap and become one. Within fairies and habitats, it means that they often inhabit places where the elements converge, such as a forest area surrounded by two rivers—where the element of earth meets that of water. Traditionally, the water in this relationship represented protection. This was exemplified by castles, which in ancient times were surrounded by moats of water that provided an obstacle for potential invaders.

Earth Fairies

With skin that radiantly sparkles like flowers in the light, dryads are described as being incredibly tall, slender, and beautiful. Their body is said to extend on one side with an intricate pattern that represents the trunk and roots of the "parent" or "mother" tree. Their hair in shades of green, brown, and rust, highlighted with gold and white, is thick and wild, and often longer than their bodies. Dryads are nymphs of the forest in the same manner as the nappees are said to be nymphs of the meadows. They are both examples of earth fairies.

The earth is the main elemental habitat for fairies because that is where they all began as part of Sidhe. As a result, all elves and fairies have an innate connection to the earth. The majority of fairies are earth fairies. From these beginnings, they branched out into all of the many aspects of earth.

In a mythological sense, the earth fairies are connected to the Mother Goddess, and all of the implications therein. These are the characteristics of creation, strength, stability, fertility, solidness, and fruitful rewards. The Greek goddess Demeter represents this divine energy. When she's happy, all of creation smiles on you, and when she's sad, there's nothing you can do but please the goddess, and give her what she wants—to be acknowledged, honored, and respected.

Earth fairies can be found in a variety of locations—from forests, where trees are the main focus, to monoliths, where stones pinpoint the movement of the sun and the seasons. The more remote and private the forest or meadow, the more chance you have of finding an earth fairy.

- Elemental habitats where you might find earth fairies: forests, mountains, glens, meadows, fields, rock outcroppings, monoliths, gardens, fruit orchards, berry patches, thickets, caves, and mines

- Names of different kinds of earth fairies: elves, dwarves, gnomes, trows, dryads, green men and women, pillywiggins, nappees, knockers, buccas, and spriggins

Water Fairies

In *The Sea Fairies*, L. Frank Baum tells the story of Trot (Mayre) and Cap'n Bill's visit to the underwater palaces of the mermaids. In describing how they move through the water, the queen of the fairies explains, "Your bodies have been made just like those of the mermaids, in order that you may fully enjoy your visit to us. One of the peculiar qualities is that water is never permitted to quite touch our bodies, or our gowns. Always there remains a very small space, hardly a hair's breadth between us and the water, which is the reason we are always warm and dry. The air space is constantly replenished from the water, which contains air, and this enables us to breathe as freely as you do upon the earth."

On Guard!

It is wise to be wary of water fairies because quite a few can be treacherous. An example is the sirens, whose sweet voices were almost the end of Odysseus on his return from the Trojan War in Homer's *The Odyssey*.

After the fairies of the earth, water fairies are next in prevalence. Ever since people sailed the seas in search of new adventures, they have told tales of the water fairies, who can either help or hinder their voyages. These fairies are sometimes described riding water horses known as kelpies, and other times as sirens who can capture lovers by singing to them, touching them, or brushing against their hair. Once captured, the unsuspecting lover is dragged to the depths of sea and an untimely end.

As shape shifters, one of the forms that water fairies like to take is that of swans. Within Norse mythology, the first swan pair lives in the Mimir's well, located beneath the roots of Yggdrasil, the world tree. The other fairy swans were reported to reside in a palace suspended in the clouds by four golden chains. Because they fly as well as swim in the water, swans connect the water element to that of air.

By accounts in folklore, the nixies are an ancient race of beautiful English water fairies said to have translucent white skin and long green hair. Undines, also known as "water elven," live in crystal palaces in the deepest lakes. A legendary fairy lives in the fountain of Chancela, in the region of Berry in France. According to

Pierre Dubois in his book *The Great Encyclopedia of Faeries*, "The fairy of the fountain of Chancela (Chance La) walks on the Lady's Meadow and the Maiden's Field: At night the white figure of a woman would be seen to rise above the spring and disappear into time."

Fairy Tales and Legends

The fairy of the fountain of Chancela in France was so incredibly beautiful that the Lord of the Manor fell head-over-heels in love with her. He kidnapped her about once a year, but as soon as he squeezed her and went to put her on his horse, she disappeared in his arms. She left such a dreadfully cold feeling when she disappeared that it froze out any feeling of love the Manor Lord had for her. It took him about a year to get over the dreadful feeling, and then he would think about kidnapping the beautiful fountain fairy once again. For all of his misguided efforts, he never did catch her.

Both merrows and water sprites live in watery residences and are known to wear red caps. The difference is that merrows use their caps to swim between their underwater world and our world. Folklore says that if a mortal takes the cap, the merrow cannot get home, and often becomes betrothed to the mortal who possesses the cap. In the case of the selkie, it is a sealskin that can tie it to the terrestrial world and a mortal mate. If the fairy regains the cap or skin, she or he is free again to return to the kingdom under the waves. The same is true of the swan maiden's cloak of feathers.

Water sprites can move from one world to the other without the aid of red caps, skins, or feathered cloaks. They wear headgear such as red caps purely for decoration. When on land, water sprites sometimes shape shift into tiny red cattle that have no horns.

◆ Elemental habitats where you might find water fairies: oceans, rivers, lakes, creeks, wells, wetlands, and springs

◆ Names of different kinds of water fairies: water sprites, merrows, mermaids, mermen, and alvens

Fire Fairies

Like fireflies on a hot summer night, fire sprites travel through the air as sparks of light. Within folklore and literature, two different types of fire fairies appear. The first are those such as fire sprites, who give off immense amounts of light. The second are those fire fairies related to dragons. These are magical beings and creatures that use the heat and the burning aspect of fire to derive their magical power.

Compared to their water counterparts, fire sprites are fairly uncommon. The main example is the shining ones, who are usually described as being luminescent and glowing. The light or fire element in this case is bright rather than being hot. Within the metaphysical and spiritual, this light is equated with the divine.

In the PBS series *Dragon Tales*, a sister and brother have an amulet that allows them to visit the realm of dragons. Rather than being scary, the realm is a magical place where dragons and humans both learn about their worlds. Like fairy swans that connect air with water, dragons connect the space between the elements of air and fire as they fly through the air, breathing giant plumes of flame and smoke out their nostrils and mouth.

Through the Ages

Author J. R. R. Tolkien believed that dragons were an important part of fairy tales and the fairy realm. In his own words, "I never imagined that the dragon was of the same order as the horse. And that was not solely because I saw horses daily, but never even the footprint of a worm. Dragons had the trade-mark of 'Faerie' written plain upon them. In whatever world they had their being it was an Other-world."

Dragons and their relatives are found in cultures throughout the world, from China to Europe. Dragons are usually associated with serpents in the following ways:

- ◆ They have a serpent head and tongue.

- ◆ They have scales that protect their skin.

- ◆ They have an elongated body with a serpentlike tale.

Within folklore and literature, dragons live in caves within the earth. Often they are portrayed as beasts that terrorize people, but also as allies that can help us overcome our fear and anger. This illustrates the dualistic nature of the fire element. On one side it is destructive and all-consuming and on the other side, it is regenerative—the forces of rebirth and the burning desire that keeps us all passionately racing toward the future.

- ◆ Elemental habitats where you might find fire fairies: deserts, volcanoes, hot springs, mountain lakes, remote wooded areas, sand and rocks in the sun, and places with geothermal activity

- ◆ Names of different kinds of fire fairies: fire sprites, salamanders, dragons, fire drakes, drakes, drachen, draks, shining ones, and fire feys

Air Fairies

Artists often draw elves and fairies with wings almost as an explanation for the way fairies effortlessly glide through the air, moving through space in the blink of an eye. Contrary to this conception, air fairies use thought to fly. The wings are almost always for ornamental purposes only. They can go wherever they desire by simply thinking it.

As with the deities Mercury (Roman) and Hermes (Greek), winged fairies are often energetic messengers that fly between our world and the Otherworld. Because of this, air fairies have a transcendent quality about them. When you become lighter than air, the transition is symbolic of moving from the physical to the spiritual, from the mundane to the divine.

Within nature, hummingbirds, dragonflies, and butterflies are representative of air fairies. They all generally avoid human contact, but at times when you least expect it, a dragonfly lands on your arm, or a butterfly flutters slowly up over your head and then flits away. These fairy forms can act as signposts, and often point the way to new horizons. When you spread your wings, you push the envelope of your existence, opening doorways to new worlds and realms of beings.

> **Fairy Tales and Legends**
>
> In Irish folklore, whirlwinds or fairy winds are made by the passing of troops of fairies. Whenever you see a fairy wind, it is important to quickly bless yourself or else you might suffer the consequences of being carried off by fairies.

Owls, swans, eagles, and ravens are the closest of all birds to the fairy realm. They are also often the forms that fairies take when they shape shift. The ganconer or ganconaugh is an air sprite that is known as a charmer. All winged fairies have the characteristics of being quick, subtle, and flowing.

Shifting light, emotion, and energy are what form fairy wings. They represent the ability to transcend the mundane, a visual expression of the ethereal forces that flow through their bodies. They symbolize the transmutation of thought, as it becomes physical form. This is the metaphysical basis for magic of any kind.

- ◆ Elemental habitats where you might find air fairies: anywhere the breeze blows, windy coves, canyons, mountaintops, hilltops, wind tunnels, tornados, and the eye of a hurricane

- ◆ Names of different kinds of air fairies: ganconers, ganconaughs, sylphs, corrigans, and the seelies

In the Presence of Elves and Fairies: An Exercise

The following is an exercise for helping get in touch with the different elemental fairy energies. You can either choose four different places that each exhibit one of the elements or you can find one place, such as the beach on a breezy, sunny day, that exhibits all four elements. If you choose one place, make sure that it strongly reflects all of the elements in order for the exercise to be effective.

This exercise moves through each fairy element in the traditional order of earth, air, fire, and water. You can change the order of these elements if you like or as circumstances dictate, such as being someplace where one or two of the elements predominate over the others. An example would be sitting on a large rock in the afternoon sun. The rock connects you to the earth element and the sun connects you to the fire element, but unless there is a breeze or water nearby, the elements of air and water do not come as much into play.

Earth

Go outdoors in nature. Sit or lie down on the earth element whether it is earth, rock, or wood. Also put the palms of your hands on something signifying the earth element. One suggestion would be to sit on the ground and put your palms on the trunk of a tree. You can either close your eyes or leave them open, depending on your own preference.

Next take several deep breaths while beginning to move your awareness into the earth energy that touches your body. Let all of your senses in on the process by being aware of how it feels, what aroma it gives off, and what tone it emits. In a metaphysical sense, everything emits a tone or vibration that can be sensed by your body on a deeper level. The earth element generally has a stabilizing nature to it; it supports your body as you sit or lie down. Use the palms of your hands to sense this stabile and grounding energy that's being generated by the earth element.

Give yourself the suggestion to expand your awareness even further outward until the energy field resonating from your body meets and melds with the earth energy. For a moment imagine becoming your favorite earth spirit, whether it is an elf, a dwarf, or a dryad. Sense what it is to be this energetic being, moving around and through the earth, rocks, and trees.

Afterward, sit and reflect on your experience and what it felt like to be an earth fairy. Before beginning to get up and move around, stretch your muscles and be aware of what you are doing.

Air

You should be someplace outdoors where you can feel the movement of the air on your skin. You can either sit down or you can slowly move and dance around with the breeze. Whether sitting or moving, spread your arms and hands out so that they can catch the wind.

Take several deep breaths, and begin expanding your senses, becoming acutely aware of the air element all around you. Sense how it moves, and feel how it touches your skin. What aroma does it have, and what sound does it make? Sense how it flows and connects to your breath each time you inhale and exhale. Become aware of your breathing for a few minutes.

Expand the energy field around your body until it meets and melds with the energy of the air element. Sense yourself becoming an air fairy. Imagine having fairy wings, and flying up on the breeze. You can go wherever your imagination takes you. For a moment feel as though you are flying between worlds, the mortal world and the Otherworld of the fairies.

Afterward, sit and reflect on what it is like to be an air fairy. These reflections will prove handy the next time you encounter one of these kinds of fairies.

Fire

To better connect to the fire element, go outdoors on a sunny day and spread your body out so that it gets maximum exposure to the heat and the light. Sand, rocks, and earth all have a tendency to heat up in the sun, which is why fire fairies like to hang out in these places. Spread out your arms and face the palms of your hands upward so that they receive the most amount of sunlight.

Take several deep breaths and expand your senses, becoming aware of every way that the fire element moves into your personal space. Sense the bright light spreading out across your body and feel its warmth caressing your skin. Become aware of how your own inner light connects to the light of the fire element, and how the warmth of your body connects to its heat.

Using your mind, move your senses out a little further until they meet and then meld with the fire energy. Imagine yourself becoming a dragon or some other fire fairy. Imagine having a thick, scaly body, massive wings, and breathing fire. You are filled with energy waiting to be released so that you can realize your full potential. You are the light that shines divine from both the earth and the heavens.

Afterward, sit and reflect on your experience as a fire fairy. How can you bring a little of this fire into your own life? It could be that little bit of extra energy you have been wanting.

Water

The best way to connect to the water element is to go outdoors and actually be in water of some kind. You can either stand still or move around like you did with the air element. This is because both water and air have a tendency to be dynamic elements. Spread your arms out and put the palms of your hands down on the surface of the water.

Take several deep breaths while at the same time moving your senses outward and becoming more aware of the water element. Be aware of how it feels on your skin, how it smells, whether it's warm or cold, and any sounds it makes. Sense the connection between all the fluids in your body and the water element.

With the intention of your mind, expand the awareness of your senses until you meet and then merge with the energy of the water element. Sense its fluidness as you imagine yourself becoming your favorite water fairy. Imagine gracefully gliding through the water to your crystal palaces.

Afterward, sit down and reflect on your experience as a water fairy. Like all of your elemental fairy adventures, these reflections give you an idea of what it is like to be a fairy moving through a particular element. This information should help you the next time you're out wandering in nature and wondering where to find some elves and fairies.

The Least You Need to Know

- As shape shifters, elves and fairies can be found everywhere.

- Earth fairies are the most numerous and can be found in gardens, meadows, and just about anywhere on land.

- Air fairies can be found in the wind and breeze.

- Fire fairies can be found anywhere there is an abundance of heat and light.

- Water fairies are numerous and can be found in rain, snow, hail, the morning dew, and any body of water.

- You can get in touch with different fairy energies by connecting with the four elements of earth, air, fire, and water.

Chapter 11

The Best Times to Meet and Celebrate with Elves and Fairies

In This Chapter

- ◆ When the veil between our world and the fairy realm is thinnest
- ◆ What times of day and night are preferred by elves and fairies
- ◆ Magical days of fairy celebration
- ◆ Creating your own fairy celebrations
- ◆ Making Fairy Sweet Bread and other projects

At dawn when the dewdrops sparkle in the sunlight, for a moment you can see the flicker of movement as the elves and fairies play in the fields and meadows. At dusk when the last trails of sunlight stream down through the branches of the trees, you can glimpse their shadowy images as they scamper behind trees and bushes.

Now that we have an idea as to how elves and fairies look and where they live, let's explore the best times for meeting and celebrating with them. You'll also learn how you can create your own celebrations to honor these magical beings.

When the Veil Between the Worlds Is Thinnest

The fairy realm is just a blink or shift of the eyes from this world. This is why you often catch glimpses of it out of the corner of your eye. Then you blink, and it's not there anymore. The fairy realm isn't really invisible so to speak; it's just not visible to most people most of the time. But then again, there are times when the veil between the worlds becomes so thin that even those not gifted with second sight are able to see elves and fairies.

Magical Meaning

Great Days or **Sabbats** are the names that the ancient Celts gave to times of the year when the sun and Earth are aligned in particular positions, such as the solstices and equinoxes. The early druids viewed these as times of high magic when the divine forces of the Earth Mother were particularly active.

As the sun and moon progress on their daily and yearly paths, they present moments when it becomes easier for fairies and humans to move back and forth between the worlds. It's interesting to note that these are the same times that ancient druids considered the *Great Days* or *Sabbats*. These are astronomical times when the polarities of light and dark as viewed here on Earth essentially cross and spiral forth in the other direction.

Everything in our world is perceived in terms of polarities—from hot and cold, hard and soft, to light and dark, good and evil. Like alternating current, the energy seems to fluctuate between the poles, creating energy as it moves back and forth. In terms of life, we see this change as the difference between good days and bad days. Sometimes everything goes right and we feel we can do no wrong, and other times everything goes wrong and we feel we can do no right. When the experience is happening, the distance between the two seems astronomical, but in energetic terms, it's only a matter of perception, something that can—and often does—change in the blink of an eye. It is a moment when our perception is suddenly and forever changed, so that we are aware of the alternative reality that exists alongside our own.

The fairy world represents a realm where polarities and even dimensions, such as time and space, come together as one. This is why those times when polarities momentarily cross each other are times when the doorway to the Otherworld opens up. These are the best times for meeting elves and fairies.

When Dark and Light Converge: Sunrise and Sunset

The times when the division of day and night, dark and light come together represent the best times for meeting elves and fairies. The day symbolizes the seen or manifested world, and the night symbolizes the unseen or unmanifested world. These worlds live side-by-side, only occasionally converging.

In terms of the daily cycle, the main changes of polarity happen at sunrise and sunset. These are the times when the veil between light and dark becomes thinnest. Numerous accounts exist that give evidence to this idea. This is particularly true of the days of celebration and full moons.

Within the yearly cycle, the solstices, equinoxes, and in-between points (the celebration days that are between the solstices and equinoxes), are the times when the dark/light cycle comes together. These are times when the magic of elves and fairies is at its highest. They are also the best times for meeting elves and fairies.

> **Fairy Tales and Legends**
>
> Legends say that every nine years selkies come out and gather on deserted beaches when the moon rises on midsummer eve. They play on the sand and show their classic beauty and their supple hairless bodies with silvery skin.

The movie *Ladyhawk* epitomizes this idea. It's the tale of two lovers—the woman who is a hawk by day and the man who is a wolf by night. For a brief moment at dusk and dawn, the lovers are given the opportunity to briefly view one another in their human forms, before they once again change shapes. The human and fairy worlds are very much like the two people in *Ladyhawk*. The worlds are always a step apart except for the two times each day when both sides can sit and look at one another for a brief moment before they shape shift again.

The early morning hours as the first vestiges of light stream down through the trees is one of the best times to meet elves and fairies. The dawn offers a window into the fairy realm, just as the last moments of darkness fade into the first moments of light. In the morning, you can catch glimpses of elves and fairies who have been out all night and are getting ready to move back over into the Otherworld. Open your senses to otherworldly experiences, and your chances of meeting elves and fairies increases considerably.

> **Through the Ages**
>
> At dawn, the dewdrops look like pearls glistening in the first rays of light. The fairies were said to go about in the morning collecting them, as described in a line spoken by the fairy in Shakespeare's *A Midsummer Night's Dream*: "I must go seek some dewdrops here, and hang a pearl in every cowslip's ear."

Dusk is the time when the fairy troops move from the fairy realm to this world. Within the moment when the polarities of light and dark change places, the doorway to the fairy world opens and out comes a parade of spirits who move into our world. Under cover of evening, they dance, sing, and celebrate the night away. They particularly like it when the moon is rising in the sky, illuminating their gaiety and merriment.

As the last rays of the sun slip down amongst the hills and oceans, the ever-shifting shapes of the elves and fairies begin taking form. To those humans who show them kindness or indifference, they give back the same. To those humans who are angry, greedy, and petty, they also give these energies back, by shape shifting into a bogey beast and spreading mischief—or if the person is really bad, into a troll and wreaking pure havoc.

Evening is generally a special time for elves and fairies because they are less likely to be seen under the cover of darkness. Many a fairy tale is filled with the stories of mortals walking home at night and encountering fairies and other magical creatures en route. This is why it's so important for people to be careful when venturing out at night. Sometimes one might find himself taking an unexpected detour into the fairy realm.

Wizardly Wisdom

Noon, when the sun is at its apex in the sky, is another magical time of day. This is a time when the light cycle is strong, and even though it may not be as common a time of day to encounter magical beings, it is still a good time for experiencing the magic of elves and fairies, especially garden and fire fairies.

Midnight is the time of the evening with the strongest magical implications. It is the witching hour and the time when Cinderella's coach turned back into a pumpkin. Midnight is also important on various magical days of celebration, which will be covered in the next section.

Magical Days of Celebration

Just as dawn and dusk are the two times during the daily cycle when the polarities of light and dark meet, the magical days of celebration are times in the yearly cycle when this same thing happens. As the earth moves around the sun, there are times when, from our perception, the light and dark cycle changes. These traditionally have been times of magic when the doorways to the fairy realm are briefly open.

Within the yearly cycle, the times when the polarities of light and dark change are at the solstices and equinoxes. The winter solstice is the shortest day of the year and signals the time when the days will begin getting longer; the summer solstice is the longest day, known in fairy lore as midsummer. The equinoxes are the two times when the light and dark cycle is in balance, and the length of the day equals that of the night. In modern times, the vernal equinox is the first day of spring and the autumnal equinox the first day of fall.

Besides the solstices and equinoxes, the other times of fairy celebrations are at the halfway point between the solstices and equinoxes. Examples of this are Beltane, which is halfway between the vernal equinox and summer solstice; and Samhain, which is halfway between the autumnal equinox and the winter solstice. Unlike our current habit of beginning the seasons on the solstices and equinoxes, the Celts and early Gaelic people began their seasons earlier: Beltane represented the beginning of summer and Samhain the beginning of winter. This explains why they called the summer solstice midsummer, because to them summer had begun back at the beginning of May. Because these in-between days represented the beginning of the seasons, they traditionally were given more importance as times of celebrating the fairies. Let's look at these magical days of celebration.

> **Through the Ages**
>
> According to poet W. B. Yeats, in his book *Fairy and Folk Tales of Ireland*, "On Midsummer Eve, when the bonfires are lighted on every hill in honour of St. John, the fairies are at their gayest, and sometimes steal away beautiful mortals to be their brides. On November Eve they are at their gloomiest, for according to the old Gaelic reckoning, this is the first night of winter."

Samhain/Halloween

Occurring at the end of October or beginning of November, this magical time of celebration traditionally represents the end of the light or warm half of the year and the beginning of the dark or cold half of the year. As such, the doorways from this world and the fairy realm are said to be wide open for those who wish to visit one or the other. It is an excellent time to visit the fairy realm or to meet fairies in this world.

In the fairy tale "Jamie Freel and the Young Lady," W. B. Yeats gives this description of Jamie: "He was extolled by his neighbours as the best son ever known or heard of. But he had neighbours, of whose opinion he was ignorant—neighbours who lived pretty close to him, whom he had never seen, who are, indeed, rarely seen by mortals, except on May eves and Halloweens."

Yeats goes on to describe the scene: "An old ruined castle, about a quarter of a mile from Jamie's cabin, was said to be the abode of the 'wee folk.' Every Halloween were the ancient windows lighted up, and passers-by saw little figures flitting to and fro inside the building while they heard the music of pipes and flutes."

The traditional Halloween customs of wearing masks and carving scary-looking jack-o'-lanterns represent ways for keeping the spirits of the Otherworld away. It is a time when, like Jamie Freel, you can go looking for the fairies, or a time when you need to protect you and your space from unwanted spirits. (For techniques on attracting good fairies and protecting yourself from bad fairies, please see Chapter 12.)

Yule

Occurring at the winter solstice, usually on or around December 21, this time of celebration lives on in our current holiday of Christmas. Complete with a magical being who delivers presents to the children with the help of elves and flying reindeer, Yule embodies many of the elements of the fairy, including rewarding the good for deeds throughout the year and the idea that magical beings and creatures right the wrongs of the world.

As the shortest day and longest night of the year, Yule also represents a time when the polarities of light and dark cross one another, providing a point of contact between our world and the fairy realm. Traditionally, people not only gave each other gifts, but also gave gifts to and received gifts from the fairies. The lore of leaving milk and cookies out for Santa Claus is an example of this two-way exchange.

Rituals such as decorating an evergreen tree with ornaments and lights and honoring the holly king have long been a part of Yule. Mistletoe, still hung over doorways as both a love charm and symbol of protection against bad luck or misfortune, was long revered by the ancient druids for its magical powers. Yule has long been a time for celebrating the birth and renewal of life. It is still a time of the year when the magic of children, elves, and fairies is alive and well.

Imbolc/Candlemas

Occurring at the beginning of February, this time of celebration marks the time when the milk of the ewes and other barnyard animals begins to flow. This marks the beginning of the spring cycle when food starts becoming more plentiful, ending winter's fast.

Also known as Bridget's Fire, traditionally the Irish would dance around a fairy mound, circling around it until reaching the top, where a huge bonfire was waiting to be lit. They would finish by all throwing their torches on the stacked wood, lighting the fairy fire. Afterward the flame was carried into every home's hearth, and was kept burning until the next year.

Bridget was the ancient Celtic goddess of fire, symbolizing the will and determination of the people with the help of the fairy to bring the light back into the dark land. Calls of "Bridget, Bridget, sacred name; Bridget, Bridget, sacred flame" echoed around the bonfire and throughout the houses of the community as people summoned the goddess and one of the queens of the fairies.

Ostara

Occurring at the spring equinox (around March 21), this is a time of celebration when the powers of light and dark, represented by the day and night, are equal and in balance. Traditionally, trees and seeds are planted with the blessings of the elves and fairies for a good growing season.

The Easter Bunny is a magical creature that within mythological terms has become comparable to Santa Claus. Traditionally, eggs represent fertility and new life. When the Easter Bunny fills each person's basket, it is giving the fertility of creation and the magic of life. As with eggs, rabbits also represent fertility and the renewal of life. This connection to the cosmic order is the reason Alice followed a white rabbit with pink eyes down the rabbit hole into the fairy realm in Lewis Carroll's classic tale *Alice's Adventures in Wonderland*.

Beltane/May Day

Occurring at the beginning of May, this time of celebration has been characterized by "May poles" and "May flowers," as evidenced by the folk saying, "April showers bring to May flowers." Beltane is the flipside of Samhain in that Beltane ushers in the light half of the year much the same as Samhain opens the way for the dark half. Both represent times when the veil between our world and the fairy realm is at its thinnest.

On Beltane, elves and fairies mix barley with dew gathered at midnight to make a very potent brew. Traditionally people left gifts of food and drink out for the fairies, hoping to win their favor, particularly in matters of the heart. Beltane has long been a time when lovers would encounter one another in search of their compatibility.

Flowers and love are favorites of the fairies, giving Beltane its special quality. When you give someone flowers or a plant, you are giving a fairy gift. It is a piece of nature that represents the larger whole. Love is a beautiful fairy flower that must be nurtured and cared for if it is to survive and grow to its fullest potential. To settle for anything less is to deprive yourself of the breath of life.

Midsummer

Occurring at the summer solstice, this time of celebration happens on the longest day and shortest night of the year when again the separation between the worlds becomes almost nonexistent. Made famous in Shakespeare's *A Midsummer Night's Dream*, midsummer was traditionally one of the most widespread celebrations throughout Europe. The celebrations often climaxed with a midsummer bonfire. People in Ireland give accounts of fairy rings appearing where none were before the morning after midsummer night's eve.

"Hand in hand, with fairy grace, will we sing, and bless this place," proclaims the fairy queen Titania as she blesses the bridal chamber of Theseus and Hippolyta. *A Midsummer Night's Dream* superbly mimics the basic theme of midsummer complete with a fairy queen and king, love potions, and the magic of the evening. In the end love prevails as told in the lines, "The iron tongue of midnight hath told twelve. Lovers, to bed; 'tis almost fairy time."

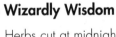 **Wizardly Wisdom** _____

Herbs cut at midnight on midsummer's eve are said to contain more potent properties because they contain the power of the fairy. Divining rods cut on this night are more able to foretell and all natural waters are said to have special medicinal powers on this day. At midsummer, the magical spirits of the fairies are strong; hence the folk term "midsummer madness," referring to the effect elves and fairies can sometimes have on mortals, particularly when they try to help in matters of love.

Lughnassad

Occurring at the beginning of August, this time of celebration signals the end of summer and beginning of fall. *Lughnassad* literally means "Lugh's wedding feast," which in Christian celebrations has come to be called *Lammas*. Traditionally, this was when people gave thanks for the first of the new grain and for the first fruits. Loaves of bread were baked from this grain, and blessed by the divine spirits of nature.

Lugh is the Celtic god of the setting sun who rules the part of the year when the days get shorter. Lugh's wedding feast was in celebration of his marriage to the beautiful fairy queen, Rosemerta. Traditionally people would climb mountains, hills, or other high places and leave offerings for both Lugh and the elves and fairies. Afterward, there were large feasts celebrating the divine marriage of the god and goddess as well as the beginning of the harvest.

People climb mountains on "Garland Sunday," which is the Sunday before and after Lughnassad, and leave flower offerings at the top as well as other offerings such as wheat. Another name was "Bilberry Sunday," which came to be because people picked little blue berries known as bilberries or whortle-berries as they climbed the mountain or hill. The berries were sometimes strung on bracelets and given to lovers as a sign of love. The berries were also said to bring luck.

Harvest

Occurring on the autumnal equinox (around September 22), this is the time of year when the harvest of summer is celebrated. Lovers of good food and drink, the elves and fairies are particularly active during this time. Brownies have been known to help with the harvest, and pixies have at times been said to ride the farm animals wildly around in circles, creating fairy rings.

During the traditional celebration, the last sheaf of the harvest was made into a figure, complete with a woman's dress and ribbons, symbolizing the spirit of the harvest. Known by a variety of names that included "harvest queen" and "barley mother," this figure also represents the goddess or fairy queen, whose connection to creation made the harvest possible. In later celebrations, a young maiden was selected to be the harvest queen, who as before represented the goddess and the spirits of nature, often referred to as elves and fairies.

Harvest celebrations were usually concluded with a feast, giving thanks to the divine forces of creation and magical spirits of nature. Offerings of drink and food are left out for the elves and fairies, not only giving them thanks for the present harvest, but also ensuring their help in the coming year. A time of plenty, harvest festivals are symbolized by a horn that is forever full, much like one of the four ancient treasures of the Celtic Tuatha De Danann, "the cauldron of plenty" that was always magically replenishing itself, and thus could never be emptied.

Celebrating with Elves and Fairies

Elves and fairies like being honored on the magical days of celebration. The other major time of fairy celebrations are on the full moons. These are times when troops of elves and fairies can be seen in the bright moonlight, singing and dancing in the fields, forests, and lake areas. During a full moon, on the wind lilting through the trees, you can hear the faint sounds of exquisite fairy music unlike any music you have ever heard before.

> **Wizardly Wisdom**
>
> Each year usually has twelve full moons, except for every so often there is a thirteenth moon, known in Celtic traditions as the "oak moon." Years when thirteen moons happen set up a scenario where two moons happen in one month, which is called a "blue moon." Blue moons are times when the magic of elves and fairies is especially strong.

Celebrating is one of the things that elves and fairies most like to do. Fairy circles and such are often the by-product of these magical beings celebrating and dancing the night away. They gladly welcome humans into their merriment, and in turn, often like to join in on human festivities. Days of celebration and full moons offer times when the division between worlds breaks down and the two worlds celebrate together the magic of life.

When we celebrate with elves and fairies, we acknowledge the spirit and life force of nature, as well as our inherent connection to it. Celebrations are naturally times when people and energies come together to acknowledge and strengthen the bonds they have with one another. Traditional rites and ways of doing things present a means for connecting not only with the spirits of the land, but also ancestral spirits.

Party Traditions and Lore

Throughout the world, especially in the United States, Canada, and Europe, fairy celebrations are customarily comprised of people coming together and performing various rituals that enact their spiritual relationship with nature. These rituals, usually done in circles, honor the fairy queens and kings who rule the different times of the year, such as Bridget on Imbolc and Lugh on Lughnassad. In addition to honoring the fairy spirits, these circles ask for their blessings in the coming year.

After the rituals, fairy celebrations normally include a feast that adds to the bond between fairies and humans while at the same time strengthening the bonds between humans and humans. Feasts were traditionally times when people came together, each bringing a food and/or drink that they had grown or made to add to the whole of the celebration. The food was laid out on tables for everyone's enjoyment, including the elves and fairies who were always offered their own portions.

Wizardly Wisdom

When you are celebrating, remember that fairies prefer to be called the "gentry" or "gentle folk." Calling them thus will bring you good fortune and good luck.

Fairy celebrations sometimes include some or all of the participants dressing up in costumes, such as harvest festivals where young girls dressed up as harvest queens and the Halloween celebrations where everyone comes dressed as a variety of magical beings and creatures from folklore and literature. Stage plays are modern examples of people dressing up and acting out the fairy celebrations, such as Shakespeare's *A Midsummer Night's Dream*, in which a portion of the cast dress up in the costumes of fairies.

Modern-day potlucks, masquerade balls, and Halloween parties are versions of fairy party traditions. Costumes give us an avenue for acting out our elf and fairy nature that we usually have problems expressing. Exchanging food, particularly when you grow it or make it, gives people an opportunity to share a part of themselves with the group. This is also a way of expressing your thanks to the energies of nature that made it possible.

Making Your Own Fairy Fun

The following are suggestions for things you can make to enhance your fairy celebrations or just to have fairy fun. I include a recipe for making Fairy Sweet Bread (good for spring celebrations) and simple directions for making a harvest box and a Yule log. (See Chapter 21 for other magical recipes.)

Fairy Sweet Bread

This bread is not only good to take to potlucks after fairy celebrations, but can also be used as a goodwill offering to the elves and fairies themselves. Fairy Sweet Bread is one of their favorites! This recipe makes one loaf.

> 1 package yeast, active dry or compressed
>
> ¼ cup warm water for dissolving yeast
>
> 4 cups flour
>
> ¼ cup sugar

¾ cup brown sugar

1 teaspoon salt

1 cup milk, scalded and cooled to lukewarm

1 egg, slightly beaten

¼ cup butter, margarine, or oil

1 teaspoon vanilla

1 cup raisins

1 cup nuts (such as almonds, cashews, or walnuts)

Dissolve the yeast in the warm water. In a bowl, combine the flour, sugar, brown sugar, and salt. In another bowl, combine the lukewarm milk, beaten egg, butter, margarine, or oil, and vanilla. Now combine the dry and wet ingredients along with the dissolved yeast mixture. Stir in the raisins and nuts. Knead the dough until it is moist but doesn't stick to your hands. Put the dough in a well-oiled bread pan in a warm location and wait for it to double in size. Punch it down and let it rise one more time. Transfer the mixture to a glass loaf pan and bake the loaf at 350 degrees for 30 to 35 minutes or until done and lightly browned on top. Don't overbake the bread; that makes it dry.

Harvest Box

Like the harvest doll that represented the spirit of the harvest, including the fairy energy, your harvest box represents the spirit of one of your "harvests" in life. This can be a relationship, maintaining a healthy body, a business success, a spiritual experience, or anything else in your life that represents you putting in the effort and reaping the rewards. You will need:

A box of wood or cardboard

Harvest objects to put in the box

Paints, colored pens, fabric, pictures, glue, and other decorating supplies

The box should be big enough so that all the objects—things that represent your harvest—will fit in. This could be pressed flowers, ticket stubs, pictures, and so on. The paints, colored pens, and other things are for decorating the outside of your box. How you make the box look is totally up to you. Don't be afraid to be creative and express your inner self.

Your harvest box can either be a permanent fixture, symbolizing something such as your primary long-term relationship, or you can change it from time to time, to represent new harvests you have made in life. Every time you look at or into the box, you remember something positive that worked out and in some way made your life better. You also remember the energy of elves and fairies, and how it can help you create anything you want in life.

Yule Log

A small piece of the burned Yule log kept in your home, specifically on the mantle, protects your family and attracts abundance and prosperity to you.

Begin by selecting a dry log that can easily fit in your fireplace. Traditionally, Yule logs were made from a hard wood such as oak so that they would burn a long time. The log was also doused in cider and ale. You can adorn your Yule log with a variety of things from pine, fir, and cedar boughs, pine cones, and grapevines to colored ribbon, yarn, and beeswax. Wheat and corn flour can also be sprinkled on the log. Do not use paint or products that give off toxic gas when burned on your Yule log. The idea is to make it decorative while at the same time embodying your perceptions of life and how it connects to nature. As you decorate the log, think about all the good things that happened throughout the past year and imagine all the great things that are going to happen in the coming year.

After you are done decorating it, put your Yule log in the fireplace. As you light it, give your thanks to the elves and fairies by saying:

> To the gentry I give thanks for their blessings,
>
> May the coming year be even more magical and fruitful.
>
> Blessed Be!

Let your Yule log burn to ashes in the fireplace. Each time you look at it burning, imagine that the flame is the light of the elves and fairies shining its good luck down on you and your loved ones. If you decorated your log with only natural things, then after the ashes are cold, spread them underneath a tree, preferably an oak or evergreen.

The Least You Need to Know

◆ Dawn and dusk are the times of day when the veil between this world and the fairy world is the thinnest.

◆ Days of celebration represent times when the doorway to the fairy realm is open. Many traditional days of celebration are still celebrated today in one form or another.

◆ Elves and fairies like to celebrate and be honored by humans.

◆ There are many ways of having fairy fun, including making Yule logs, a harvest box, and Fairy Sweet Bread.

Chapter 12

Methods of Attraction and Protection

In This Chapter

- ◆ The differences between good and bad elves and fairies
- ◆ How to attract good elves and fairies
- ◆ Becoming familiar with bad fairies—and how to protect yourself from them
- ◆ Your secret name and how it can help to magically protect you

The battle between good and evil is sometimes overrated as far as its significance in people's lives. Usually life becomes a balance between the two that sometimes requires our constant attention and effort. Other times life seems to flow as if guided by an unseen hand that ensures that everything flows in the right direction. Ultimately this points to the forces that push and pull at everything, giving life definition and boundaries.

In this chapter, I'll show you how to attract the energies that help expand your boundaries and avoid becoming waylaid by the forces that would shoot you down. The idea is to attract the good elves and fairies and to protect yourself from those who would do you harm. As a result you'll create a life that is more creative and positive.

The Good, the Bad, and the Indifferent

In an Irish fairy tale, "The Fairies' Dancing-place," a man builds a house for his family on a fairy circle, actively used by the fairies for dancing on moonlit nights. The fairies let him know that they are going to tear it down, and he strikes a bargain by telling them he will tear it down and move to another spot away from their dancing place. When the man digs the foundation for the new house, he finds a chest filled with treasure, all compliments of the elves and fairies.

What's interesting about this tale is that the person in the story initially raises the ire of the fairies to the point where they're going to tear his house down. Only when he decides to begin working with the fairies rather than against them does his luck and direction in life start to change its course. In the closing words of the tale, "So that in leaving to the fairies their play-ground, he became a richer man than ever he otherwise would have been, had he never come in contact with them at all."

Wizardly Wisdom

Listen to the fairies! At Knowle, in Warwickshire, England, the fairies chose the site of the church. The mason began to build it on the hill above St. Anne's Well, but every night the fairies came and carried the stones to another site. Finally the mason took the hint and built the church at the location the fairies wanted, where it still stands today.

As shape shifters, elves and fairies have three faces that they show humans—the good, the bad, and the indifferent. They generally reflect and give back the energy that is shown them. To humans who give them respect and act in a happy and loving manner, they show their good face. This is the face that can bestow good luck and worldly treasures to those deserving humans.

Like Santa Claus at Christmastime, the elves and fairies keep lists of who treats them well and who treats them badly. To those who treat them well, the fairies show a face that is forever helpful. In this guise, they are happy and capricious, singing, dancing, and bringing good luck and wealth to those they favor.

When a bad elf and fairy energy comes into your life it's usually a portent that is trying to tell you something about your life. These come in the following general forms:

- Something you are doing that needs to change
- Something someone else is doing (usually to you) that needs to change

- Something that is going to happen in the future, such as disease and death

- You are being energetically attacked and need to implement some protection

When you are visited by a bad fairy, either in a dream or in your everyday travels, it's often a sign telling you something about who you are and what's happening in your world. This is a common theme in mythology, fairy tales, and literature. An example is the bean nighe or "Washerwomen at the Ford," which is described in Celtic mythology and folklore as being a woman who could be found at the side of desolate streams and pools washing the bloodstained clothes of those who are about to meet their end. Dressed in green with webbed feet, she did not always signal one's own death, and if you could get in between her and the water, she would be forced to grant you three wishes and three questions that she must answer truthfully.

As well as having good and bad dispositions, elves and fairies can be very indifferent when it comes to humans. This is particularly true of solitary fairies, who often like being left alone or like being the ones who initiate contact and interaction. In terms of indifference, the best thing to do is to leave the elf or fairy alone; when he or she is ready to interact with you he or she will make the motions.

Good Elf, Good Fairy

In *The Lord of the Rings*, J. R. R. Tolkien writes about an ancient alliance forged in the beginnings of the races of elves and humans. This is similar to the alliance that the fairies had with the early inhabitants of Ireland. Although through the epochs of time these alliances have become strained, they nonetheless still exist and are part of our heritage.

The following elves and fairies are known to be friendly and helpful to humans:

- **Blue Ladies**—With skin and hair sparkling like ice and snow, these fairy maidens plant wild flowers on the hillsides of mountains. They've been known to save humans from avalanches as well as teach mortals about the benefits of unconditional love and medicinal plants for healing. Wherever the grass in meadows is long with a vibrant green color, it's a sign the blue ladies have been around.

- **Brownies**—Often shy and prone to stay out of sight, brownies have long helped farmers and their wives in both the fields and the home. They have been known to thrash the grain, winnow it, and tie it up in bags before washing the clothes,

Through the Ages

In *Favorite Fairy Tales Told in Scotland*, Virginia Haviland writes, "Indeed, like all good brownies that are properly treated and let alone, the Brownie o' Ferne-Den was always on the lookout to do a good turn to those in need of his help."

working the churn, and weeding the garden. All a brownie wants in return is a place to stay undisturbed and a bowl of new milk with maybe a bit of Fairy Sweet Bread (see Chapter 11 for the recipe). Do not try to give them gifts of clothes or pay them wages; they will take this as a sign to leave.

- **Seelie**—An example of a trooping fairy (one that always travels in groups, usually on the wind, rain, snow, starlight, and moonbeams), seelies are known for having a good-hearted and benevolent nature. Riding the wind, they radiate light as they search for humans in need of help. The troop as a whole is known as the seelie court (seelie meaning blessed), and has been known to give seed and food to those less fortunate.

Bad Elf, Bad Fairy

Because of people's nature and experiences, the bad faces of elves and fairies are sometimes perceived as having more forms and aspects than the good faces. In reality, the good, the bad, and the indifferent usually balance themselves. Here are some examples of some of the so-called "bad" elves and fairies. (The term *bad* is used loosely and is only from the human perception.)

Bad fairies are usually unpleasant, often ugly, and generally destructive. Just before they appear, you may sense a foreboding or feel the hairs on your neck stand up. Sometimes bad fairies appear as beautiful good fairies. But once they speak or act, you will know immediately that something is wrong.

- **Boggarts**—Possessing the opposite temperament of brownies, boggarts are ill-tempered, mischievous practical jokers who love to break things. Living in old homes, they are known to pull covers off people when they are sleeping, rearrange the furniture, and knock on the door or ring the telephone at odd hours with no one there. If you let them, they will slowly but surely drive you crazy in little ways that continually disrupt your life. When a boggart enters your life, it's time to seek some kind of protection to rid yourself of it (which I'll discuss in a few pages).

- **Sirens**—With their beautiful voices, sirens lure sailors into their watery depths only to be drowned. From afar you see their beautiful green eyes and their bodies, naked except for their coral and seashell necklaces. As they move closer, the sirens become hideous women with eagle's bodies and claws, with long fishlike tails covered with scales. They are also known to foretell the future and to sing songs warning of bad weather to those they like, which are few. They can shape shift into either a bird or a fish, depending on their needs. As with trolls, sirens do not like the fire element.

- **Trolls**—In Scandinavian mythology, trolls were powerful fairies. Through time they became a magical race and were a cross between dwarves and giants. They are very unfriendly, and if tampered with they can be downright deadly, like a hive of hornets. They can run faster than all humans, but at the same time, exposure to sunlight turns them to stone.

> **CAUTION   On Guard!**
>
> Like a bean nighe, a banshee is a fairy woman who groans and screams. Banshees are a sign that something bad will befall a household. Seeing, hearing, or dreaming of a banshee is a very bad sign, most often a portent of death.

Attracting Good Elves and Fairies

Probably the first question you need to ask yourself is, "Do you want to attract elves and fairies into your life?" If the answer is yes, then the next question becomes, "Why?" There are many good reasons for wanting to attract this energy into your life and an equally long list of reasons for avoiding this energy all together, particularly after reading the list of bad elves and fairies.

Some of the reasons you might want to attract helpful elves and fairies are:

- To help you grow plants, flowers, and trees in your yard, garden, and home, as well as help you draw wildlife to your area

- To show you how to gather and direct elemental nature energies and use them to benefit the greater good

- To bring a little childlike whimsy, magic, brightness, humor, and playful mischief into your life during the holidays (and every day!)

- To protect you and your loved ones from negative energies such as bad fairies, negative people, and negative thoughts

- To help you attain your personal and professional goals

- To help you better understand your ancestral connections and proclivities

- To help you expand your psychic abilities and intuition

- To create a heightened spiritual connection with the divine mother, Mother Nature, that sacred feminine energy that is the mother of us all, whether we are human, elf, or fairy

Some of the reasons you want to avoid attracting bad fairies and elves are …

- They generally create chaos in your life and make everything go wrong!

- They disrupt and destroy all of your goals and dreams.

- They will give you nightmares; tempt you; entice you into darkness, depression, and evil; and will harm, maim, and kill you and those you love.

> **" " Through the Ages**
>
> Irish poet W. B. Yeats described one of the greatest appeals to elves and fairies when he wrote, "Come fairies take me out of this dull world, for I would ride with you upon the wind and dance upon the mountains like a flame."

You don't even want to go there, not even for a split second!

If you decide you want to attract the energy of elves and fairies, you need to decide what kinds you want to attract into your life. As with any magic, the idea is to be as specific as possible. Being too general leaves you open to attracting the wrong kind of energy, such as a boggart instead of a brownie. Then, instead of getting help around the house and yard, you get an energy that's trying to add to your problems.

Elves and fairies are nature spirits, and as such have a vested interest in what happens to the natural environment. Because of this, it is very important when attracting elves and fairies to be respectful of both them and nature. When out walking around in their habitats, be careful not to disturb the natural surroundings. By respecting nature, you are taking a big step toward attracting elves and fairies into your world.

After you have decided what kinds of elves and fairies you want to attract into your life, you should begin learning what these fairies like and dislike. Knowing the proper protocol and learning about their ways will help you attract good elves and fairies. It also helps you to stay on their good side, and keep them helping rather than hindering you.

Methods for Attracting These Magical Beings

Overall, elves and fairies prefer to be called "the good people," "the good folk," or "the gentry." They like to initiate contact with humans, and love gifts of fresh bits of food and drink. They also like music, dancing, and celebrations of almost any kind. With a little effort they are easy to please, and as such can be of a tremendous help in your endeavors, no matter what they are.

Besides creating a fairy ring as described in Chapter 6, you can plant a fairy garden. This creates an environment that fairies can frequent. Any garden that attracts hummingbirds, butterflies, and dragonflies is a place that elves and fairies will like. The idea is to plant lots of flowers and to create habitats where the fairies will feel at home. Full instructions for planting a fairy garden are given in Chapter 20.

> **Fairy Tales and Legends**
>
> You can attract a selkie by shedding seven sincere tears into the sea, where magically he or she will appear and please you. If you take a selkie's seal skin, then he or she must remain with you as your husband or wife.

When you harvest your vegetable garden, elves and fairies like to be rewarded for their efforts in the process. Fairies are believed to control crops, including the ripening process. This is why the first and/or last piece of fruit is traditionally given to them as a gift.

You can leave your gifts of fruits, vegetables, nuts, berries, flowers, and the like on the plants and trees if you prefer. When doing this, say aloud that they are intended as heartfelt gifts to the helpful, friendly elves and fairies of earth, air, fire, and water. Or you can leave these natural gifts in small baskets, on platters, plates, or in bowls as offerings. Use your imagination when presenting your gifts; they represent your sincere efforts to communicate and work with the elves and fairies.

Magical Foods and Beverages

Elves and fairies like food and drink that is fresh. Don't try to give them something that is stale, because they will take it as an insult. After being left out all night for the fairies, food should not be eaten by humans or animals. Bury it the next day or put it in your compost pile. The food is said to have no substance left in it. The idea is that "the fairies extract the spiritual essence from food offered to them, leaving behind the grosser elements."

Some of the general foods and beverages that are favorites of elves and fairies include:

♦ **Fresh milk and butter.** Traditionally, any milk spilled on the ground or butter left on the knife after churning was given to the fairies. Their love of butter is so great that on May Day or Beltane, they are known to steal any butter left unattended by humans.

♦ **Fresh fruits, vegetables, breads, and cakes.** It is customary to reserve a piece of bread or cake for the fairies after it is baked. This is particularly true on days of celebration in their honor.

♦ **A good brew or mead.** This is particularly true during times of celebration. For an extensive listing of the elf and fairy foods and beverages, please see Chapter 21.

Protecting Yourself from Bad Elves and Fairies

Having someone or something energetically attack you can result in your feeling depleted and in time becoming ill. When this happens, it is important to protect yourself and stop the negative effects. Feeling energetically depleted and ill are two of the symptoms of being attacked by bad elves and fairies.

Some of the signs to let you know you are being psychically attacked include …

♦ Feeling sad and depressed all the time.

♦ Having a complete lack of energy and ambition.

♦ Feeling ill, particularly when around certain people or situations.

♦ Having frequent bad dreams and nightmares.

♦ Continually perceiving images of bad fairies.

♦ Feeling lost and out of control with your world and life.

On Guard!

Watch out, travelers! Pixies enjoy confusing travelers and helping them to become lost. Wearing your clothes inside out when traveling will protect you from this mischief.

After you become aware that you are being energetically attacked, it's important to do something about it before you start being pixilated to the point where it drives you crazy—little by little, bit by bit.

How to Stop from Being Pixilated

Pixilated means to be somewhat mentally off balance along with whimsical and be-mused. The word itself is a derivative of *pixie*, a kind of fairy known for its playful and mischievous ways. You know when your life starts behaving like a slapstick comedy, verging on tragedy (depending on your perspective) that maybe you are being pixilated. It can make you laugh, cry, or scream in frustration. Here are a few traditional methods for stopping the work of pixies before they become too ingrained in your life:

- On dark nights when you feel pursued by an energy that means you no good, go to a body of water such as a creek or stream and cross over it. The water protects you by stopping evil from crossing it.

- If you feel a fairy wind when walking, it is best to bless yourself lest you be swept away by a troop of fairies to the Otherworld. Their intention is not necessarily bad, but the effect is to move you off your path and deter you from what you are doing. A fairy wind stirs up unexpectedly, often when there is no apparent breeze. It feels warm, almost prickly, and other times cold like a winter's draft. The fairy wind sweeps swiftly across the land, often mysteriously toward you, even when you attempt to avoid it and go the other way. The best way to withstand the fairy wind is to stand perfectly still, take a deep breath, and say a simple prayer.

> **Fairy Tales and Legends**
>
> An old folk remedy instructs a mother to take some bindweed and place it burnt at the ends over her baby's cradle. This is said to render the magic of the bad fairies powerless over the child. It also protects the child from being kidnapped by bad fairies and a changling being put in the child's place.

- If you build on a fairy fort or trod (a fairy path), the outcome will be that your house will always be pixilated and in turmoil. (Remember the Irish fairy tale from earlier in this chapter?) The only solution to this problem is to build in a new location. Elves and fairies are often only too happy to show you a new, more suitable, location for your dwelling. The idea is to listen when advice is being given, whether it is wanted.

Basics of Magical Protection

When negative energy imprints your personal space or body, the idea is to remove it or balance it as soon as possible. If left alone, it will fester into something much more than what it was when it started. Within magic, there are a few basic methods that you can use to clear and protect your space.

Clearing your body and space of negative energy can be achieved in several different ways, including using sounds such as bells and drums, using crystals, and invoking the divine god and/or goddess. Traditionally, Christians used a cross as a mode of divine protection and pagans used the goddess. A traditional invocation would be either of the following:

> In the Lord's name, all evil and foulness be gone from this place.

or

> In the Lady's name, all evil and foulness be gone from this place.

Another method of protection is to imagine an energetic net that encircles you and your space. You can use trees, the roof of your house, and the stars in the night sky as ways of adding energy to a protective net. I'll often set up an energetic net with the intention of letting in good energy, but repelling negative energy, sending it back where it came from—usually at least ninefold.

You set up the protective net by imagining bright gleaming crystals on all the leaves on the trees, or the roof shingles or tiles, or the stars in the night sky. Next, imagine a net connecting all the crystal lights together into one gridlike network, like weaving a fabric of light. Say aloud that the crystal net of light repels all negative energy and protects you from bad fairies and any kind of psychic attack. Also state aloud that the crystal net of light allows all the positive, loving energies to pass through the net and flow into your life.

Crystals and gemstones are other great tools for protection. Different stones have inherent properties that can be programmed for more specific needs. When using stones, you can invoke elf and dwarf energies to make your protection even stronger. Please consult my *Pocket Guide to Gemstones and Crystals* (see Appendix A) for a listing of the magical and metaphysical qualities of each stone.

Create a simple protection grid with four clear quartz crystal points, each about the size of your finger. Before you position the stones, be sure to clear them by rinsing them in cool water for at least a minute, pointing the tip down as you do so. Next, hold each of the crystal points in between your hands and charge them with protective white light. (Or if you prefer, charge them with helpful elf and fairy energies, using the elements of earth, air, fire, and water. Just imagine that energy instead of or in addition to the white light.) Start charging the stone by imagining or feeling bright white light flowing out of your hands and forehead and flowing into the crystal. To reinforce the protective light with which you have imbued the stones, say a prayer for protection and divine guidance.

Position the crystals pointed outward, indoors around your home, at the north-, east-, south-, and west-most points. Strengthen the protective crystal energy by turning your mind toward the stones each day for a few minutes as you imagine filling them with more bright white, protective light. You can also add other gemstones and stones you find in nature to your grid to strengthen its power.

Wizardly Wisdom

Certain metals are used to repel bad elves and fairies. In general, elves and fairies don't like iron, steel, lead, or any metal that contains these alloys. The traditional way to keep bad fairies from harming you is to carry a nail in your pocket. But remember, carrying these metals on your person also keeps the good fairies and elves away.

Secret Name Technique for Protection

Personal or secret names have long been a source of magic for not only elves and fairies but humans as well. In terms of elves and fairies, each one has a common name, such as *leprechaun*, but in addition they also have individual or secret names. By knowing this name, you can make it so the magic of the elf or fairy has no effect on you. The classic fairy tale "Rumplestiltskin" is an example of this idea: The woman has to guess the fairy's name before the spell is broken and she is able to keep her firstborn child.

Not only does each elf and fairy have a secret name, every human has one. Secret names are powerful tools for protection. Just as knowing someone else's secret name renders his or her magic ineffective against you, having your own secret name that no one knows makes it so that the negative magic of others, such as bad fairies, can't get through your protective shield—no matter who they are, human or otherwise.

The following technique helps you find your secret name, and the second shows you how to use and protect this name. The first thing you need to do is discover your secret name. In many ways it's more a matter of remembering than anything else. Your secret name is your true name that transcends this lifetime, connecting you to the divine. For this reason, it's important to work with divine energy when trying to discover your secret name. Here are some things you can do to help this process:

- ◆ Declare your intentions to discover your secret name aloud to yourself. Do this at regular intervals during the day, such as when you wake up, when you take a break from what you're doing, and when you go to sleep.

- ◆ Give yourself the suggestion when you go to bed to remember your secret name in your dreams.

- ◆ Every morning when you get up, give yourself a moment to remember your dreams and your secret name.

- ◆ Work with divine energies that you have a rapport with to help you in your efforts.

It might take a day, a week, or a month to discover your secret name. When you discover it, you should know in your heart that it is your true name. Use your intuition to make sure. There should be no doubt; otherwise, you need to go back to it until it does feel right.

When you discover your secret name, keep it to yourself and *never* tell anyone. Also, *never* write it down anywhere. If you tell others your secret name, you are magically giving them power over you. This would be very foolish, because you would also be doing away with your best tool for protection against the negative energy of others, including bad fairies.

Set up a fairy ring as described in Chapter 6. Afterward, sit down in the middle of the circle and begin by stating aloud all the names you have been known by in the past, and how these are not your true name. Repeat, "Only one name represents the true me, and that is my secret name." Next say your secret name aloud three times. Finish by saying:

> No one can ever harm me with any negative work of magic,
>
> Unless they discover my secret and true name;
>
> No one can use my secret and true name against me,
>
> Without first counting every elf and fairy in the cosmos
>
> Forward and backward, forever and a day.

Any time you feel like any elf, fairy, or person is energetically attacking you, draw your fairy ring and repeat these words as a way to reinforce the protection of your secret name.

The Least You Need to Know

♦ Elves and fairies often mirror the energy we give to them.

♦ Good elves and fairies can help in a number of ways.

♦ Bad fairies can be a portent of something going wrong.

♦ The best way to attract elves and fairies is to treat them with respect.

♦ Sometimes you have to energetically protect yourself from those who mean you harm.

Part 4

The Spiritual Aspects of Elves and Fairies

In this part, we look at the extraordinary and supernatural qualities of elves and fairies. You learn how the Celtic Tuatha De Danann traveled into the Otherworld and became the divine spirits of nature as well as gods and goddesses. We end with a sampling of elven and fairy magic rituals, meditations, and blessings. The spiritual world of elves and fairies blossoms with magical folk who are particularly talented at shape shifting, flying, and living immortal lives. Come then, and continue the adventure by entering this world and discovering the spiritual aspects of these enchanting beings.

Immortality and Supernatural Powers

In This Chapter

- A closer look at the similarities and differences between fairies and humans
- Shape shifting and other supernatural powers of elves and fairies
- Are elves and fairies immortal—or do they just live for a really long time?
- The mythical world of elves and fairies, whose names include Tir-na-n-Og

In the fairy tale "The King of the Golden River" or "The Black Brothers," written and then first published by John Ruskin in 1851, there is a place known as Treasure Valley that is blessed by the spirits of nature in that severe weather patterns always move away from the valley, and as such it is always fertile with plants and animals. The three Black Brothers live and prosper in Treasure Valley. The two older brothers, Schwartz and Hans, are greedy and ill-tempered, whereas the youngest, Gluck, is the opposite. When a nature spirit comes to visit in the form of an old man, Gluck welcomes him in, but when Schwartz and Hans return home, they throw him out. The old man warns them of their misdeed, but the two older brothers laugh it off. In the morning, they awaken to find Treasure Valley has been destroyed by a massive wind. On the kitchen table they find the old man's (nature spirit) card, which reads, "South West Wind Esquire."

This story shows the tremendous and extraordinary power that nature spirits can wield, in this case as the wind. Because elves and fairies are spirits of nature, it's only normal that they would have supernatural powers. As spirits of nature, elves and fairies are very much rooted in what's natural, but at the same time they take the concept of nature and move it a step further, giving rise to *super-nature* and the term *supernatural*. In this case, the word describes elves and fairies perfectly as they do indeed take nature to a higher level, particularly with respects to its spiritual aspects. These are some of the characteristics that make them different from humans.

What Makes Elves and Fairies Different Than Humans?

Originally elves, fairies, and humans were all stardust. We all come from the same cosmic source. As essence and spirit, we are the same, but our physical manifestations have through time become different from one another. We as humans have sought our meaning and substance in the physical and material world. Elves and fairies focused their energies on the magical world. These choices of worlds have made the separation between the fairies and humans much more pronounced, particularly as humans forlornly and foolishly encase themselves in more plastic, concrete, and steel.

Humans now rely on technology for magic. As such, the magical powers of humans have become much different than those of elves and fairies, who change shape at will, move through space in an instant and never seem to grow old. Humans by contrast resist most forms of change, rely on mechanical means for rapid movement, and are continually worried about their age and mortality.

In time, the world of mortals and the world of elves and fairies have become more separated. For a while, most people ignored the magical world of fairies by constantly telling themselves that it wasn't real. Scientists spent years trying to disprove the notions of magic, but no matter how hard they try, it keeps

> **Through the Ages**
>
> Poet William Butler Yeats gives his insights as to the differences between the fairy and human worlds: "The land of faery, Where nobody gets old and godly and grave, Where nobody gets old and crafty and wise, Where nobody gets old and bitter of tongue."

showing up again. This is because ultimately elves and fairies represent aspects that are both similar and different to mortals, and some of those differences are very extraordinary indeed!

In one way, elves and fairies are very humanlike: They like to celebrate, sing, dance, love, and eat good food, and for the most part they have a human appearance (eyes, head, arms, legs, ears, mouth, and so on). In another way, fairies and elves are beings that have extraordinary powers in terms of the human world. These powers are called by names such as *magic*, *enchantment*, and *glamour*.

Mythology and folklore abound with stories of elves and fairies teaching mortals the ways of magic. Through time, we have forgotten some of these magical ways, but fortunately the elves and fairies are still around to remind us of them—if we are open to listening. We sometimes get so absorbed in our own microcosmic world that we forget to stop and savor the beauty and majesty of nature. Elves and fairies are here to remind us of the magic that exists and to nudge us toward a more natural lifestyle.

Exploring the similarities and differences between elves and fairies and humans offers insights into the spiritual nature of everyone. After all, one of the explanations of elves and fairies is that they are manifestations of our spirituality and how it relates to nature. Almost like a psychological exercise, they allow us to work out our basic issues with our environment and ourselves. We can both confront and come to terms with those energies that give us the drive to continue our magical adventure in life.

Each sunrise is the beginning of a new and more magnificent chapter that unfolds with the turn of every page. The more experience you put into each chapter, the longer and more fulfilling the book that is your life seems. The depth of your experience comes through your senses—to see, to smell, to touch, to taste, to hear—and into what is called extrasensory perception. Each is a layer that adds more depth and meaning to the story of your life.

They're Like Us ...

Elves as described in both Norse mythology and J. R. R. Tolkien's *The Lord of the Rings* are very similar in appearance to humans. They also have many of the same needs as we do, including the need to love and be loved, and the need to move toward the light rather than the dark. This tendency to gravitate toward the light, to be optimistic, and to seek the positive is inherent. Ultimately humans and elves both want the same things; it's just that they have different ways of getting them.

Fairies, as you know, like to sing, dance, eat, drink, play games, and celebrate whenever they can. In many ways, this is much like mortals at their best. In their contented state, fairies symbolize humans having fun. When annoyed and feeling slighted, they symbolize humans at their most ill tempered. If treated with disrespect, they are like a scorned woman whose fury knows no end. Put a supernatural twist on that, and you can have an extremely dangerous fairy on your hands.

Like most mortals, elves and fairies prefer working in some way for their food and lodgings. They like to be acknowledged for the ways they help—around the house, in the garden, and bringing good fortune to the family. When you give them a piece of bread, a few berries, or a saucer of milk and honey, you are returning the favor.

> **Wizardly Wisdom**
>
> The Norse rune Gebo symbolizes the basic exchange in life in regard to giving and receiving. Written X, it represents two lines (the giver and the receiver) crossing at an in-between point that indicates both their exchange as well as their divine connection.

As previously mentioned, elves and fairies are mirrors in which humans can see themselves both at their best and their worst. At times, humans are so nice, to the point of being almost angelic; other times, humans can turn into mega-beasts. These polarities represent the dichotomy, and often paradoxical nature, of human existence. It gives us a source of constant anxiety and insanity while at the same time giving us a lot freedom to become anyone we want to be—as long as it doesn't go against what the fates have threaded into the fabric of our life. As usual, everything is double-sided and in deep need of balance.

... And Yet, They're Not

In the fairy tale "The Legend of Knockgrafton," a young man named Lusmore helps the fairies finish one of their songs, and as a reward, the fairies relieve him of the hump he had carried on his back since birth. In contrast, another young man named Jack Madden insults the fairies by being impatient and singing over their song. They punish Jack by giving him two humps, Lusmore's as well as his own.

Not only does this fairy tale show how elves and fairies reward those who they favor and show them due respect, it also shows how they can affect the physical form of mortals—in one case healing someone and in another adding to someone's diseased condition. Healing someone by taking the hump off his or her back is not a trait normally ascribed to humans, but in contrast, it is a supernatural characteristic attributed to elves and fairies. As a whole, their supernatural healing or harming powers are part of their extraordinary nature, and one of the things that make them very different from mortals.

As intermediaries between the divine and humans, elves and fairies move back and forth between the two worlds. From the perspective of mortals, elves and fairies appear to be immortal because they never seem to age. That is, they age so slowly that in human perception, they seem not to age at all. This contrasts with humans, who move through life as children, adults, and then seniors, also depicted as maid, mother, and crone, and son, father, and grand-father.

Fairy Tales and Legends

In the Irish tale "The Mountain Elf," the storyteller describes meeting what he calls "a wee boy," who was left by the fairies. He says, "This boy could do any-thing. He could go out and fly from one house to another, rise up and fly as far as he liked. He was seen here, and he was seen there, miles and miles away."

Besides healing people and seeming immortal, elves and fairies are known to move across great distances of space in a short amount of time and are able to shape shift, becoming any form they desire. Their ability to shape shift also includes changing the shape of others.

Superheroes and Their Special Powers

In the movie and television show *Star Gate*, characters use a circular gate to enter a wormhole—a kind of pathway through time and space—that can take them through great distances of space in an instant. Essentially this is a great analogy for the way elves and fairies move through space, but instead of moving through a technologically created wormhole, they move into the fairy realm and from there they can go any-where they want in the blink of eye.

The supernatural powers of elves and fairies come under the following categories:

♦ The ability to move quickly through space (flying)

♦ The ability to shape shift, including shifting people's state of wellness

♦ The ability to age slowly in the human world and be immortal in the fairy realm

The fairy realm exists beyond the borders of time and space and as such, time moves relatively much slower than it does in the human world. Like the mythical land of

Shangri La, no one who resides there grows old and dies. In addition, those who reside in the fairy realm are able to move anywhere on the earthly plane. In the flicker of a moment, they move across the globe from Tibet to North America. In addition, elves and fairies are said to have the ability to be in several locations simultaneously.

Shape shifting, as you know from earlier chapters, is the ability to change form at will—to appear as anything to anyone. Reality, with regard to form, is permeable, meaning that it can inherently change shape. Elves and fairies can change form just by thinking about it, just like you and I would by getting up and physically doing something. Mind produces thought, which is energy, and intention moves this energy from the magical into the physical realm.

Some smaller fairies such as skillywiddens do not have the power to shape shift, and others such as the eash uisge only shift into two different shapes—a young man or a horse. In contrast, brownies, boggarts, and hobgoblins are known as adept shape shifters. The coomlaen or elven steeds normally appear as tall, thin, white or silvery horses, but can take the shape of anything they desire. The only catch is that they have to return to their original shape of a horse once a day for at least six hours.

A Basic Shape-Shifting Exercise

Elves and fairies and trees have always gone hand in hand. For elves and fairies, trees are sacred. They embody the three worlds of subterranean (roots), Middle Earth (trunk), and celestial (branches and leaves). In this way, they are a bridge to the Otherworld of the fairies.

Your natural instincts and intention, together with your imagination, a living tree, and a magical fairy dryad help make the following exercise an empowering shape-shifting journey. If you like, enhance your experience by putting a few drops of the matching essential oil of the tree on a cotton ball, and breathing in its scent. For example, use pine essential oil if you sit next to a pine tree, cedar essential oil if next to a cedar, apricot oil if next to an apricot tree, and so forth. If you select a bay tree, pick a couple of the less than perfect leaves, tear them slightly, and inhale their fragrance.

The purpose of this exercise is twofold: First, it empowers you by connecting you to the energy and spirits of trees, some of the longest-living entities on this planet. Second, it lets you experience what it's like to shape shift—a power that elves and fairies possess. Overall, it lets you sense what it's like to be an elf or fairy.

1. While outdoors in nature, somewhere you will be undisturbed for a few minutes, sit by a favorite tree or one you feel a connection to. Select a tree you like the look and feel of, one you admire in some way, one that seems to have a special spirit or energy within it.

2. Gently rest your back against the tree and get as comfortable as possible. Notice the environment around you, the plants, animals, sounds, and other sensations.

3. Take a deep breath in and fill your lungs with fresh air and exhale completely. Do this a few times to relax and center your awareness.

4. Now imagine breathing in white light for a few breaths. As you breathe in, say, "I am the tree." As you breathe out, say, "The tree is me." Continue doing this for a few minutes.

5. Imagine becoming one with the energy, the fairy spirit or dryad of the tree. Extend your mind a little more and shape shift into the tree itself. Become its roots, and feel their strength and power and the cool earth all around you.

6. Take a few more slow, deep breaths, and imagine becoming one with the tree trunk, standing tall through time and the seasons. Continue taking deep, complete breaths, and imagine shape shifting into the tree branches and leaves, your arms reaching out to the heavens.

7. Take another slow, deep breath in and out, and allow the light, power, and wisdom of the tree and its magical fairy dryad to fill you completely.

8. After a few minutes, slowly stand up, and kindly thank the fairy dryad of the tree.

Elves and Fairies as Immortal Beings

In *The Lord of the Rings*, the elven princess Arwen decides to be with her true love Aragorn, and in doing so gives up her immortality. Because she chose to live as the bride of a human, she would live in the human world and suffer the eventual fate of all mortals—death.

This story splendidly depicts the relationship of elves and fairies to immortality. As long as they stay in the fairy realm, they remain young and never age, but once they move into the human world, the aging process slowly begins. But even in this mortal world, fairies don't age as quickly as humans, and often when they reach a certain age, they move permanently into the fairy realm. This allows them to suspend the aging process and become immortal.

The reason that elves and fairies move into the mortal world in the first place is because their interaction with our world moves them forward spiritually, while at the same time moving us forward. We make them aware of their extraordinary abilities, and they make us aware of our environment, in terms of both nature and magic. As with Arwen and Aragorn, sometimes elves and fairies fall in love with a human and choose to stay in the mortal world.

Fairy Tales and Legends

The seven-pointed star is known as an elven or fairy star. Each point represents the seven stars of the Pleiadean Star System, known in mythology as the seven sisters, who were the center of the universe, living in the land of immortality and the home of the divine.

In Andrew Lang's *Crimson Fairy Book* (Dover Publications, 1966), there is a tale entitled "The Prince Who Would Seek Immortality" that speaks of the relativity of time, particularly with respect to elves and fairies. In the story, a young prince sets out for the "land of immortality," and in the process encounters an eagle who is tearing down a giant tree. When the prince arrives, the eagle shape shifts into a king, who offers to let the prince live in his kingdom, where no one can die until the tree is completely torn down—a task that will take at least six hundred years. Telling the king that six hundred years is not immortality, the prince moves on to the next place.

Next the prince meets a man who is digging up the top of a mountain. The man implores him to stay in his kingdom, where no one can die until the entire mountain is dug up—a task that will take eight hundred years. As before, the prince turns him down and continues his search for the land of immortality.

The prince then meets a young woman who has just become queen. She asks him to stay, telling him that no one in her kingdom can die until she has used a whole roomful of needles in sewing—a task that will take a thousand years. Once again, the prince declines and continues his adventure.

In the end, the prince does indeed find the land of immortality, where he marries the queen and lives there for eternity. At some point during his stay, he wants to venture back out into the mortal world. Before he leaves, the queen gives him the power to bring things back to life. As the prince travels back through the world he meets each of the three people. The tree has been torn down, the mountain dug up, and all the sewing needles have been used. He brings them all back to life before returning to his queen and the land of immortality.

The story is an interesting metaphor that again depicts the relationship of elves and fairies to immortality. In the mortal world, some of them live to be six hundred years, others eight hundred years, and others still a thousand. Although these are all a long time, they are ultimately not immortality.

Both this story and the sequence from *The Lord of the Rings* show the fragile balance that elves and fairies maintain when they move between and exist in both the mortal and immortal worlds. Although a reflection of one another and at times quite close together, the two worlds are very different in terms of the dimension of time. The human or mortal world experiences time in a linear way, meaning everything moves from point *a* to point *b* to point *c*, and so forth.

In the fairy realm linear time doesn't exist, but instead everything exists simultaneously. Because of this there is no linear movement of time, meaning that things don't age because they are continually in the state of the perpetual now. In this state, there is no past or future, only the experience that is happening to you right now.

From Other Worlds They Come

Folklore, mythology, and literature have given a variety of names to the fairy realm. Some of these names include the Otherworld, the "other side," alfheim, Avalon, the Land of the Blessed, and Tir-na-n-Og. Though it has several different names, ultimately all of these refer to the same basic place. It is the land of immortality and home of the divine. It's a place where everyone is forever healthy and happy.

Within Celtic mythology, Tir-na-n-Og is the home of the gods and goddesses, and as such, is the divine land of immortality. Its name means "country of the young," a reference to the fact that age and death have no power there.

Known in folk tales and mythology as the realm of the fairies, Tir-na-n-Og is also the divine world of the goddesses and gods and the place where both King Arthur and Merlin the wizard went when they died. It is a mystical place hidden within the misty veils of time and space, a place where the dead go to become immortal and the immortal go to become divine.

Fairy Tales and Legends

The only mortal known to have gone to Tir-na-n-Og is the bard Oisin, who rode there with his fairy Niamh on a white horse that moved on the surface of the foam brought by the waves as they stroked the sandy shore. He lived there for three hundred years, at which time he returned to the mortal world searching for his friends, who had all long since died. When he touched the shores of the mortal world, he, too, turned old and showed his true age.

In its more modern incarnation as Heaven, Tir-na-n-Og is a place where all the spirits of the good go when they pass away from this mortal world. As in the Celtic scenario, it is a place where the divine dwells and stays eternally youthful.

Elves and fairies have the innate ability to move from world to world with great ease. It is one of the powers that make them distinct from humans, who have a tendency to dig in and stay in the same place unless there is a stick with a carrot on it waving in front of their face. Humans are always trying to find patterns that work and then exclusively use these patterns to move throughout the world. Elves and fairies often use their supernatural powers to help break us free of these culturally imposed shackles.

This is one of the major ingredients in spiritual development; moving beyond your social conditioning and pushing the magic envelope. Our social conditioning is what makes us act the way we do, which is sometimes good and sometimes bad when it comes to elves and fairies. The time when it's bad is when we can't seem to move beyond our conditioned minds. We are taught at an early age that such things don't exist, and that those who believe in them are somehow crazy or "pixilated." The idea is to learn and move forward beyond your social conditioning.

The Least You Need to Know

- Elves and fairies have needs that are similar to humans, but their extraordinary powers make them different than humans.

- Elves and fairies have the supernatural powers to move rapidly through space and shape shift into any form at will.

- Elves and fairies are immortal as long as they stay in the fairy realm.

- The fairy realm is called by many names, including the Otherworld, Avalon, the Land of the Blessed, and Tir-na-n-Og.

- Tir-na-n-Og means "country of the young" and is the divine home of the gods and goddesses.

Chapter 14

A Treasure Trove of Myth from Ireland and Britain

In This Chapter

- ◆ A glimpse into the mythical and magical history of Ireland
- ◆ The four magical objects brought by the Tuatha De Danann
- ◆ The magical legends surrounding King Arthur
- ◆ The ongoing battle between light and darkness
- ◆ How elves and fairies can help you connect with your innate divinity

When you learn about the history of Ireland, filled with its mythical and magical wonder, then you begin to understand how the traditions of elves and fairies flourished there in the past as well as they still do today. The history of the British Isles, complete with the stories of King Arthur and Merlin the wizard, provides clues as to why elves and fairies are so prevalent in these regions.

Sit back and enjoy as your adventure leads you through the many mythical invasions of Ireland. Learn how fairy encounters can help you to realize your innate connection to the divine.

Brief History of Ancient Ireland

Because of their location as islands on the western coast of Europe, Ireland and Britain have been subject to a series of invasions. In the history of Ireland, these invasions take on a mythical quality. This becomes immediately evident when you learn the first invaders were the Cesair, who were descended from the daughter of Bith who was a son of Noah, the mythical Hebrew character associated with the Ark and flooding of the Earth. Myths tell of how Bith built his own ark with his two companions Fintan and Ladra, and after sailing around for seven years came upon the shores of Ireland. In the story, Fintan is the only one of them to survive the flood, which he does by shape shifting into a salmon, thus beginning a long tradition of magical elf and fairy lore.

The major invaders of Ireland are as follows:

◆ The Cesair—The descendents of Noah came to Ireland via Egypt.

◆ The Partholon and Nemed—They were both descendents of Magog, son of Japhet, who was another of Noah's sons. Magog was the grandson of Noah. When the Partholon and Nemed invaded, they encountered fierce resistance from the Formorii, mythical undersea dwellers who are usually portrayed as dark and sinister. After the war, the Partholon and Nemed did not stay in Ireland.

◆ The Fir Bolg—These Nemedian survivors returned to Ireland after traveling to Greece, where they had been enslaved and made to carry earth in bags (Fir Bolg means "men of the bags"). According to mythological accounts, they were the first inhabitants of Ireland, and were by today's standards giants.

◆ The Tuatha De Danann—They came from the fabled northernmost isles, north of Greece. Some say they came from Hyperborea. When they invaded Ireland, the Tuatha De Danann came down from the sky on May Day, and defeated the Fir Bolg, who fled to the Aran Islands. Their name means "Tribe (People) of Danu or Anu," a Mother Goddess whose roots extend into the fertile Danube area of modern-day Germany. This is a place that many of the Germanic tribes, including the Celts and Norse, migrated to and resided in.

◆ The Milesians—Known as the "Sons of Mil Espane," they came from Spain. Ancestors of the Gaels, they defeated the Tuatha De Danann in several major battles. They set the stage for the Celtic tribes and the magic of the druids. It is at this time that the extraordinary Tuatha De Danann merged with the land.

This succession of invasions brought with it a tradition that was continually connected to mythology and magic. The first two groups of invaders had blood ties to Noah, who in biblical terms had one degree of separation to communicating with God. The Fir Bolg became both the giants of mythology as well as a type of fairy. The original members of the Tuatha De Danann and the Milesians became associated with the shapes and forms of the countryside as well as with different types of fairies. In particular the bean nighe, ominous fairies of portent, have lineage descended from the original Sons of Mil.

The Tuatha De Danann and Milesians began the tribal traditions that then carried through Irish history. The word *tuatha* means "tribe" or "people," and throughout Ireland there came to be several different tuathas; for example, the bardic Tuatha De Kerridwen. Each tuatha had its own mythical fairy queens, kings, and magical ways of doing things. Besides this, each tribe began to spawn a magical tradition whose priests, known as *druids*, were shamans of nature and learned in the ancient art and craft of magic.

Magical Meaning

Druids were priests of nature who were knowledgeable in the ways of magic, including being masters of invisibility and shape shifting. They were also herbalists, bards, and officials within the tribes. Druids often advised the tribal leaders (queens and kings), and acted as their emissaries to the Otherworld.

One of the most notable druids was Merlin (Myrddin), who advised King Arthur and acted as his mediator between the Otherworld and this world. He is credited with many uncanny prophecies, and helped with some of Arthur's successes, such as making all the tents of Arthur's adversaries fall down at the same time, thus enabling Arthur to seize control during the resulting melee.

Not only did the druids plant and harvest the magical traditions of fairies, but they also seeded the many Celtic traditions that continue into the modern era. Certain personages have become elevated to a higher and sometimes divine status, as with Japhet, the son of Noah, who has roots to both the Partholon and the Nemed. Later on, Magog, the grandson of Noah, became divine within Celtic and fairy spiritual traditions as a god in his own right.

Into the Hills They Go

When the people of the Tuatha De Danann moved or merged into the hills, they transmigrated from the physical to the spiritual. Their essence imprinted every rock, stream, tree, and plant within the countryside. Like all living things, they did not die, but instead became transformed from the experience, propelling them into a higher state of being, into light.

Everything about the Tuatha De Danann has a mythical and magical quality to it, beginning with their arrival. Legend has it that they landed in Connaught on May Day, sailing ships in the sky. They brought a mist with them that is said to have blotted out the sun for three days while they took Ireland from the Fir Bolg with their magic.

The Book of Invasions says about the Tuatha De Danann, "Their intelligence and skills make it likely that they came from the heavens." With them they brought knowledge of science and magic that exceeded the previous inhabitants. They brought the druids, the priests of nature, who moved between this world and the Otherworld. (Ireland was invaded by successive Celtic tribes. The details are found in *Leabhar Gabhála* or *Lebor Gabala Erren*, translated in English as the "Book of Conquests" or the "Book of Invasions of Ireland.")

> **Through the Ages**
>
> Beginning with Nuada, the kings of the Tuatha De Danann ruled from Tara. In her *Dictionary of Celtic Myth and Legend* (Thames and Hudson, 1992), Miranda Green writes, "The high kings of Ireland were also frequently called 'King of Tara,' the sacred stronghold situated in the middle of the five provinces. On the feast of Samhain, they all gathered for fairs, markets, horse races, and agricultural rites."

In addition, the Tuatha De Danann brought four magical objects with them when they came to the shores of Ireland:

- Cauldron of Dagda or Inexhaustible Cauldron of Plenty—Dagda was also one of the great kings of the Tuatha De Danann who later became a Celtic god. Also known as the Cauldron of Rebirth, it came from Murias and had the magical power to feed an army, heal the sick, and bring the dead back to life. Legend says that only a righteous person could benefit from its powers.

- Spear of Lugh—It was forged by the smith of Falias for Lugh, one of the original great kings of the Tuatha De Danann and later a Celtic god. Sometimes referred to as the victory lance (and in some stories it is a slingshot), it came from Gorias and had the magical power to be victorious in battle and make its owner invincible.

- Stone of Fal (Lea Fail) or Stone of Destiny—It came from Falias to a location near the Hill of Tara. It magically keeps Ireland above the waves, and when a true king of Ireland touches it, the stone shouts out to tell everyone.

◆ Sword of Nuada or Infallible Sword of Light—Nuada was the original king of the Tuatha De Danann. The sword, whose name was Fragarach (The Answerer), came from Findias, and when it was magically drawn from its sheath, no one escaped from or resisted its blade.

Just as their original appearance in Ireland had been both mythical and magical, so was the Tuatha De Danann's exit. When they were defeated by the Milesians, they deprived the Gaels of corn and milk, and used this as bargaining power. The Tuatha De Danann and the Milesians agreed to separate Ireland into two halves: the upper half and the lower half. The Milesians took the upper half and the Tuatha De Danann took the lower half, which was a magical mirror to the upper world. This is the Otherworld of the fairy. Upon their defeat by the Milesians, they wove a permanent veil of invisibility. This divided Ireland into two worlds—the seen (ordinary) and the unseen (magical). When they moved into the hills, they became the spirits that inhabited the various aspects of nature. They moved into the Otherworld or fairy realm, where they remain to this day.

So what became of the Tuatha De Danann? In terms of mythology and legend, the Tuatha were magical beings who were described as descending from the heavens. Essentially they came from the magical world of spirit, and when the Tuatha left, they moved back into the spirit world. But when they moved back into the spirit, they kept their love and energetic connection to the earth. They did this to the point where their spirit became one with the spirit of the earth.

The different members of the Tuatha De Danann spread throughout Ireland, and in time they became the many spirits and aspects of nature that now inhabit every dale, glen, meadow, valley, hill, mountain, and forest land. The various members of the Tuatha De Danann inhabited the different regions and counties of Ireland. In time, they became fairy queens and kings who are still celebrated today.

On a spiritual level, the Tuatha De Danann's invasion, lives, and merging with the land represents the metaphoric transition of the soul from the physical to the spiritual. When people die, their being moves from the physical world to the world of spirit. In the philosophy of the ancient Irish, the soul of a person then becomes part of the land. In time the land is enlivened with the energies of your ancestors. This includes every tree, rock, hill, spring, and creek.

After this ancestral energy becomes part of the land, it can be called upon and used by future generations. This energy continued with the Tuatha De Danann, whose members became divine energies of nature that could be called upon in times of need, and

Magical Meaning

The **sleeping king** is a familiar theme in mythology and fairy tales. It involves a king who, when he is defeated or dying, merges with the land. Sometimes the place where this happens becomes a mountain or hill, where the spirit of the king waits to be called in times of need by future generations.

continued on to the later kings of Ireland and England. Irish kings include Finn mac Cumhaill and Conchobar mac Nessa, whereas the most renowned English king is Arthur, hero of Camelot and the mythical round table. King Arthur is the classic example of the *sleeping king*, a common motif in folk tales and mythology.

Myth and Magic of King Arthur

The son of Uther Pendragon, Arthur was a prince of one of the tribes of Britons known as the Silures, who occupied the land around South Wales. He rose to the level of Pendragonship, meaning "of dragon blood," and he ruled over the many kings of Britain. In that role, he is credited with twelve victories over the Saxons, who after the Battle of Badon, ceased to be a problem to the Britons. There were twenty years of peace that were broken by the revolt of Arthur's nephew, Modred. At the battle of Camlan in Cornwall, Modred was slain and Arthur mortally wounded.

As with the Tuatha De Danann, the fairy tales and legends surrounding King Arthur have a mythical and magical quality to them. One of them involves his sword Escalibore (Excalibur). Legend has it that after a religious ceremony, the bishop asked for a divine sign. Afterward, on the front door of the church, they found a stone with a sword stuck in it. On the hilt of the stone read the words, "I am hight Escalibore, Unto a king fair tresore (treasure)." The people took it as the divine sign they had been looking for, and each nobleman and knight took up the challenge to pull the sword from the stone. Looking for a sword for Sir Kay to use in a tournament, Arthur pulled the sword from the stone and became the true king of England. This compares to the Tuatha De Danann's magical Stone of Fal, which in its own right, proclaims the king of Ireland.

Another of the magical legends surrounding King Arthur has to do with his relationship with Merlin the wizard. Merlin was instrumental in helping Arthur become king, and then uses his magic to ensure Arthur's rule over Britain. This sets the stage for the mythical tale of Camelot, where knights were "all for one, one for all."

In particular, Merlin is said to have had a fairy mother, and so came about his magical abilities quite naturally. He was a master of animals and a shape shifter. Two of

Merlin's students were Morgan le Fay and Vivian. Both later became living symbols of the sleeping queens or priestesses. Like the sleeping kings, their energy could be called on in times of need. Morgan le Fay and Vivian are associated with the fairies and the power of the land. Like the members of the Tuatha De Danann, they eventually became elevated to Celtic goddess status.

Fairy Tales and Legends

Many legends exist regarding the sleeping kings such as King Arthur. One such legend is about the Germanic Emperor Frederick Barbarossa and how he sleeps inside Kyffheuser Mountain, where he sits on a bench at a round stone table, asleep with his head in his hands. One legend says that his beard has grown so long that it encircles the table twice. When it grows so that it reaches around three times, he will awaken. In another tale, a dwarf led a shepherd into the mountain, and after the shepherd played a beautiful tune for the sleeping king, he awoke to ask, "Are ravens still flying around the mountain?" When the shepherd answered "yes," the king responded, "Then I must sleep for another hundred years."

When King Arthur is mortally wounded after his battle with Modred, Morgan le Fay, Vivian (also known as the "Lady of the Lake"), and the queen of North Galis, take him to the Isle of Avalon. Another name for the Otherworld paradise and fairy realm is the Land of Apples. King Arthur is taken there to be healed by the magic of the fairies so that he might once again be ready to carry on the fight against darkness. The inscription on King Arthur's tomb reportedly reads, "Here Arthur lies, King once and King to be."

The Battle for Middle Earth

In *The Lord of the Rings*, the members of the magical world and the human world fight side-by-side to defeat the forces of darkness. This battle between "light and dark" and "good and evil" is fought on many fronts. Middle Earth was the ancient Norse name in mythology for our sometimes wonderful, sometimes fragile and tragic, mortal human world. Sometimes we go out and are victorious in our fight against the orcs, trolls, and hobgoblins. And at other times they seem to make our life utter chaos and confusion. The idea is to keep your wits about you. That's the real magic!

For the Irish, the invasions continued on from the Milesians to the Norse, the Romans, and the Christians. The people preserved their spiritual heritage by practicing it in secret. The magical tradition preserved by the druids remained alive during the dark ages, when the forces of evil reigned supreme. Since then, the age (cycle) of light has begun again and we are all part of that progression. As such, it is the time of the good elf and fairy.

This battle between darkness and light is one that every spiritual tradition addresses and often is their primary theme. The struggle of these primary polarities happens on all levels and in all aspects of life. It happens in nature; it happens in groups of people; and it happens within each individual. Accordingly, this struggle carries out into the divine and fairyland as evidenced by good and bad goddesses and gods as well as good and bad elves and fairies.

Within mythology and fairy tales, the mortal world (Middle Earth) seems to be particularly the place where the battle between light and darkness is waged. Good elves and fairies continually help people who are good-hearted, creative, and in need. Bad elves and fairies like to throw barriers in people's way, disrupting their patterns and movement toward the light and compassion. Creating disruption and chaos is a common characteristic of the polarity of darkness. An example in popular culture is in the 2002 animated movie *Sinbad: Legend of the Seven Seas*, with Michelle Pfeiffer as the voice of the Goddess of Chaos, who hopes to steal the Book of Peace and send the world into perpetual war.

> **CAUTION**
>
> ## On Guard!
>
> In the battle for Middle Earth, evil and darkness are continually trying to create chaos and disruption to further their aims. When you feel the moment dissolving into chaos, it's time to sit back, relax, meditate, take a walk in nature, sing a song, listen to your favorite music, work out, dance, do a little gardening, or just collect your thoughts. The worst thing you can do is to give in to the darkness and get upset or angry.

Elves, fairies, and humans are ultimately engaged in the same battle between the forces of light and the forces of dark. It is a battle that affects every level of your being: body, mind, and spirit. Each time you go out in the world, you are forced to choose between the two opposing forces. Oftentimes they disguise themselves so it becomes harder to discern which one is light and which one is dark. You have to trust your intuition and what you know to be true within your heart and the energetic essence of your spirit. Trust your hunches—if something feels right in your heart, head, and spirit, then go with it, and if it doesn't feel right, then steer away from it, and find something that does feel right to you; find the things that bring light into your life.

On Becoming Divine

At the end of *The Lord of the Rings*, Frodo accepts the invitation of the elves and accompanies them on the ship sailing to the land of immortality. It is at this point in the story that Frodo moves from the mortal and human world to the world of the divine. As with the Tuatha De Danann, he makes the transition from the physical to the spiritual.

This parallels the progression of people and events as they move through the cycle from history to fable to mythical. It is at this point that people and events begin taking on magical qualities that transcend the everyday occurrences of the mortal world. When people reach the mythical level, they become divine energies that can be summoned when needed in the battle between light and dark.

At some point within our development as spiritual beings, we have to come to terms with and fully realize our divine self. Within Eastern traditions, this would be called enlightenment, a state of being where the polarity of darkness ceases to exist. It's all about the ongoing battle between good and evil, which at times seems highly overrated, particularly as you are trying to find a parking place in a crowded city garage five minutes before you're supposed to be at an important appointment. As Einstein said, "It's all relative."

> **Wizardly Wisdom**
>
> In Herman Hesse's *Siddhartha*, a retelling of the life of Buddha, the main character seeks meaning in many different physical ways without success. Eventually he achieves meaning and enlightenment when his spirit connects to the spirit of nature (the river) and they become one. Connecting with nature is one of the best ways to realize your divine self.

When we realize our divine self, then we finally become aware that each one us is a reflection of the divine light, just as the earth and moon reflect the light of the sun. The divine experience then is felt both outwardly, like when you go out to places in nature and encounter elves and fairies, and inwardly, where you become aware that you are completely at one with the divine. The divine is you, and you are the divine. The magic is within you! It has always been so.

Elves and fairies offer a way for you to get in touch with the divinity within. When you encounter one of these magical beings, you are connecting with something that instinctually moves from the physical to the spiritual. The contact propels your energetic self or spirit self into the Otherworld of elves and fairies. The experience makes you aware that you are more than just your physical self. At this point, it is a matter of following the stepping-stones leading you to your divine self. Suddenly your perception alters, and you begin sensing things with a second sight that enables you to see things in both the seen and unseen worlds. When this happens, elves and fairies abound and your adventure takes a magically enchanting turn.

The following magical meditation can help you get in touch with elf and fairy energy. The best place to do this elf and fairy encounter meditation is outdoors, in a spot you will not be disturbed. But you can also do this meditation while sitting in front of a window or on your balcony. If you like, before you meditate, turn on some soft, magical music to set the mood and help you relax even more.

1. Get as comfortable as you can, either sitting or reclining, and breathe in deeply and exhale completely.

2. Close your eyes and imagine breathing in a magical, warm, white light and breathing out bright white light. Do this several times.

3. Now imagine breathing in the magical green light of the fairies and elves, and then breathe out bright, emerald green light. Continue doing this for a few minutes to relax and center your awareness.

4. In your mind's eye, imagine encountering a friendly and playful fairy or elf. See and sense the magical being in front of you as clearly as you can. Use deep, complete breaths to help you imagine the fairy or elf in front of you in your mind's eye.

5. Respectfully and politely greet the fairy or elf. Do so from your heart. Kindly ask what the fairy or elf's name is. Make a mental note of his or her name.

6. Pay close attention and notice if the fairy or elf has a message or special gift for you. Allow your deep breathing to help you see and sense this experience even more clearly, more completely.

7. Thank the fairy or elf for his or her message or gift. Imagine breathing the magical, warm, white light in and out again. Do this for a few minutes, allowing the divine light to empower and magically refresh you from the tips of your toes to the top of your head. Know that you can visit with your magical friend any

time you like by simply closing your eyes, saying his or her name, and breathing deeply for a few minutes.

8. When you're ready, open your eyes, and come back to the present time and place. If you like, make a few notes about your meditation experience in your journal or a special fairy adventure notebook.

The Least You Need to Know

- The history of Ireland included a series of mythical invasions.
- The Tuatha De Danann brought four important magical objects with them.
- King Arthur is a sleeping king, waiting for the call to action.
- The powers of light and darkness battle for Middle Earth.
- Communing with elves and fairies helps you realize your divine self.

Chapter 15

The Empowerment of Nature

In This Chapter

- ◆ The cosmic tree of life and how it connects you with creation
- ◆ How elves and fairies repay kindness and punish contempt
- ◆ The karmic implications of our relationship with the earth
- ◆ Becoming whole again through nature

When the Tuatha De Dannan moved into nature they empowered it with the energy of their spirits. Being magical beings, the energy they imparted to the land had a magical quality to it. The beings of the Tuatha De Danann became the Irish and Celtic gods and goddesses. At the same time, this magical energy gave birth to a host of nature spirits. Being excellent shape shifters, these nature spirits can appear in any guise they choose, including the many varieties of elves and fairies.

One of the important things these nature spirits do is maintain the basic balance of nature. As elves and fairies, they act as instruments of karma in that those who respect and live in harmony with nature are rewarded, whereas those who defile and plunder nature are penalized for their actions. An example would be a garden. If you compost and fertilize it, the soil becomes rich and fertile, whereas if you grow things and never give anything back to the soil, it will eventually become barren and not grow much of anything. In the following chapter, we will learn the ways for creating and maintaining a harmonious relationship with nature as a whole as well as with individual elves and fairies.

Divine Creation

In the Danish fairy tale "The Tree of Health," three sons are left an apple orchard, where one of the trees bears the apples of health. The problem is that the sons don't know which tree bears the fruit. The two eldest brothers divide the orchard in half, leaving the youngest a single tree. They even own the land under this tree just in case it turns out to be the tree that grows the apples of health.

Soon thereafter, a call goes out through the land that the princess is gravely ill, and that her father the king is offering a reward of his daughter and half his kingdom to anyone who can heal her. The two older brothers gather up their apples and head for the castle of the king. On the way there, they each meet an old woman, who is secretly a fairy. She asks them what they have in their basket. The first brother replies, "Frogs and toads, if it's any business of yours!" The old woman responds, "Frogs and toads it is, and shall be." The second brother says, "Snakes and worms." And the old woman answers, "Snakes and worms it is, and shall be." When the two brothers reach the castle, they are turned away and whipped by the sentry for having frogs and toads and snakes and worms.

Fairy Tales and Legends
In folktales, when you've got apples, you know you've got magic! Apples are a magical food that has the power to heal. In "The Arabian Nights," Prince Ahmed possesses an apple that can cure any disease. Besides their curative association, apples are also linked with the Otherworld, immortality, divination, and the divine gift.

The younger brother gathers up several apples from his one tree, and heads for the castle. When he meets the fairy disguised as an old woman, and she asks what he has in his basket, he replies that he has apples of health. The fairy replies, "Apples of health it is, and shall be." On his way to the castle, the younger brother helps a fish, a swarm of bees, and a raven, and in return, they each say they will help the young man sometime in the future when he needs their help.

The young man arrives at the castle, and his apples do indeed save the princess's life. But instead of marrying him, she insists that her father put her suitor through several tests to prove his worthiness. In the first test, he must retrieve from the bottom of the sea a ring the king lost 24 years before. The young man performs the test by calling in his favor with the fish. In the second test, he must build a castle of wax that shines golden. This he does with the help of the swarm of bees. The third test involves bringing the three oldest coals of the underworld, which he does with the help of the raven. Finally the princess admits to being duly impressed by him and they are married and he receives half the kingdom.

This fairy tale has three basic concepts that are important in terms of elves and fairies and the empowerment of nature:

1. The tree is the source of cosmic order in the universe and the apple is a symbol of health.

2. Elves and fairies are often sources of instant karma in that humans get back when they give in the interaction.

3. Nature is magical and can be a powerful ally when humans gain favors from it.

Let's take a closer look at each.

The Tree of Life

Several spiritual traditions throughout the world allude to a "world tree" or "tree of life" that grows at the center of the universe. In its branches are the many worlds and levels of existence. Also called the "shaman's tree," the world tree is a great flowering tree that contains all knowledge. As the tree of life, it is forever green, flowering, and bearing fruit. When someone eats the fruit, he or she becomes immortal.

In Norse mythology, the world tree is a giant ash tree known as Yggdrasil.

It is the cosmic axis that holds each of the nine worlds, including that of the elves and dwarves. It is the tree of divine creation that has existed since the beginning of the universe. One of its roots is fed by Mimir's Well, the source of all wisdom and knowledge.

In Celtic traditions, the tree of life or "crann bethadh," as it is known in Ireland, is generally an apple tree. Its fruit represents a divine gift that brings good health and knowledge. Also known as the "mother tree," the tree of life represents the connection between the worlds because its roots descend down into the depths of the underworld and its branches rise up into the heavens.

Within this concept, trees overall are perceived as living, magical beings, who bestow blessings from the Otherworld. Because trees have their roots and branches in the lower and upper worlds of spirit, they are doorways into that realm. Legends speak of those who have entered the Otherworld by the door of a sacred tree. The thirteenth-century bard Thomas the Rhymer reportedly sat under an Eildon tree and the queen of Elfland took him away. The Eildon tree is another name for the hawthorn tree, a sacred tree of elves and fairies.

Love Your Mother

The second significant concept in "The Tree of Health" is the concept that elves and fairies mirror our own behavior back at us. In the story, the two older brothers were rude to the fairy as an old woman, and in return the fairy was rude back. In contrast, the younger brother was courteous and nice to the fairy, and she in turn was nice to him by making his wishes come true. His apples did indeed become the apples of health, as he so desired.

This idea that elves and fairies repay kindness with kindness and contempt with contempt is a common theme that is replayed over and over again in fairy tales. This is true in both "The Fairy" and "The Legend of Knockgrafton." In both cases the kind person is rewarded and the greedy person is thwarted in their attempts to gain favor among the fairies. And not only are they thwarted in their attempts to gain unwarranted riches, they are also ultimately punished for being nasty people.

In a sense, these encounters with elves and fairies have an air of *karma* about them, in particular *instant karma*. Karma is basically the idea that whatever actions you take in one lifetime have an effect on future lifetimes. In other words, if you act badly in one lifetime you might have to come back and atone for these actions, oftentimes with the same spirits in different guises and situations. Instant karma is when this effect takes place almost instantaneously in the same lifetime.

Magical Meanings _____

Karma is the basic idea that everything we do in life builds up either good or bad consequences, depending on our intentions and actions. Karma generally carries over from one lifetime to another, and in Eastern spiritual philosophies, such as Buddhism, it's a way for an individual to evolve as a spiritual being. **Instant karma** is when the result of your actions comes back to you very quickly within the same lifetime. Elves and fairies fit these criteria because they use magic, which has a tendency to change things quickly.

In Celtic and fairy traditions, the concept of the mother goddess is synonymous with the earth as a divine being. The spirit of the mother goddess lives within the soul of the earth as displayed by the many magically divine aspects of nature. In the spring her seed sprouts and she comes shooting out of her shell. In the summer her flowers, fruits, and other foods come alive with a vitality that sustains all life on the planet. In the fall her branches fill with the last of the year's harvest before generating the seeds necessary for the spring. In the winter her form looks brown and wrinkled against the backdrop of the ice and snow as her spirit hibernates, awaiting the return of spring when the warmth of the sun again germinates the seeds of life.

Nature spirits, such as elves and fairies, embody the many aspects of the mother goddess and, in turn, the many aspects of the earth. They become the trees, the hills, the rocks, the flowers, the rivers and streams, and everything else in nature. They also become the watchers and protectors of Mother Earth, because what is done to her is also done to them.

Returning to the idea that elves and fairies act toward humans in the same way humans act toward them opens the way to elves and fairies responding positively or negatively toward humans depending on how humans treat the earth. Again, the effect can be like instant karma in that certain actions can produce very immediate and sometimes extreme results that can be either positive or negative depending on the intentions and actions of humans toward nature.

This means that we as humans need to be loving and caring in our relationship with Mother Nature. As a result, she will also be more loving and caring toward us. The idea is to plant gardens and places that attract elves and fairies rather than create wastelands, where elves and fairies have moved out and have no immediate plans to return. We have to treat nature as the living spirit that it is. We need to make peace with the elves, fairies, and other magical nature spirits, and to learn to love our mother, the earth. The following is a fairy prayer for the earth to help with this process.

> CAUTION
>
> **On Guard!**
>
> People have the ability to do some very harmful things to nature, such as clear-cutting trees in the forests, polluting the waterways, depleting nutrients from the soil, and throwing trash everywhere. In these instances, Mother Nature responds by not providing food and a livable environment. If these abuses to Mother Nature continue, most likely people will be replaced by a more earth-friendly species.

Fairy Prayer for Mother Earth

This prayer can be done anyplace and anytime, but is best performed in a beautiful natural setting with either the rising or setting sun in the background. Wherever you decide to be, begin by taking several deep breaths. Use your thoughts combined with your inhalations to invite and bring the elf and fairy energy into your space.

Recite the following fairy prayer aloud three times, each time building the energy. When you have spoken the prayer the third time, raise your hands in the air and feel the energy being released. Afterward, resoundingly clap your hands three times. This sets the prayer in place.

> Divine Mother of creation
>
> You who are all things
>
> I join with the spirits of nature
>
> In seeking to nurture and heal the earth;
>
> Elves and fairies of the sacred land
>
> Come and take me by the hand
>
> Together we will plant our seeds
>
> So that love grows forever on the earth.

Magic All Around You

The third important concept arising out of "The Tree of Health" is that nature is magical and can be a powerful ally when humans gain its favor. In the story, the younger brother first helps a giant pike that has beached itself on the shore. Rather than let it die, he helps the fish back into the water and is given a favor in return for his kind deed. Second he comes upon a swarm of bees and a raven who are fighting one another. The young man succeeds in stopping the fight by convincing the bees and raven to go in separate directions. As a way of saying thanks, both the bees and the raven offer up a future favor.

As with most fairy tales, the animals in this story are magical and most likely elves and fairies in shape-shifting disguise. This becomes particularly evident later on in the story when the fish is able to go to the bottom of the sea and retrieve the king's ring, the bees build a beautiful golden castle made of beeswax, and the raven is able to go into the underworld and return with the three oldest coals. Obviously these are in no way ordinary animals by the fact they talk to humans and do magical things. Instead they are evidence of the magic that is inherent not only in the spirits of nature, but in all nature.

Fairy Tales and Legends

In the European fairy tale "The Language of Animals," a father sends his son Jack to school. When Jack returns home, his father asks, "Well, Jack, what have you learned at school?" Jack replies, "I know what dogs mean when they bark." Unimpressed, his father sends him back to school, and when he returns, asks him the same question. Jack answers, "Well, father, when frogs croak, I know what they mean." Again Jack is sent back to school, and the third time he is asked the question, he replies, "I know what all the birds say when they twitter and chirp, caw and coo, gobble and cluck." The father angrily sends Jack away, but in the end Jack's magical talents for talking with dogs, frogs, and birds helps him reap great rewards, save a princess, and eventually become Pope, at which point his father is finally impressed.

As the spirit of elves and fairies inhabit all the aspects of nature, they accordingly enliven all of these aspects with their magic. In this way, all of nature becomes magical. Everywhere you go magic abounds all around you—from the meadows covered with bright yellow mustard flowers and vibrant red tulips to creeks and streams whose picturesque waterfalls playfully spill down into pools, brimming with life in every imaginable form.

Elf and Fairy Energy in Nature

In Chapter 10, we looked at the many ways elf and fairy energy abounds in nature. Elves and fairies inhabit each of the four elements of nature—earth, air, fire, and water. Not only do they inhabit these elements, but they also bring them to life. When a water nymph parades her blue-green form lightly over the top of the water, you sense that the element of water has been brought to life. As you gaze into her eyes, you feel a fluidness and emotion that washes like a wave over your entire being. At this point, you have been touched by the elf and fairy energy in nature.

As shape shifters, elves and fairies can become anything they desire, a power they like to use to reward deserving humans, help the undeserving see the error of their ways,

Through the Ages

"Over hill, over dale,
Thorough bush, thorough brier,
Over park, over pale,
Thorough flood, thorough fire,
I do wander everywhere,
Swifter than the moon's sphere,
And I serve the fairy queen,
To dew her orbs upon the green,
The cowslips tall her pensioners be,
In their gold coats spots you see,
Those be rubies, fairy favours,
In those freckles live their
 savours."

—From *A Midsummer Night's Dream*, William Shakespeare

or in those few times when someone shows no re-deeming qualities, to punish. But punishing people is usually not their first choice. In the long run, elves and fairies are much more interested in helping people to connect with the energy of nature and helping to nurture and heal it.

The other thing they do as spirits of nature is help people discover who they really are as spiritually evolving beings who exist on many levels simultane-ously. Besides existing on a physical level, we have energetic aspects, such as our spiritual self. Our spiritual self has to do with our continually evolv-ing relationship with the divine. Because elves and fairies exist on a level somewhere between the physical and the divine, they are in a perfect position to help us with respect to our divine rela-tionship.

Becoming One with Nature

Originally we humans sprang from the same cosmic soup as the rest of creation, including the spirits of nature. At that time, we were connected to and one with nature. Many early mythological tales tell of a time when humans and animals could talk to one another and treated each other as equals. Humans could also see and talk to the spirits of nature, including elves and fairies.

Through the ages, we humans began separating ourselves from nature until soon there was very little of the ancient connection left. People began thinking they were smarter and better than nature. We started perceiving nature as primitive and the spirits of nature as the ridiculous fantasies of children. We saw ourselves not as being connected with nature, but as being apart and sometimes above it. Nature became something that we thought we could control and manipulate with our own will and greed. Eventually the chasm between humans and nature became great.

Now as we move into the twenty-first century, we have begun to re-examine our relationship with nature. We have come to realize that by separating ourselves from nature, we have also separated ourselves from an essential part of who we are. As a result, we have started to reconnect and become one with the energies of nature. In doing so, we are realizing that it helps us become whole again.

Nature Oneness Exercise

During this exercise you will go out in nature and practice becoming one with all the natural and magical aspects. Begin small and move up from there. Also, as you name each aspect, take the time to really become that aspect for a moment and sense what it feels. The following example is fitted for the forest, but you can adapt it to any natural surroundings by naming and becoming one with all of the things around you. The more times you do this exercise, the more you will become connected and one with the spirits and whole of nature. It's an exercise that can help you move forward with your own spiritual development.

Begin by finding a comfortable spot among the trees and grass. Breathe deeply for several moments. Each time you breathe in, imagine taking the natural energy inside your lungs and then moving it throughout your being. As you exhale, sense your awareness expanding outward from your physical being into the natural surroundings. While doing this, open your senses up to every smell, sound, sight, and sensation.

After a few deep breaths, begin repeating the following verse. If you need to, adapt it to your surroundings. The idea is to become one with everything around you. Move from each individual component of nature to the whole of nature.

I am the green grass; the green grass is me.

I am the dew drops on the grass; the dew drops are me.

I am the tree roots; the tree roots are me.

I am the tree trunk, the tree trunk is me.

I am the squirrel; the squirrel is me.

I am the rocks; the rocks are me.

I am the flowers; the flowers are me.

I am the branches of the tree; the branches are me.

I am the leaves of the tree; the leaves are me.

I am the whole tree; the whole tree is me.

I am the clouds; the clouds are me.

I am the blue sky; the blue sky is me.

I am the elves; the elves are me.

I am the fairies; the fairies are me.

I am the earth; the earth is me.

I am the cosmos; the cosmos is me.

I am oneness, oneness is me.

Discovering Your "Wild Side"

When you take the time to discover and connect with the spirits of nature, you open up a whole other area of your being. It's that part of you that likes to run barefoot through the grass on a summer's day, to stand beneath a waterfall and feel the cascading water rush down the length of your body, and to smell the fragrance of a Tropicana Rose as it fills your senses with an indescribable ecstasy that pales in comparison to anything you have experienced previously.

> **Wizardly Wisdom**
>
> The Aborigines' concept of Dreamtime has similarities to elves and fairies. Dreamtime refers to the time before memory when ancestral spirits roamed the earth and in the process formed its natural features. These ancestral spirits imbued each hill, rock, and other natural feature with their spirit. By meditating and connecting with these aspects of nature you become one with the energies of creation and oneness.

Many New Age and self-help books and workshops devote themselves to discovering and releasing your "wild side." This refers to the part of you that was around at the time of creation when humans and nature were connected as one. Sometimes referred to as the animal or primal part of you, but more appropriately, it is your "nature self," that part of you that is like elves and fairies.

By taking the time to explore and connect with the spirits of nature, you begin discovering layers of your being that you didn't previously know existed. Each animal and plant you encounter shows you a different part of your self. This is also true of the various kinds of elves and fairies. Sometimes you might feel like an elf—mostly friendly, helpful, and full of positive magic. Other times you might seem like a boggart—mostly unfriendly, disruptive, and full of negativity. Although these magical creatures seem like poles apart, they nonetheless represent various parts of who you are as a person. (I'll discuss this more in Chapter 23.)

By moving through the separation between humans and nature, you begin to reconnect with a part of your being that has recently seemed alien. You release your feelings and emotions from the box where you house them. You open your self up to a higher power that is in everything and everyone. No one is dispossessed and condemned, but instead they are enlivened and empowered to go into world and spread the seeds of their creation and existence. You become empowered by the energies of nature, and in turn they become empowered by you. The relationship is mutual and beneficial to both you and nature.

The Least You Need to Know

♦ The cosmic tree of life represents our connection with creation.

♦ Elves and fairies repay kindness with kindness and contempt with contempt.

♦ Our relationship with the Earth and nature has karmic implications.

♦ The spirits of nature are magical and everywhere around you.

♦ By spending time meditating on and experiencing the many aspects of nature, we become whole again.

Chapter 16

Elven and Fairy Magic Rituals, Meditations, and Blessings

In This Chapter

- ◆ Connect to elf and fairy energy using rituals, meditations, and blessings
- ◆ The power that can be generated when doing ritual
- ◆ How to perform some simple rituals, meditations, and blessings
- ◆ Getting in touch with the Otherworld

Mythologist Joseph Campbell describes ritual as the enactment of myth. What we act out in ritual is our mythical connection to the Otherworld. When we open the sacred circle, we open an energetic portal into the realm of gods and goddesses, elves and fairies.

As you'll discover in this chapter, rituals, meditations, and blessings offer a means for direct communication with these spiritual energies. In the process, we empower ourselves as well as the spirits of nature, no matter what form they take.

The Power of Rituals, Meditations, and Blessings

The power of rituals, meditations, and blessings comes from their ability to act as positive change-agents within life. They offer a way for focusing energy and directing it toward a specific intention. They also provide a means for enlisting the help of divine energies (such as gods and goddesses) and nature spirits (such as elves and fairies).

Rituals, meditations, and blessings give us an opportunity to create a sacred space, where we can go to practice our spirituality and to connect and be one with the whole of creation. They are methods that have been practiced since the dawn of humankind. In the words of Joseph Campbell, "The idea of a sacred space where the walls and laws of the temporal world dissolve to reveal wonder is apparently as old as the human race."

They let us connect to the spiritual side of our being. When we make this connection, magic starts happening on every level. We clear away the old patterns, changing in positive ways. The change comes from our intention to move our life in directions that are in alignment with our personal ideal of who we want to be. Rituals, meditations, and blessings help us realize this goal of making our dreams come true.

Divine Power of Rituals

Rituals are a systematic way of doing things. They are procedures that produce the results you desire. Besides being a forum for honoring the divine, rituals also provide a way for directing and influencing energy, in particular, the magical energies of the elves and fairies. Certain words and rhyming phrases, coupled with the basic steps of intention and expectation, desire, and merging can open the right windows and let the magic enter your life.

Through ritual you can fill each day with magic. You become much closer to the divine energies of the universe. When you perform a ritual, you call upon divine powers. This divine connection is the key to empowering communication and rapport with the elves and fairies.

Rituals use *focals*, such as candles and incense, to give sensual form to them. Wands, swords, chalices, candles, incense, crystals, and scented oils are all ritual focals that can be used to enhance your experience. Music is one of the most powerful focals. Use melody, rhythm, and song to empower your rituals.

Magical Meaning

Focals are items that give rituals more of a sensory focus. They include everything from ritual tools to music to aromas.

Focals add a sensual quality to rituals. Whether visual, auditory, kinesthetic, olfactory, or gustatory, they trigger your senses and help you focus more intently on the experience. They also add a sense of adventure and fun.

The Fairy Circle

The fairy circle acts as a bridge of light that ties the human and fairy worlds together into one. Each time you do a ritual, you need to first draw a fairy ring, as explained in Chapter 6. To create a fairy circle, sprinkle water from a cup or chalice clockwise all around the inside of the fairy ring. Then hold your *power hand* outward. You can use a fairy wand if you prefer. (For complete instructions on making or purchasing a fairy wand, please refer to my book *Faery Magick*; see Appendix A.) Face east, and slowly spin in a clockwise circle. As you do this imagine a bright, blue-white fairy light flowing from your hand and creating a circle of radiant light all around you. Trace a clockwise circle of bright, elven green light with your power hand, over the blue-white circle. Stand at the center of the light circles and say:

> May the helpful elves and fairies bright
>
> Bless this circle with their starry light.
>
> Blessed be! Evo-He!

Magical Meaning

Your **power hand** is the hand you use to direct energy or power. If you are right-handed, this is your right hand. (Your **receiving hand** is the hand you receive energy or power with. If you are right-handed, this is your left hand.)

The Seven Fairy Guardians

After you have created the fairy ring and magic circle, call the fairy guardians to protect the elemental gates of your sacred space. They are also called the Watchers; they watch the thresholds of the seven directions, and remain in place until you release them.

Stand at the center of your circle and face east. Ring the bell three times, raise your arms upward, and say:

> Star Finder, Fairy Watcher of the east,
>
> Guardian of the air, dawn, and knowledge,
>
> I now invite you into this circle.

Face south, ring the bell three times, raise your arms upward, and say:

> Shining Flame, Fairy Watcher of the south
>
> Guardian of fire, noon, and truth
>
> I now invite you into this circle.

Face west, ring the bell three times, raise your arms upward, and say:

> Water Maker, Fairy Watcher of the west
>
> Guardian of water, twilight, and love
>
> I now invite you into this circle.

Face north, ring the bell three times, and say:

> Black Mother, Fairy Watcher of the north
>
> Guardian of earth, midnight, and wisdom
>
> I now invite you into this circle.

Go to the center of the circle, ring the bell three times, raise your arms upward, and say:

> Heaven Shiner, Fire in the Earth, and Star Goddess,
>
> Fairy watchers and guardians
>
> Of above, below, and center
>
> I now invite you into this circle.
>
> Blessed be! Evo-He!

The fairy guardians are now in place.

The Little Fairy Gate

After you have called the fairy guardians into your circle, create a little fairy gate. This is an energetic gate through which you can enter and exit the fairy circle without disrupting its energy flow. Draw the energetic gate at the east point of your circle. If you prefer, draw the fairy gate at the actual doorway in the room for practical purposes. Use your power hand to trace the gate. When you need to exit and reenter your fairy circle, open and close the fairy gate with a sweeping motion of your power hand.

A Sampling of Rituals

Now that you have learned the basics for setting up a ritual, it's time to apply these concepts to a sampling of elven and fairy rituals. Included in the following sections is a ritual for finding your elven name, a holiday ritual, and an elvenstar rose ritual.

Elven Name Ritual

Names are chosen for the qualities they embody. Originally they were a pattern of sounds and symbols that had magical significance. To better understand the elves, I invite you to discover your own elven name.

The elves are powerful spirits of nature. They are the firstborn, also called the speakers, the elder (eldar) people, and the folk of the wood. They are the fairest of all earthly creatures and love the wonders of nature, especially the waters, woods, flowers, and stars. Their senses are much keener than those of humans, they can communicate telepathically, and their curiosity is insatiable. They don't necessarily sleep, but rather rest their minds in waking dreams.

Your elven name reveals something about you, something magical and mysterious. Use your elven name when doing rituals and working with the elves. In this way, your name's creative power will unfold within you. Some examples of traditional elven names are Eglantina (wild rose), Ellette (little elf), Titania (fairy queen), Alfred (elf friend), Aubrey (elf king), Dain (mythical dwarf), and Oberon (fairy king).

To discover your elven name, follow these steps:

1. Go outdoors on the night of a full moon and find a private spot where you can see the moon. If this isn't possible, sit next to a window where you can see the moon. Draw a fairy ring, a fairy circle, and call in the fairy guardians.

2. Stand, sit, or recline comfortably where you can see the luminous moon. Focus your awareness on the moon as you breathe in and out, deeply and completely. Say aloud:

   Moon of magical white light,

   Illuminate my elven name tonight.

3. Now imagine that you are breathing the bright white light of the moon and stars into your being. Breathe in light and imagine the light surrounding you. Keep focusing on the moon, and in your mind's eye imagine being in an old-growth forest with the magical elves. Say aloud three times:

   Folk of the wood, blessed be

   Please reveal my eleven name to me.

4. Visualize the bright light of the moon illuminating the forest and see your elven name shining in the night sky as you look up at the moon. Make a mental note of the name that comes to mind. Often it's a name that creates joy within you, seems somehow familiar, or gives you goose bumps. State your elven name aloud three times. Then say:

   May the grace of the elves

   Pass to me, blessed be!

5. When you are done with your ritual, bid farewell to the fairy guardians. Go to the center of the circle, ring the bell once, and say:

   Fairy Watchers of all directions

   I bid you farewell

   Please depart in peace and love

   Thank you for your presence.

   Ring the bell once more, and say:

   Blessed be! Evo-He!

6. Pull up your fairy circle and ring by facing east and holding your power hand outward. Slowly turn in a counterclockwise circle. As you do this, imagine the blue-white light of the circle being drawn back up into your hand. Then do the same thing with the green light circle. Scatter the flowers in the ring and erase the ring mark with your shoe or hand. Do this in a counterclockwise motion. When you are done, face center, ring the bell once, and say:

   Blessed be! Evo-He!

Merry Elf and Fairy Holiday Ritual

Green is the favorite color of the elves and fairies because it embodies the color of nature. The elves and the fairy nation of the Daoine Sidhe of Ireland all dress in green. And as you well know, green is one of the best colors for the holiday season. The other most popular color among the elves and fairies is red. And red is another perfect color for the holidays!

This ritual is designed to honor the elves and fairies by dressing in green and red. You will also create a special tree of silver and golden bells as an offering to the Yuletime elves and fairies such as Santa, as well as send a cone of white light greeting to fairyland. In this way, you are more apt to gain the rapport and favors of the merry elves and fairies.

You will need green and red clothes, some fun and uplifting holiday music, a small tree in a flowerpot, a spool of silver ribbon, and a package of 12 gold-colored bells.

1. Do this ritual at twilight 12 days before Yule (winter solstice) during the holiday season. Turn on some merry holiday music and get dressed in your green and red clothes. As you dress, chant:

   As I dress in red and green, may the merry elves and fairies bless me.

2. Draw a fairy ring (use acorns or small white stones to mark your ring), draw the fairy circle, and call in the fairy guardians. Put the tree in the center of your circle and decorate it. Tie a bell with a piece of ribbon. Ring the bell on the tied ribbon seven times. Fasten the ribbon and bell onto the tree. With each of the 12 bells and ribbons you ring and then tie onto the tree, repeat aloud:

   May the merry elves and fairies bless me.

3. When you are finished decorating the tree, hold your hands about an inch above the top of it, palms toward the tree, and become one with the tree for a few moments. Repeat three times:

   I am the tree. The tree is me. We are one.

4. As you take a deep breath, imagine breathing in bright, blue-white fairy light. As you exhale, imagine breathing out blue-white light for a minute or two. Now imagine breathing in bright, elven green light, and breathing out green light for a minute or two.

5. Extend your power hand over the tree, palm toward the tree's top. Imagine the tree being a direct communication link with the elves and fairies. See and sense a bright white light coming out of your power hand and filling and surrounding the decorated tree as if it were enveloped in a bright white cone of energy. Now move your power hand in a clockwise circle again and again, as if you are stirring up the white cone light into a swirling ball of energy. Continue doing this until the cone gathers intensity and brilliance. Now touch the cone of light with your mind. Feel it moving faster and faster, stronger and stronger, brighter and brighter.

6. Move the cone with your mind and intention upward into the heavens. Imagine sending the bright cone of light directly to the elves and fairies as a radiant, holiday greeting. As you do this, actually use your hands to throw the light into the heavens, and say a resounding, "GO!" This moves the light to where you want it to go. After you send the cone of light outward to the elves and fairies, clap your hands loudly three times.

7. When your ritual is complete, bid farewell to the fairy guardians by standing or sitting at the center of the circle, ringing the bell once, and saying:

Fairy Watchers of all directions

I bid you farewell.

Please depart in peace and love.

Thank you for your presence.

Ring the bell once more, and say:

Blessed be! Evo-He!

8. Pull up your fairy circle and ring. Face east and hold your power hand outward. Slowly turn in a counterclockwise circle. As you do this, imagine the blue-white light of the circle being drawn back up into your hand. Then do the same thing with the green light circle. Scatter the flowers in the ring. If you are doing this ritual outdoors, erase the ring mark with the heel of your shoe or with your hand. Do this in a counterclockwise motion. When you are done, face center, ring the bell once, and say:

Blessed be! Evo-He!

9. Put the decorated tree in a special spot outdoors where you will frequently gaze upon it during the holidays and throughout the year. Care for it well. This will draw the joyful and divine favors of the elves and fairies to you and your home.

Elvenstar Rose Ritual

The elvenstar or septagram is a star with seven points. The points represent the directions of east (air), south (fire), west (water), north (earth), plus above (the stars above us), below (the stars below us), and center (the spirit within). Seven is also the number of the visible colors of the rainbow, the seven basic body chakras, and the notes to a musical scale (do, re, mi, fa, so, la, ti).

Fairy Tales and Legends
In "The Medieval Chronicles," Ralph of Coggeshall tells the story of a boy and girl with green skin who were found near a pit in Saint Mary of the Wolf-Pit. They ate only green food and spoke in a foreign tongue. The boy died quickly, but the girl learned to talk and she spoke of a land very much like fairyland.

The fragrance of roses is a powerful fairy-attracting force. So bring the helpful rose fairies into your garden, and watch your daily life blossom with positive magic and joy. You will need a bell, a young rose bush, a shovel, and water for this ritual.

1. Do this ritual at noon during the spring or summer in your garden or yard, or you can use miniature roses and a large flowerpot and soil. Draw a fairy ring and circle around the area you are planting the rose bush in, and call in the fairy guardians.

2. Use a sharp rock or stick to draw a seven-pointed elvenstar in the ground (or top of the soil if using a flowerpot) where you are going to plant the rose bush. Ring the bell seven times. Use the shovel to dig a hole for the bush at the center of the elvenstar. Plant the bush inside the star. Ring the bell three times. Plant your young rose bush in the ground. As you plant the bush, chant:

   Blessed be the sweet rose fairies.

3. After you are done planting the rose, water and fertilize it according to the planting directions. Put seven small stones around the base of the bush. Ring the bell seven times. Walk clockwise around the bush, and say:

   Blessed be the sweet rose blossom fairies

   Please watch over this young rose as it flowers

   At dawn, noon, dusk, midnight, and all hours.

4. When you are done with your ritual, thank the rose fairies. Go to the center of the circle, ring the bell once, and say:

Fairy Watchers of all directions

I bid you farewell.

Please depart in peace and love.

Thank you for your presence.

Ring the bell once more, and say:

Blessed be! Evo-He!

5. Pull up your fairy circle and scatter the flowers in the ring and erase the ring mark with the heel of your shoe or your hand. Do this in a counterclockwise motion. Face center, ring the bell once and say:

Blessed be! Evo-He!

6. Water and tend the bush so that it thrives and blossoms.

Meditating on Elves and Fairies

Eastern spiritual traditions such as Buddhism and Hinduism have long advocated meditation as a means for becoming one with the divine. Because of its health benefits such as lowering blood pressure and lessening stress and depression, meditation has gone mainstream. It is rapidly gaining popularity throughout the world.

Wizardly Wisdom _____

While meditating, turn off your cell phone, turn the volume all the way down on your phone machine. Better yet, just unplug your phone. Let any other people in your home know that you will be meditating and that you do not want to be interrupted. Also put your pets out of the room so they can't interrupt the process.

While meditating, you are in a very relaxed state of awareness. You open yourself up to experiencing each moment as itself with a more centered awareness. The positive effects of meditation include deeper inner knowledge, clear insight, and a state of deep relaxation. Your heartbeat rate, oxygen consumption, perspiration, muscle tension, and blood pressure all decrease. You feel calm, yet your mind remains alert. Your brain waves move into alpha, which is the state in which you are more likely to encounter otherworldly beings such as elves and fairies.

Read the following elf and fairy meditations to yourself, one sentence at a time. Take time to understand the meaning of each sentence, and then move to the next, and the next, and so on, until you complete the process. I suggest that you read a sentence at a time, close your eyes, and then imagine it in your mind's eye.

If you prefer, record the meditations in your own voice. In a quiet location, turn on some soft, fairylike music, and read the meditation aloud slowly into the tape or CD recorder, pausing between sentences and paragraphs. Play the recorded meditation back as often as you like.

On Guard!

When you meditate you are in a very relaxed state of mind. Don't do things that require your attention, for example, drive a car, jog or work out, watch television, ride a bike, work, or talk on the phone. It's always best to focus completely on the meditation process.

To enhance your elf and fairy meditations, create a fairy ring and circle in which to meditate. This will intensify the meditation experience. These meditations are in the form of guided visualizations that can be done as often as you desire.

A Sampling of Meditations

The following meditations offer you a means of connecting with the divine and magical aspects of elves and fairies. Included in this sampling is a magic garden meditation, a one ring meditation, and a fairy castle meditation. The more often you do these meditations, the more rapport you will gain with the energy of elves and fairies.

Magic Garden Meditation

Sit or recline comfortably in a private, peaceful spot, preferably outdoors in your garden or in the woods. When doing this meditation indoors, use a picture of a beautiful garden. Put the picture in front of you where you can see it.

Take several deep and complete breaths. As you inhale, imagine breathing in pure white light. As you exhale, just let go of any tension you might be feeling. Focus your awareness on your surroundings if you are outdoors. If meditating indoors, focus your attention on the picture of the beautiful garden in front of you. Take a deep, complete breath, and as you exhale, close your eyes. Continue breathing deeply and rhythmically.

In your mind's eye, imagine being at the top of a flight of natural earthen steps. Move slowly down the steps, one at a time, down to a beautiful magic garden. It's a place of enchanting adventure and joyful whimsy surrounded by green mountains and filled with magical elves and fairy beings. In this garden are flowers of every color and vegetables of every kind, as well as fruiting trees and splendid old-growth trees. A silver stream flows from the waterfall upon the hill above you, and feeds a small, glassy pond in the center of the magical garden.

You come to a large, low branching tree, and sit upon one of the smooth branches. You can feel the power of the gnarled tree supporting you, and you can feel the energy from the earth beneath your feet. You connect with the essence of the tree. Your roots are your ancestors, your trunk is your life's foundation, and your branches are your many aspects. Your leaves are like your thoughts, which act as light receptors.

You become aware of the dryad of the tree, a tall, green and brown tree spirit, and then you become aware of the dwarves and gnomes who live underground in caves, caverns, and great stone mountains. You see leprechauns and brownies dash about and winged brown, green, and multicolored garden fairies flash about in the flowers and shrubbery. Woodland elves dance in and out from behind a thick grove of oak trees in the near distance, and you can hear the sound of enchanting music floating toward you.

As the music grows louder, you see lovely winged fairies surrounded by a radiant glow, and wind fairies with wings larger than their bodies, moving about the magic garden. You also see salamanders in the silver stream, and red newts on the stream bank. The entire garden seems to be enveloped in a beautiful light that brightens all the dark corners and make the colors in the garden sparkle with an otherworldly radiance.

As you breathe in the beauty of the garden and relax even more, imagine the stream speaking to you in an ancient voice, a voice that goes beyond sound. Somehow you understand that ancient voice. You see water fairies in the pond, beautiful and dreamlike undines with enchanting voices. You listen to their song and it fills you with joyful wonder.

Continue enjoying the magical beauty of the garden for a few more minutes as you breathe in and out, completely and deeply. When you are ready, imagine seeing those natural earthen steps in front of you, this time leading upward. Slowly ascend the steps, one at a time, feeling more and more energized and refreshed as you move upward. Now start moving your hands and feet, slowly opening your eyes, and coming back to the present moment and place.

One Ring Meditation

You don't have to necessarily become a ring bearer like Frodo in Tolkien's *The Lord of the Rings* to experience mysterious adventures. The following meditation takes you on a journey to the Otherworld while you sit or recline in the comfort of your own home. To do this one ring meditation, turn on some soft instrumental music. Sit or recline comfortably, and loosen any clothing that might be binding you. Take a deep breath and count three heartbeats, still your breath for three heartbeats, and exhale for three heartbeats. Do this several times to relax and center your awareness.

In your mind's eye, imagine two trees in front of you. To your left is a tree the color of silver, and to your right is a tree the color of gold. Between the two trees, you see an unusual golden ring on the ground. You put the ring on the middle finger of your left hand, and a large chasm abruptly appears in the ground.

Climbing down into the chasm, you follow a long, steep, winding passageway. Moving to the end of the passageway, you enter a bright Otherworld, a fairyland of color and light. There are rings of colored flowers in this Otherworld. They are red, orange, gold, green, blue, purple, rose, silver, and white. As you gaze upon the flower rings, you ponder the many rings—the circles and cycles in your own life—for a minute or two.

At the center of this fairyland is a fountain that dispenses the waters of life. Water spills out of the Dragon's Mouth of the fountain. You look upward to see a large winged dragon flying toward the fountain. Its wings gleam in the strange light of this Otherworld, shining with the colors of the rainbow. The dragon glides down, sparkling all over, and settles upon the ground a short distance from the fountain. The dragon mindspeaks to you:

> Your mind has a will, just as your body has a will.
>
> Your heart has a will. Your spirit has a will.
>
> Each and every person has the power
>
> To change the course of the future.

The dragon flies away, softly and without a sound, and a delightful blue mist pours over the fairyland. The mist feels warm like a soft blue flame. Everything is covered in the mist, and you feel as though you are afloat in a vast blue ocean of fairy light. You feel the bright blue mist flowing over your skin, through you, and energizing your entire body, from the top of your head to the tips of your toes.

> **Fairy Tales and Legends**
>
> Andrew Lang's *Yellow Fairy Book* (Dover Publishing, 1966) contains the story "The Magic Ring," about a young man named Martin who is rewarded by the king of the underworld with a magic ring for saving the king's daughter. His reward? Whenever Martin tosses the ring from one hand to the other, twelve young men appear and do his bidding, no matter how difficult, in a single night.

Now imagine gathering the blue mist into your hands and shaping it into a ball of blue light. Shape it into a bright blue staff of light that you hold between your hands. Allow the staff's light to surround you completely, breathing it in and out. Continue doing this for a few minutes.

In your mind's eye, move back over to the passageway by which you entered fairyland, and slowly go up the winding passageway into the ordinary world. Imagine taking off the ring and placing it between the golden and silver trees. It remains there for you to take it up again whenever you want to. Move your hands and feet, and slowly open your eyes and return to the present time and place.

Fairy Castle Meditation

Turn on some fairylike, instrumental music. Sit or recline comfortably. Loosen any clothing that might be binding you. Breathe deeply for several minutes to relax your body and quiet your mind.

Now in your mind's eye, imagine a magical fairy castle. It can be in any world or realm you can imagine. Shape and fashion it from anything you like; crystals, gems, trees, flowers, water, or pure starlight. This magical fairy castle is a place where you can go to energize yourself with the magic of fairyland, even if it's for just a few minutes.

Take a deep breath in and out. In your mind's eye, step over the threshold of the castle, and enter it. As you step inside, your senses seem to come alive as you can almost see, touch, smell, hear, taste, and intuit the inside of the magical fairy castle. You notice that the castle is filled with friendly fairies of all different types. There are flower fairies and woodland elves, winged fairies and will-o-wisps. Take a few minutes to explore the castle and all the fairies within it. Enjoy the joyful sensations that accompany the adventure.

When you are done meditating, bring your attention to the present time and place. Move your toes and fingers and slowly open your eyes. Clap your hands three times. You can repeat this meditation as often as you like.

Blessings for All Occasions

To *bless* means to hallow or consecrate by spiritual rite or word. This includes the invoking of the divine for the care and protection of your personal and professional patterns. Accept divine blessings of the helpful elves and fairies whenever they are offered and you will draw their magical energies, a little playfulness, and most likely some adventure into your life.

When you wake up in the morning, your mind is still partly caught in the dream world, making it more open to suggestion. By doing affirmations, prayers, and blessings before your mind has a chance to fully awaken, you have a wide-open route into your sub-conscious.

A blessing is a suggestion you give yourself, as well as a request for divine help. Repeated, the blessing's meaning penetrates your psyche, setting the stage for transformation. The helpful fairy and elf energy you call upon when you say a blessing positively influences your empowerment process.

Magical Meaning

A **blessing** is an approval or encouragement that is conducive to your happiness and well-being. The word *bless* comes from the Old English word *bletsian* and French *blod* meaning blood, deriving this from the blood kinship humans hold with the sacred earth.

When you say a blessing, an energy field is created. When you do this when you first wake up or before you go to sleep, this field carries over into the dream world. When this happens, divine guidance in the form of helpful fairies, elves, and magical creatures begins to occur in your dreams.

A Sampling of Blessings

The following sampling of blessings is intended to bring the energy of elves and fairies into both your waking and dream worlds. Included is a flower fairy blessing, a fairy dream blessing, and an elven starfire blessing. These blessings should be repeated as many times as it takes to bring the elf and fairy energy into your personal space.

Flower Fairy Blessing

Go outdoors and focus your attention on some beautiful flowers. Choose someone you would like to send healing blessings to via the gentle flower fairies. Sit or stand, and focus all of your attention on the flowers in front of you. Notice all the different qualities of the flowers, the way the petals and stems are shaped and their colors. Take a deep breath, and smell the fragrance of the flowers. Feel the texture of the flowers.

Now imagine the flower fairies, the divine spirits that inhabit the flowers and help keep them healthy in front of you. These fairies might look like winged beings, tiny white, pink, gold, blue, or green spheres or dots of light, or they might look like large elflike beings that seem to flow from the flowers themselves. You might actually see the fairies, or you might sense them in another way. Just keep breathing deeply and turn your awareness toward the flower fairies.

Now imagine the person to whom you want to send the flower fairy healing blessings. Ask the flower fairies to fly to that person and fill her or him with all of their healing blessings. Take a deep and complete breath, and as you exhale, actually imagine them all flying to and filling the person with divine healing light. Keep using your breath to move more and more healing flower fairy blessings to the person. Do this for at least five minutes. Keep focusing on the flower fairies and send their healing blessings to the person. You can also send flower fairy blessings to those who have passed on.

Fairy Dream Blessing

You need a small cloth pouch for this blessing, a 5'×5' piece of paper, a pen with green ink, and a small stone from nature. Using the pen, write down one of your dearest dreams on the piece of paper. Make it a dream that is actually attainable. Fold the paper three times and put it in the pouch. Hold the pouch in between your hands, and ask for the fairies' blessings by saying three times:

> Helpful fairies, please bless me with my dream.

Put the pouch by your bedside, for example on a bedside table or in your bureau drawer. Each night just before you go to sleep, and every morning just after you wake up, hold the fairy pouch and repeat:

> Helpful fairies, please bless me with my dream.

Focus your attention on your dearest dream as you hold the pouch for a few minutes. Know in your heart, believe with all your being, that your dream is coming true. Continue doing this every morning and every night until you attain your dream.

Elven Starfire Blessing

At midnight, send your awareness into the night sky. Imagine transforming your awareness into a luminous star. Move as a star on the surface of the sky, spinning softly as you fly out across the dark expanse. See and sense yourself being filled completely with white starlight, with starfire. Breathe this light into your being to the count of three, hold your breath for three counts, and exhale slowly. Repeat this three times, and then say this blessing for someone you love:

> May the blessing of the elves
>
> And all friendly folk go with you, (say the person's name).
>
> May the starfire shine upon your face
>
> And illuminate you with eternal grace.

The Least You Need to Know

- ◆ Rituals, meditations, and blessings are powerful tools for positive change.
- ◆ Rituals are systematic ways of doing things that produce results.
- ◆ Meditations have long been a way to become one with the divine.
- ◆ Blessings are ways of asking or thanking the divine for help.
- ◆ There are many different kinds of rituals, meditations, and blessings, but all connect you with the Otherworld.

Part 5

Connecting with the Spirit of Nature

Elves and fairies are an essential expression of the spirit of nature. They are part of an unseen realm inhabited by the various manifestations of this spirit. These manifestations include elves, fairies, elementals, devas, and divine gods and goddesses. This part of our elf and fairy adventure is about connecting with the spirit of nature. This includes exploring the world of nature devas and how people around the world have learned how to work with the nature devas, with miraculous results.

I also give suggestions on planting your own fairy garden. One of the best ways to connect with the spirit of nature is to go outside and experience it firsthand as often as you can. Not only is it a great way to connect with your natural self, it's also a great way to forget all of your troubles and relax for a brief interlude with elves, fairies, and their good relations—the nature devas.

Chapter 17

Nature Devas

In This Chapter

- The world of nature devas, an essential creative force of nature
- How nature devas can help you become one with the animals and plants in your world
- Living in balance and harmony with the energies of the earth
- Clearing and energizing techniques for connecting with nature devas

As spirits of nature, devas have an energetic kinship with elves and fairies. They come from the creative energies of the universe and have an essential connection with every living thing. Like elves and fairies, devas emanate from the unseen realm of the Otherworld, and are perceived by mortals as being spirits. This means we perceive them as we want to and as they want us to. As essences, they can help us relate and connect with the world of plants and animals. In addition, devas facilitate the perception that every living thing is connected in an energetic web of oneness.

Through this oneness, we are part of the divine spirit of nature. By becoming more aware of this spiritual connection, we can learn to live in balance and harmony with the energies of the earth. In this chapter, I'll share some techniques that will help you balance and harmonize your energy with nature devas and the divine spirit of the earth.

What Are Nature Devas?

When you take a seed and plant it in the ground, you begin a process that is magical without any stretch of the imagination. When gifted with water, the seed then germinates and sends out its first sign of life. From an embryo, the sprout continues to grow larger by generating a root and stalk, one that moves down into the earth and one that moves up toward the light. It's at this point in the life cycle that things begin taking on individual characteristics that then determine what that life energy will become. More than the physical DNA, this life energy has to with the creative essence of everything.

Fruit trees and vegetable plants all go through a metamorphosis that starts with a flower and then magically changes into an apple, peach, tomato, or green bean, depending on what type of plant it is. If you could sit back and watch this whole progression from seed to fruit or vegetable, you would be watching the physical evidence that happens as a result of Earth spirits. These spirits come under three basic headings:

- Elementals
- Devas
- Elves and fairies

Magical Meaning

In Hindu mythology, **devas** are nature divinities or spirits. In Sanskrit, the word deva means "a being of brilliant light," referring to their role as the shining ones of the Vedas. Within the Hindu cosmology, there are 33 devas, eleven for each of the three worlds.

Elementals spring from the basic elements and have the role of being creators of form. They work as connecting points between creative energy and physical form. *Devas* work with and give direction to the elemental energy. For example, where an elemental might have responsibility over a pine seed, the overseeing deva has a connection to the essence and spirit of all pine trees.

Every species of plant and animal has a nature deva that embodies its essential energy and spirit. Elementals move energy from the unmanifested into the manifested world. Devas in turn direct what form that energy will take as well as act as the connective thread that weaves all those particular energetic forms together into a web of oneness. In terms of pine trees, it means that the pine deva ensures that all the creative energy within the seed goes to creating the form of a pine tree. It also means that by energetically connecting to one pine, you are connecting to all pine trees in the spirit of the pine deva.

I used to raise beagles, and every puppy that I came to know had a distinct and individual personality. In fact, I was always amazed at how early on each developed its own personality. Usually within an hour or two after being born, they exhibited characteristics that made one distinctive from the rest of its littermates. One pup, for example, would be more active, one more mellow, one more friendly, and another louder.

Although each puppy had its own individual personality, there were overall character-istic that they all exhibited as part of their beagle-ness. Their curiosity, affection, keen sense of smell, and ability to bugle so that they're heard from great distances away are characteristics they share. These are manifestations of the beagle deva, who is closely related to the dog deva.

How Devas Impact Your Life

People blessed with a proverbial green thumb have a special rapport with plants. It seems that every plant they come into contact with grows to its fullest potential. Knowledge and care of the plant is definitely part of what having a green thumb is about, but the concept goes deeper. Like the concept of the "horse whisperer," some-one with a green thumb has an energetic connection with plants that essentially lets them nonverbally communicate and be one with plants.

> **Through the Ages**
>
> Monty Roberts, author of *The Man Who Listens to Horses* (Ballantine Books, 1998), says, "I don't whisper, I communicate with a horse in the language of the horse. It has a very effective, involved, and discernible non-verbal language. The incredible thing about this language is these animals need no interpreters. Around the world, they all communicate in one common language that has been around for millions of years."

Television's *Crocodile Hunter* Steve Erwin was in a movie called *Collision Course*, in which he does several sequences with extremely venomous snakes. During a particular segment, Erwin describes how he becomes one with the essence of the snake, and that's how he handles the snakes with the ease that he exhibits. His calmness then appears to carry over to the snakes. They seem to innately know that he doesn't want to harm them. When he handles them, it is like he is connecting and becoming one with the snake deva, and in return the deva seems to protect him. This protection will remain as long as he stays in a spiritual state of oneness with the deva.

Some tribal people have what it known as "totems," which are kindred relationships with a particular species of animals. These relationships often extended to the point where the deva of these animals would protect the members of the tribe. In return, the tribal members protected and honored this totem animal, for example, by not eating them.

No matter how isolated we become from nature, ultimately we can no more cut ourselves off from nature than we can cut off our oxygen supply. As if coded into our innate programming, we are connected to the realm of elves, fairies, elementals, and nature devas.

As energies, these nature spirits affect us in subtle and spiritual ways. From the spiritual, energy then moves into the mental and physical; it starts having an effect on our mental process, and as a result, an effect on our physical body. This progression from the energetic and spiritual to the mental and physical is the normal pattern for both healing techniques and illness. Nature spirits begin in the energetic part of your body and from there move to the physical.

Bringing Deva Energy into Your Life

The best way to bring the energy of nature devas into your life is to understand and work with the natural energies of our planet Earth. As with elves and fairies, these natural energies have a spirit that gives them a sense of life. This practice of working with the earth's energies is called geomancy.

Geomancy melds scientific knowledge together with ancient spiritual practices that stressed being in balance and harmony with the energies of the earth. Scientific inquiry and research has opened up doors to understanding people's relationships to animals and to their environment. This includes understanding the effect of the energetic fields that move throughout both the earth and the human body.

Much scientific research investigates how archetypal shapes affect all these relationships. This study is called *sacred geometry*, also known as the "language of light" and "language of creation." The basic idea is

> **Through the Ages**
>
> In his article "The Power of Place and Human Environments," Richard Anderson writes, "Geomancy may be described as an ancient, holistic, integrated system of natural science and philosophy, used to keep human activity in harmony with natural patterns: from seasonal cycles to processes that maintain the balance of nature, to the geometrical proportions found in the way all organisms grow."

that energy fluctuates and moves in certain predictable patterns. These universal patterns affect every aspect of energy as it becomes physical form. Just as waves of energy are generated by the earth, waves of energy are also created by the human body. The waves emitted from the human body work best when they are in harmony with the energetic waves coming from the earth.

Sacred geometry and devas both rely on the concept that there is a universal oneness quality that permeates every aspect of what we know about our world. Cause and effect is built on the idea that when you perform a certain action, it results in a particular effect that is a direct result of the original action.

Also from the study of geomancy comes the idea that lines of geopathic energy exist that affect the human body. These lines of energy are similar to the earth's network of natural ley lines that crisscross the globe. The difference is that this geopathic energy can be harmful to humans. It creates a situation of geopathic stress, which means that these energy fields create an imbalance in the human energy system. This creates stress, which can compromise the immune system and lead to physical and mental illness.

> **Magical Meaning**
>
> **Sacred geometry** is founded on the premise that certain archetypal shapes exist everywhere in our universe, and as such, influence everything we do. Sacred geometry revolves around the idea that energy moves in these universal patterns, which, as a result, influences the form of everything.

The four basic lines of geopathic energy are …

- **Hartmann grids**—Discovered by German medical doctor Ernst Hartmann in the 1950s, these lines form a grid around the earth. The worst place a person can sleep or work is at places where the lines cross one another, creating a knot of energy that can be very disruptive to the human energy system.

- **Geopathic zones**—These electromagnetic fields of energy can be either generated by the earth or artificially generated from electrical towers, high voltage wires, fuse boxes, and microwave ovens.

- **Personal zones**—These are energies that affect humans on a personal level. Personal zones often manifest themselves as an energy that is grating, annoying, and irritating. People coming and bringing their energy into your personal space is often what causes these zones. These zones also affect animals.

◆ **Interference lines**—Lines of energy that interfere with someone's personal patterns. They can come from people's thoughts and energies. This thought energy creates lines of energy that can go out and create interference and disruption.

These geopathic lines of energy have similarity to fairy trods. In fairy tales and legends, these are the paths that troops of elves and fairies take on their nightly excursions from the fairy realm. The problem with building on these paths or any areas used extensively by the fairies is that the energy in these places is always unsettled, and creates stress on our human energy system, which affects our physical, mental, and spiritual health.

In the discipline of feng shui, the ancient Chinese practice of arranging your living space to promote health and harmony, these geopathic lines of energy are called *shars*. Shars are created when energy flows badly or becomes stagnant and doesn't flow at all. In feng shui, energy is called *chi*, and when it flows in balance, it brings good health and fortune. When chi doesn't flow, it brings bad health and misfortune. This is why it is important to always keep energy cleansed and moving.

The wonderful thing about the lines of energy that create geopathic stress is that their effect can be neutralized. The best way of neutralizing geopathic stress or bad chi (shars) is by connecting with nature devas and using their inherent energy to clear and energize any space.

Techniques for Connecting with Devas

The first technique gives instructions on how to clear your outside space of unwanted energies, and the second technique lays out the steps for energizing your outside space with energy that is conducive to devas, setting up an area where you can connect with them.

The reason that you want to connect with nature devas is so that you bring more natural energy into your cleansing and energizing process. The reason you want to clear your space of any bad chi or energy is because this energy can be detrimental to your health. The reason you want to energize your space is so you feel empowered every time you are in the space. In other words, it naturally energizes you and makes you feel good.

These techniques should be done in order, anytime you sense that the energy in your space has been compromised by bad chi or energy. On the whole, you should clear and energize your space at least once a month. Full moons are excellent times to do these techniques because the natural energy of elves, fairies, and nature devas is strong. See Chapter 11 for more information on the best times for working with nature spirits.

Clearing Technique: Setting the Stage for Devas

Unless routinely cleansed, energy has a tendency to build up and polarize. The following technique is intended to help you clear the energy in your garden or any outside space where you want to attract nature devas. You can also use this technique inside the house to cleanse your personal space.

Traditionally, a variety of things have been used to energetically cleanse an area. Some common means include salt, smudging, ritual, drumming, and using the tone of a bell. To stay in the spirit of elves and fairies, this technique is going to use a bell to energetically cleanse the area. Within folk practices, silver bells were employed as a means of calling the elves and fairies.

The practice of ringing or wearing bells is worldwide, with the intended purpose being to protect the person ringing the bell from both evil spirits and bodily harm. Everyone from South American Indians to Siberian Shamans use this practice to rid an area of unwanted spirits and energy. Also, the hem of the high priest's garment in Israel was lined with golden bells as prescribed by God. The tinkling sound protected him against demons as he moved in and out of the holy place. Malevolent spirits often frequent the thresholds of spiritual sanctuaries.

Fairy Tales and Legends

Like elves and fairies, bells can sometimes become indignant at insults and injuries and as a result, seek revenge. A tale is told about a bell of singularly sweet tone that was taken by the King of France to Paris from its home in the town of Sens. When it reached Paris, the bell refused to ring in spite of all efforts to persuade it otherwise. Only when it was returned to Sens did the bell burst into glorious ringing, displaying its happiness at being back home.

Begin the clearing technique by selecting a bell with a pleasant sound that is clear and strikingly vibrant. When you ring the bell, the sound should make you feel good and peaceful. If there is any uneasiness or discordant feelings from the sound of the bell, then you need to find one that is more to your liking. You need a bell whose personality harmonically matches your own.

The idea when cleansing an area is to begin ringing the bell at a particular spot, such as the north point. From there, you move around the perimeter of the space in a clockwise direction, continually ringing the bell. While you are ringing the bell, call out:

> All misfortune and foulness be gone.
>
> I ask this in the name of the good people.

If the sound of the bell is vibrant and full of life, it will carry throughout the space, and cleanse it of any negative spirits and energies. Matched with your own energy, the sound of the bell becomes like a beacon of light that brightens the areas where darkness dwells. When this happens, you are setting up an environment where nature devas want to come and experience the natural energetic pleasure with you.

Energizing Technique: Connecting with Nature Devas

You can energize your space in various ways, as discussed in Chapter 16 on rituals, meditations, and blessings. This particular energizing technique uses a clear quartz crystal. This type of crystal has long been associated with elves and fairies because of its innate ability to tune into any energetic frequency or harmonic. This means it can be programmed to anything that you desire.

Begin by choosing a clear quartz crystal that has a comfortable feel to it. You then need to cleanse the stone by placing it in your power hand (your right hand if you are right-handed). In your mind's eye, imagine a clear mountain stream splashing down throughout the crystal. Pulse your inhaled breath out through your nose, and at the same time imagine this image of the pure mountain stream moving into and permeating the latticework of the crystal. Repeat this three times.

Next, place the crystal in your power hand and begin imagining all the things you want to empower energetically into your space. For example, sense the creative forces of the nature devas move into and permeate the crystal lattice structure within the stone.

When you sense that all this energy is moving inside the crystal, inhale and pulse your exhaled breath out through your nose. Repeat this three times. With each breath, send this energy into the programming of the crystal until the energy becomes one with the stone. When you sense this has happened, your crystal is energized.

As with the cleansing, start in a particular point on the perimeter of your space, and move clockwise from that point around the area. Hold your crystal up in your power hand, and feel the energy emanating from the crystal into the surrounding areas. Like a crystal radio, the stone transmits the energy you programmed into it throughout the area you are energizing. After you have moved through the space enough times, you can feel the energy begin to change. When this happens, you will notice that nature devas will move more into your sphere of being. At this point you have created an environment that is conducive to the energies of nature devas.

The Least You Need to Know

- Each species of plant and animal has a nature deva connected with it.
- Geomancy is about keeping human patterns in balance with natural patterns and energies.
- Personal space should be regularly cleansed of stagnant energy.
- Energizing your personal space can help you connect with nature devas.

Chapter 18

The Magical Power of Nature

In This Chapter

- ◆ Findhorn, a garden in northern Scotland that grows miraculous vegetables

- ◆ Lily Hill Farm, whose elves actively help the grape harvest

- ◆ Perelandra, an organic garden whose methods come directly from nature

- ◆ How nature spirits help restore the balance between humans and nature

Places like the garden of Findhorn in Scotland have become testaments to the power of nature devas. Whenever people can plant a garden in inferior soil in an agricultural zone that is so far up in the northern latitudes as to have a short growing cycle, it's a sign that something more than the ordinary is happening. Not only is a garden planted, but the vegetables that come out of it far surpass anything grown in a garden situated in a temperate climate with incredibly fertile soil. What's going on?

There is something more at work than what we currently believe to be "real," something that is changing faster than a chameleon on a kaleidoscope. The only way you can hope to keep up with what is happening is to flow and become one with it. This is the point where energies converge and the polarities of space and time cease to exist. You have now entered the realm where anything is divinely possible and, with the right help, probable. This chapter visits some of these places where nature and humans work together in harmony, producing results that can only be termed incredible.

How It All Began

Like most things magical, Findhorn began as a small seed that grew into something extraordinary. It began in 1962 with six people, and blossomed from there into The Findhorn Foundation. Registered as a Scottish charity, the Findhorn community has grown to several hundred people. The foundation has a college that teaches classes and has begun a project known as Ecovillage, where people live in harmony and balance with the energies of the earth.

After a career as a senior officer in the Royal Air Force, Peter Caddy came with his wife Eileen and their three sons to the town of Forres in northeast Scotland in 1957. Peter and Eileen had been hired to manage the run-down Culuny Hill Hotel. Soon after they arrived, Eileen began receiving guidance in meditation from an inner divine source she called "the still small voice within." The guidance communicated certain things that Eileen and Peter should do to make the hotel successful. Following the advice, they turned the Culuny Hill Hotel into a successful four-star restaurant.

Ending their employment with the hotel, Peter, Eileen, and their sons suddenly found themselves along with their friend Dorothy Maclean moving to the nearby coastal village of Findhorn. Up near the Artic Circle, the area is known for its long and cold winters. They all survived by living in caravans (trailers), and getting into spirituality and metaphysics. This included meditation groups and discussion groups on metaphysics.

Out of work with no discernable plans for the future, the Caddy family meditated and asked for guidance. As Peter described it, "Guidance told us to not only live in the moment, but to enjoy it! We were told that Findhorn would be of importance to the world, that there was a plan behind it."

Unable to live on the benefits they were receiving for unemployment, the fledgling Findhorn community of the Caddy family and Dorothy Maclean hit upon the idea of creating a vegetable garden. Although they had lots of enthusiasm and determination, the soil conditions—lots of sand and rock—plus the cold climate made it look like they were on a fool's errand, until they started getting help from the elves, fairies, and nature devas. Suddenly their fortunes began to take a turn toward the miraculous.

Creating the Garden

In the process of creating the garden, Peter cut back some of the bushes. This upset the elves, who then threatened to leave the garden. The group did a ritual, and Peter apologized to the elves. After it was over, the elves held a gathering and decided to stay.

Everyone in the group was meditating and praying for guidance in what they were doing. In one of her meditations, Dorothy was contacted by a plant spirit or deva. In particular, it was a pea deva, who expressed eagerness to help Peter and the group with their garden. With very little to lose and much to gain, they began following the advice of the nature devas. As Peter put it, "We knew the devas to be that part of the angelic hierarchy that holds the archetypal pattern for each plant species and directs energy toward bringing a plant into the physical plane. Now here was this pea deva offering to help us!"

The deva began to relay all the information necessary to successfully grow peas: what types of soil the plants prefer, how far apart they like to be, the amount of water they like, dealing with pest problems, and how plants do not like to be transplanted. Once the group began communicating and following the instructions of the pea deva, other nature devas couldn't wait to join in and help with the ever-expanding and blossoming garden. Soon the cabbage deva, broccoli deva, rose deva, Tibetan blue-poppy deva, rain deva, and the more encompassing landscape and ocean devas were helping to make Findhorn a virtual Garden of Eden. Each message contained instructions not only about planting and pruning, but also about how everyone needs to love one another.

With help from all of these devas, the garden soon began to flourish with incredible results. Vegetables, herbs, and flowers grew abundantly and to enormous sizes. Within months, the garden was supplying the group of six with more food than they could possibly eat.

When other people began seeing the extraordinary things that were happening at the Findhorn garden, word spread quickly. Horticultural experts from around the world came and were awed by what they saw. Huge flowers and vegetables grew in the bitter climate of the

Wizardly Wisdom

Gardening books have a tendency to divide the different areas of the world into growing zones. Generally, the colder zones are limited as to what they can grow. Also, higher latitudes, such as those close to the artic circle, get what is known as "indirect" sunlight, making it harder to grow plants in these locations. Findhorn seemed to defy this traditional wisdom in terms of gardening.

North Sea, where growing conditions are, at best, abysmal. How could it be that a garden in this harsh environment acted like it was growing in a temperate climate under optimum conditions? These were questions that defied the bounds of normal scientific inquiry. As a result, the garden at Findhorn became famous as a testament to the amazing powers of nature devas.

Extraordinary Happenings

Whenever anything defies scientific explanation, it means there is something there that we need to pay attention to and learn from. In the case of Findhorn, the phenomenon seems to stem from divine spirits, elves, and nature devas. Although traditional science normally perceives these types of events as primitive and superstitious, nonetheless there is physical evidence combined with the firsthand experiences of the people who participated in the phenomenon. They say there is a direct relationship between their communication with the different devas and the extraordinary happenings that resulted in the garden.

Given the set of circumstances, it is hard to explain what happened any other way than direct communication between nature spirits (elves, fairies, elementals, and devas) and humans. Through communication in meditation, these nature spirits gave specific sets of instructions that were then followed implicitly by the members of the Findhorn group. The result was to grow things that were extraordinary by normal standards.

At its peak in the late 1960s and 1970s, the garden grew cabbages that were over 10 times a cabbage's usual weight, broccoli so large that the plants were too heavy to lift from the ground, and flowers and herbs that grew sometimes twice their normal size. Some of the heads of cabbage weighed 40 pounds, including one that weighed 42 pounds. A single gigantic head of broccoli was said to have fed the Findhorn family of six for four months!

Other people, such as David Spangler and Ogilvie Crombie, showed up later at Findhorn gardens and continued the tradition of working with the nature devas. Ogilvie could both see and talk to the different devas. They continued to receive the directions for planting, cultivating, and managing their garden from spirits that inhabit the natural world. In the 1970s, Findhorn became a model community for the New Age, pointing to the extraordinary benefits of working with the devas of nature.

Even as Findhorn was being touted as a modern Garden of Eden, Eileen received messages from "the still small voice within" reminding her and the people of

Findhorn that what they were doing was not just about gardening and growing giant vegetables! It was also about giving the world a model that showed the cooperation between the plant and human kingdoms. In the words of Peter Caddy, "True cooperation begins when we realize that humans, the devas, and nature spirits are part of the same life-force creating together."

Other Miracles of Nature

In addition to Findhorn, people in other places have worked with nature to bring about results that are at times miraculous. But more than anything these examples show what can happen when humans live in balance with the earth and the spirits of nature, such as elves, fairies, and devas.

Lily Hill Farm

When Penny Kelly and her husband bought a piece of property in Lawton, Michigan, in 1987, they had no idea what was in store for them. Located in the fruit belt, the property came with a 13-acre vineyard that was, because of years of neglect, in need of repair. Penny's degree in Humanistic Studies didn't prepare her for the agricultural setting where she now found herself living. She knew she needed help, but she never imagined what form it would take.

During one of her long walks on the property, Penny was approached by three elves. At first she doubted her eyes, but eventually came somewhat to terms with what she was seeing. Identifying themselves by the names Mairlinna, Alvey, and Kermots, the elves scolded her for being asleep to the needs of the earth and nature and doing nothing to help heal the property. They made a deal with her that would forever change both her life and the future of Lily Hill Farm.

The deal she wound up making with the elves was that they would help her revitalize the vineyard so that it would work in balance and harmony with nature, and in return she would yield one hundred tons of grapes from the vineyard's mere 13 acres. To make her task harder,

> **Through the Ages**
>
> … Ye transferred yer magic to something outside yerself and this left ye filled with uncertainty, fear, and gloom. Ye can't give away yer power and expect to get anything done.
>
> —Alvey the elf, from *The Elves of Lily Hill Farm: A Partnership with Nature* by Penny Kelly (1997)

the elves specified that she couldn't use chemical fertilizers and pesticides. Penny took on the challenge to meet her commitments to the elves and fulfill her role in rebuilding and healing the farm.

As the realization of her deal with the elves came to be, Penny felt a lot like Alice following the rabbit down the hole into Wonderland. She suddenly found herself in the world of plants, insects, animals, devas, and elementals—a place where communication and interaction is common but, like in Wonderland, all the rules have changed. The elves were intent on teaching her a series of intense and powerful lessons regarding the struggle of survival that had erupted between humans and nature since the communication between them had been lost.

One of the first tasks Penny and her husband faced was to rebuild the soil that had been destroyed by years of poisonous chemicals. From the elves they learned techniques for creating a natural and healthy environment for the grapes. Things they found out from their experience include:

♦ Fruits, vegetables, and grains grown in healthy soil have over 22 percent more natural proteins, good levels of mineral nutrients, natural sugars used by the plants to build proteins, longer shelf life (they'll dehydrate rather than rot), and natural enzymes for digestion.

♦ Insects and pests are only attracted to unhealthy plants. Healthy plants have a high natural sugar content that give insects the equivalent of a stomachache because they cannot digest the sugars.

♦ *Heirloom seeds* and historic varieties didn't require pesticides, herbicides, and fungicides to stay alive. The plants were naturally strong.

Magical Meaning

Heirloom seeds have an original set of genes that enable them to reproduce themselves in an unbroken line and that helps them adapt to a wide set of environmental growing conditions. The fruits and vegetables produced by these seeds usually have superior color, taste, and texture.

In the process, Penny and her husband learned about the importance of biodiversity and seed gathering. The elves taught them about planting based on factors that include genetic adaptability, resistance to disease, better taste, good texture, high nutrition, and dependability from generation to generation. They also learned to use heirloom seeds, which accounted for the superior production and taste of their fruit.

Penny found her experiences with the elves both enlightening and humbling. It left her with a deeper understanding of the balance between humans and nature. She learned that once communication is restored between humans and nature, anything is possible, including growing one hundred tons of grapes on 13-acres of land. As Penny Kelly writes in *The Elves of Lily Hill Farm: A Partnership with Nature*, "Here we are, with our land, our water, and the other living creatures, large and small, plant and animal, who share that same air, water, and soil, and who make it possible for us to be here, alive and well. It is as Alvey said. We humans are at the top of the heap. We need everything in the heap underneath us, but nothing in the heap needs that human at the top."

Perelandra

In 1975, Machaelle Small Wright created the Perelandra garden, located in the Blue Ridge Mountains of Virginia. Like the people at Findhorn and Penny Kelly at Lily Hill Farm, Machaelle works with and receives information from nature spirits, or as she calls it, "nature intelligence." As with the people in the other two places, she stresses the balance between humans and nature. As she tells it, "I dedicated myself to learning about nature in new ways from nature itself. I began working with nature intelligence in a conscious, coordinated and educated effort that has resulted in a new science called 'co-creative science'."

In a 100-foot-diameter garden, she has created an inclusive environment based on nature's principles of balance. She does not use organic or chemical pesticides, herbicides, or insecticides, or chemical fertilizers. From this work, she has developed guidelines and procedures that anyone can use to establish a balanced environment for such modern areas as apartments and urban homes and yards.

Her intention in creating the garden was to make an environment where all the inhabitants, whether they are plant or animal, truly enhance the life and health of one another. In 1984, she began making flower essences, such as rose essence, as a way of bringing the gifts of her garden to the rest of world. She continues to communicate with the nature spirits and learns new ways of mending the tattered bond between humans and nature.

Through the Ages

In *Summer with the Leprechauns* (Blue Dolphin Publishing, 2004), Tanis Helliwell describes going to Ireland in search of her ancestral roots. She rents a cottage on Achill Island, in County Mayo, where on her first night she meets a family of leprechauns who tell her, "You're living on a haunted land—and not all the elementals here are friendly to humans. You humans call us gnomes, goblins, dwarfs, faeries, elves, and leprechauns, but we're all elementals. That's our race, just like yours is the humans species. There are many kinds of humans, just like there are many kinds of elementals. Now as I was saying, we'll protect you for the summer."

The Spirit of Nature

All of these encounters with nature spirits are fairly recent, and rather than being hearsay, they are all well documented by all of the original participants. They all stressed the fact that humans and nature have become out of balance and when that balance is restored, miraculous things can happen. Also, it shows that things can be grown organically without the help of chemical fertilizers and pesticides. This is not only better for the earth because it doesn't put dangerous chemicals into the environment, it's better for consumers who purchase organic because they aren't putting these chemicals into their bodies.

Each person involved with these encounters perceived the spirit of nature in a somewhat different way. The information was usually communicated during meditation. The following is a listing of people and the nature energy that communicated with them:

- Eileen Caddy—Originally she called it "the still small voice within," later termed it "God"

- Dorothy Maclean—Nature devas

- David Spangler—He called the energy or being he communicated with "limitless love and light"

- Ogilvie Crombie—She could both see and talk to nature spirits, including elves

- Penny Kelly—Elves

- Machaelle Small Wright—Nature intelligence

Living in Harmony

Each of the garden encounters with nature spirits resulted in a harmonious relationship between the participants and the energies of nature. They all warned of a widening rift between humans and nature and how this is impinging on life on this planet. Much of this rift is due to the fact that humans no longer believe in or communicate with the spirits of nature. The result is that humans have grown out of touch with and are destroying nature.

Findhorn has grown larger and more successful by all outside appearances. They continue to grow their garden, but the vegetables produced are more normal in size. Peter Caddy attributes this to the fact that none of the current residents of Findhorn continue the dialogue with the nature devas begun by Dorothy Maclean, and as a result the devas have moved on to other places.

Findhorn is an example of how we can work closely with devas, and how precious such a connection to their world is. Continual effort is needed to sustain this energy. If maintained consistently, devas can come home with you from the temple and stay at your home shrine to help, bless, and gently guide your family. If disharmony and contention are allowed to prevail, the nature spirits have no choice but to leave.

Lily Hill Farm and Perelandra have continued their communication with the nature spirits, although Penny Kelly is no longer making deals with the elves for one hundred tons of grapes. Both of these gardens continue to exhibit the ideal benefits of living in harmony and balance with nature.

Although our scientific mind tells that there is no such thing as elves, fairies, and nature devas, we are continually besieged by accounts to the contrary. In the end, it becomes hard to distinguish between fact and fiction. In the end, these natural gardens are renewing our ancient ties to the spirits of nature while at the same time showing us how to organically grow our food. In the next chapter of our elf and fairy adventure, we look at the synthesis between science and nature a little closer.

An Exercise for Connecting with Nature Devas

Begin by selecting the nature deva that you want to connect with, such as the pea deva, the rose deva, or the dog deva. Now you need something to represent the deva. If it is the pea deva, then find a pea plant, and if it's the dog deva, then find a dog. Place the thing that represents the deva in front of you so that you can easily see it.

Get in a comfortable position and take several deep breaths. As you inhale, feel your senses being energized, and as you exhale, feel all of the tension in your body being released.

Using your senses, begin experiencing the item representing the deva in front of you. Move into it, and become one with it by imagining yourself as the being. If it's a pea plant, then imagine that you have roots, a stalk, branches, and leaves. If it's a dog, then imagine your fur, tail, and keen sense of smell. As much as possible, become the object in front of you. Experience the world as it experiences the world. Be as it is.

Next, move into the energy and begin moving from the one individual to the whole deva energy. In the case of a pea plant, move from the plant sitting in front of you to the whole of all the pea plants. Imagine moving down an energetic path that leads to the deva. Become one with the nature deva. Listen and ask questions when in the presence of the deva.

Afterward, take a few moments to let your consciousness return to your body. Rubbing your body and moving around are great ways to bring your perception back to the present moment.

The Least You Need to Know

- The garden at Findhorn grew successful from communications with nature devas, who told the residents what plants like and dislike.
- Penny Kelly's deal with the elves made Lily Hill Farms possible.
- Machaelle Small Wright developed Perelandra from her communications with nature intelligence.
- All of these experiences point to the need for balance between humans and nature.

19

A Synthesis of Nature and Science

In This Chapter

- ◆ How shamans combined spirituality and science

- ◆ The separation of spirituality and science after the Renaissance

- ◆ Morphic fields and how they relate to elves, fairies, and nature devas

- ◆ Combining spirituality and science to create a fairy amulet

Shamanism and fairy traditions have a commonality in that they both see nature as being filled with a living essence. This living essence is energy fields that are inherent to not only every living thing, but to everything whether animate or inanimate. Up until recently, science has ridiculed these ideas as being primitive, superstitious, and delusional.

Now with recent discoveries, science has had to evaluate its mechanistic view of the world, and allow for the fact that everything is patterned and formed energy. These patterns can take infinite forms and shapes, moving the idea of elves and fairies from magical fantasy to scientific possibility. Some of the discoveries include quantum physics and the idea of morphic fields of energy. Creating a fairy amulet, which we do at the end of this chapter, is one of the ways of generating a morphic field—in this case for protection.

Traditional Views of Nature

Tribal societies realized that a harmonious relationship with nature was crucial to their survival. They gave the task of maintaining this harmonious relationship with nature to priests they called shamans. Shamans performed this task by contacting and communicating with the spirits of nature that lived in every animal, plant, rock, and body of water. This concept of nature spirits is very akin to elves, fairies, and devas.

> **Wizardly Wisdom**
>
> The word *shaman* comes from the Tunguso-Manchurian word *saman*, which means "to know." This gives insight into the role of a shaman as a keeper of knowledge. This knowledge was a blending of both the spiritual and scientific.

Dating back to the beginnings of human society, shamanism was practiced by different cultures throughout the world. From Siberia and Africa to North and South America, shamans used various spiritual techniques, such as ritual, as a means of moving into the realm of nature spirits. They perceived these spirits as being a combination of elementals, ancestral energies, and divine powers.

Like ancient Druids, shamans viewed nature as having both a physical form and a living essence. This living essence is the spirit that resides in everything. It is this spirit that makes nature alive and overflowing with energy. Some of the names given this energy by different cultures and spiritual traditions include …

- Mana—Melanesia and Polynesia
- Kami—Japanese Shinto tradition
- Sacredness—Aborigines
- World soul—Greeks
- Elves and fairies—Ireland

The spirit realm that a tribal shaman moves into in order to communicate with the natural spirits and maintain the harmony with nature is the same as the fairy realm that we have been exploring in this book. Rather than being in any way accidental, shamans purposely move into the spirit realm with a firm intention as to what they want from the interaction. These intentions might include asking for information that could help the welfare of the tribe and asking for healing energy to aid someone who is ill.

The traditional role of the shaman was both spiritual and scientific. Besides contacting and communicating with the spirits of nature, shamans were also doctors, astronomers, and naturalists. They knew about the healing powers of herbs, the movement of the stars, and all about the plants and animals that inhabit nature. This spiritual and scientific knowledge was passed down from generation to generation from shamans to chosen young apprentices who learned their knowledge and then became the next tribal shaman.

This combining of the spiritual and scientific was a common practice up until the Renaissance. In many cases, spiritual priests and religious leaders controlled scientific discovery. In these cases, science was not allowed to openly question the principles of the universe; instead, it was supposed to confirm and validate the prevailing religious beliefs. An excellent example of this was the early Christian church, particularly in the Middle or Dark Ages. Early astronomers were expected to build up evidence supporting the church's contention that the earth was the center of the universe. When astronomers such as Copernicus and Galileo came along with findings that indicated that the earth rotated around the sun, they were threatened with persecution and death.

With the advent of the Renaissance, starting after Christopher Columbus's discovery of the New World, the Christian church's control over the actions of scientists began to wane, ushering in a new era. Isaac Newton postulated about the laws of gravity, Thomas Hobbes wrote about the laws of nature, and René Descartes announced to the world that a new Age of Reason was emerging in which everything in nature could be explained by mechanical or scientific means.

By the seventeenth century, spirituality and science had been thoroughly separated. Religion was delegated to take on matters of morality, while science concerned itself with explaining all the parts of the universe as if they were parts of a machine. Scientists became convinced that, given enough technical information, they could explain anything. To their credit, they did wind up explaining many of the things that happen in the universe, such as how the earth is a rotating sphere that circles the sun in a yearly cycle that takes 365 and ¼ days. All of this scientific information has in many ways made us humans more secure about most of what happens around us. But at the same time, it has had a hard time explaining certain phenomena that as yet cannot be physically measured, such as elves and fairies. What science cannot explain, it has a tendency to dismiss as the fantasy of a creative or delusional mind. This is particularly true of elves, fairies, and other nature spirits.

Through the Ages

Rupert Sheldrake, author of *Seven Experiments That Could Change the World* (Fourth Estate, 1994), writes, "I think a lot of harm was done in the West by splitting apart science and religion in the 17th century. Science became very limited in its focus to mechanical, material things, and religion became very introverted; it became very concerned just with the human spirit and with morality and so forth, and so religion signed over the whole of the natural world including the cosmos to science and science signed over to religion human ethical questions and left this terribly limited domain as the sphere of religion."

In time, science took to the forefront of popular culture and began to expose the inconsistencies of religion. As this happened, spirituality and science become pitted against one another. Religious leaders saw the scientific work of individuals such as Charles Darwin as running contrary to their belief systems. The Bible said God created the world in seven days, and then Darwin came along and contradicted this by saying the world was created by evolution that took millions of years. Scientists could not fathom how priests put their fate in the hands of God, something that could not be proven or explained by scientific means. Eventually this rift between the two became so great that journalists in the 1960s were declaring that God was either dead or had been replaced by science. At that moment in history, it seemed the two would never again come together.

On Guard!

Becoming close-minded or entrenched in a particular mind-set is never a good idea. The world and our perception of it is forever in motion and changing. Tribal people once believed that evil spirits were the cause of disease, but science came along and proved that to be superstition. But now scientific research is showing that negative energies can indeed play a pivotal role in making someone ill.

When the Paths Converge

Just when it looked like God—along with elves, fairies, and all the other magical creatures—was dying just like Tinkerbell did at the end of *Peter Pan*, people's perceptions began changing and the belief in nature spirits came back stronger than ever. Plus scientific discoveries such as quantum physics and the existence of morphic fields has brought a new understanding as to how the spiritual and the physical interplay together to make up what happens in the universe. Now as we move further into the twenty-first century, the paths of spirituality and science have again begun to converse. The important difference this time is that neither is attempting to control the other as in the past.

Through research, scientists have come to the realization that the universe cannot be reduced to the mechanical parts of a machine. The earth and everything that is a part of it is alive with energy. Everything is energy, from the smallest atom to the largest galaxy. This energy is alive and always moving. It also has repetition, pattern, and form to it. From this point, it is not that big of a jump to say that some of these energetic forms include nature spirits such as elves and fairies.

Recent Scientific Discoveries

One of the concepts to come out of quantum physics is the idea that everything down to the quantum level is energy. One of the basic characteristics of energy is that it has tendencies. These tendencies are what give it repetition, pattern, and form. This idea can also be viewed in the theory of particles and waves. Particles are the individual parts, and waves are the energetic patterns that the particles make as they move around.

Quantum research also brought out the fact that researchers can have an effect on what they are researching just by observing it. This means something is happening on a very subtle energetic level that is impacting the flow and pattern of energy. The implications are that human thoughts and other external energies can influence these tendencies of energy. Thought produces energy, which then produces form and pattern. This means our thoughts are more than abstract things in our head. They are beacons of energy that we send out in the world that can have a discernable influence on other energies.

In addition to the work done in quantum physics, the other scientific discovery that has helped bring spirituality and science back together is the effort of individuals such as biologist and contemporary author Rupert Sheldrake. His research has led him to discover the existence of *morphic fields* of energy. As with quantum energy, these morphic fields essentially have to do with tendencies and patterns of energy. Sheldrake calls these

Magical Meaning

Morphic fields are fields of energy within and around units of form or organization. These units include atoms, molecules, crystals, organelles, cells, tissues, organs, organisms, societies, ecosystems, planetary systems, solar systems, and galaxies. Morphic fields include morphogenetic, behavioral, social, cultural, and mental fields of energy.

tendencies *habits*. In his words, "Basically 'morphic fields' are fields of habit set up by habits of thought, habits of activity, and habits of speech."

Morphic fields influence the shape of forms of self-organizing systems, such as the human body. This influence happens from the atomic to the holistic level. Morphic fields are also the basis for the wholeness that scientists observe, where the whole of something equals more than the sum of its individual parts. For example, the human body with its arms, legs, head, and other body parts forms something (the body and its energy) that equals more than the separate parts. The body's morphic field is created by their collective and organized form.

The morphic field of one organism can be sensed by another organism. One of the ways that Sheldrake has tested this idea is to research the energetic bond between pets and their owners. In his book *Dogs That Know When Their Owners Are Coming Home* (Crown, 1999), he cites cases in his research where dogs seem to sense the morphic field of their owners. One of the many tests he performed to prove this idea was to set up a situation where the owner is away and the dog doesn't know when he or she is going to return. What he observed is that dogs visibly start acting different in the time just before their owners return home. In one particular case, a woman was away from home and was instructed to begin returning home at a particular time. When the time arrived and she began to return home, her dog, who had been lying down, began walking around restlessly, continually directing its attention toward the front door.

When Sheldrake explains why the pet knows its owner is returning home, he writes, "Their ability to anticipate this arrival seems to depend on a kind of telepathic bond. We have found by experiment that it cannot be explained in terms of routine times, familiar sounds, or clues given by people at home. I explain this effect in terms of a morphic field connecting pet to owner, through which the owner's intentions to come home are transmitted to the pet."

Wizardly Wisdom

The idea of morphic resonance is comparable to the concepts of nature spirits and devas. Within the context of morphic fields, elves and fairies move from the realm of fantasy to the world of scientific possibility.

Just as morphic fields influence the pattern and form of the organism that is connected to it, morphic fields in turn are influenced by what is known as morphic resonance. Morphic resonance is a collective memory that each kind of thing possesses as a whole. A dog currently living in California is influenced by all past dogs, who together form the collective dog-memory. Similar to Carl Jung's theory of the collective unconscious, this collective memory or morphic resonance is an energy that can be sensed by the individual parts. With dogs, it means each dog connects to the whole of the collective dog-memory.

The concept of morphic resonance is very similar to the idea of nature devas that we explored in Chapters 17 and 18. Surprisingly, scientific research then starts providing evidence for the spiritual idea that there is an energy or spirit that surrounds every individual thing, every grouping of individuals, and everything as a whole. The energetic field that surrounds everything together as one is known as "oneness."

The Evolution of Religion

Religions originally sought to control people's thoughts and actions, including those of researchers and scientists. When the Renaissance arrived and scientific knowledge began expanding by leaps and bounds, religious leaders had to relinquish this control. They also had to come to terms with scientific discoveries in order to stay current. Science forced religion to adopt scientific ideas and evolve to the point where it had to allow for scientific points of view. No longer did the universe revolve around the earth, as was the view in the Middle Ages.

The movement of people recently has been to move more toward *spirituality* and away from organized *religions*. The infusion of Eastern spiritual ideas into Western culture has led a number of people to seek their own spiritual path. People like Joseph Campbell have shown the similarities between different spiritualities and religions, particularly in terms of creation, mortality, and the divine. These similarities have made it easy for people to combine different spiritual ideas together into something that personally works.

> **Magical Meaning**
>
> **Spirituality** is a set of beliefs that relate to the spirit, including creation, mortality, and a connection to the divine. **Religion** is organized spirituality, whose structure exerts a certain amount of control over its members.

Finding Common Ground

The combination of scientific ideas such as quantum physics and morphic fields with spiritual ideas has led to a certain amount of common ground between spirituality and science. Science is less quick to dismiss matters of the spirit and the divine. With the understanding that everything is energy, and this energy has pattern and takes form, scientific researchers opened the door to the spiritual realm. Also, the idea that thought can influence this energy and form is what traditional magic and fairy traditions are all about.

Traditional magical techniques involved the steps of intention, desire, and merging. First of all, you get a clear image of what it is you want. Second, you focus your energy on the object of your intention. Third, you merge with the divine and become one with your intention and desire. When you do this, you release the energy you have built up and send it toward the energetic or magical pattern you want to achieve.

Wizardly Wisdom

Traditional spiritualities and religions long believed that plants and animals had souls. In the Middle Ages, it was the official doctrine of the Catholic church. Even the word *animal* comes from the Latin word *anima*, meaning soul.

Spirituality and science have also found common ground in the idea that everything has a living spirit. Within spirituality, this living spirit originates from the divine forces of creation and is in everything. Within science, it is part of the energetic field that is in and around everything. These individual fields of energy then make up larger and larger fields of energy until you reach the infinite, which in spiritual terms is the divine. Spirituality and science are traveling different paths to reach the same place.

The Road Ahead

Spirituality and science need to continue to work together. They are in no way separate or exclusive of one another, and in the long run can help each other to understand the many riddles of our world. Matters of creation, mortality, and divine energies are no longer the exclusive concern of spirituality; and matters of how the universe works are no longer left entirely to science.

Elves and fairies move from the realm of magic to the world of possibilities and probabilities. As this happens, the road ahead starts looking much different. This is particularly true as new discoveries continue to move the world closer and closer to the one envisioned by fantasy and science fiction writers.

The following is a technique for creating a fairy amulet. This technique combines the ideas of spirituality, in this case magic, and science, in this case morphic fields of energy.

Creating a Fairy Amulet

Traditionally, amulets were protective charms that were usually worn in the form of a necklace or ring. Also hung in the house, they could purportedly repel or drive away negative energies such as harmful elves and fairies. Similar to talismans, amulets were normally made of metal or stone because these materials most readily hold an energetic charge.

When you make an amulet you are creating a morphic field of energy in and around a piece of metal or stone. Metals and stones naturally conduct energetic fields. You create the morphic field of energy around the object with your thoughts and intention.

Begin by selecting a piece of metal or stone that you want to turn into an amulet. Energetically clear out the object by cupping it between both your hands, and imagine in your mind the image of a clear mountain stream. Pulse your breath out your nose, and at the same time envision the image of the clear mountain stream moving through and cleansing the object of all energy patterns.

On a blank piece of paper, start listing all of the qualities that you would like your amulet to have. In this case you are using it for protection, so list all of the ways that it is going to protect you. List what types of energies it is going to protect you from, and how far the energetic field of the amulet will extend outward.

Open your fairy ring or circle as described in the section on rituals in Chapter 16. Next invite the energy of the fairy queen Anu into your circle, by saying:

> Anu, queen of the fairies,
>
> Please bless my circle with your energy.

Sit comfortably in the middle of your circle with your piece of metal or stone in the palm of your outstretched power hand (your right hand if you're right-handed). Place the sheet of paper with the qualities you want the amulet to have next to you so you can see it clearly. Take several deep breaths, each time focusing on the qualities that you want to impart into your amulet.

When the image of the protective qualities that you want to move into the amulet is firmly in your mind, then set in the pattern by calling out:

> Anu, bestow into this stone
>
> The power to repel all invaders.

Protect me from all harmful energies.

So mote it be.

Clap your hands firmly three times. Your amulet is now ready to use to protect you from harmful elves and fairies.

The Least You Need to Know

♦ Traditionally spirituality and science were intertwined together.

♦ Beginning with the Renaissance, they began to separate from one another.

♦ Every self-sustaining form has a morphic field of energy moving in and around it.

♦ Spirituality and science have once again begun converging.

♦ Amulets have a morphic field around them, which is where they derive their power for protection.

Chapter 20

Planting a Fairy Garden

In This Chapter

- ◆ Explore the magical world of fairy gardens
- ◆ Find your fairy garden's "sweet spot"
- ◆ Determining what flowers and trees to plant
- ◆ Bringing natural beauty indoors

The magical power of elves and fairies dwells in nature, be it wild and untamed or cultivated and planted. These magical beings reside in the trees, flowers, stones, mountains, and hills. They appear in meadows of wildflowers and green grass, in thickly wooded forests, in vegetable and flower gardens, as well as in fountains, wells, lakes, rivers, creeks, and oceans. They protect and regulate the abundance and fertility of the earth herself.

Planting a fairy garden is a way of bringing the elf and fairy energy into your outside space. This involves finding a "sweet spot" and determining what kinds of flowers and trees to plant that will bring enchantment to your garden. In the following sections I tell you how to make this happen.

Garden of Delight

I am always so pleased when my garden comes alive in the spring. Suddenly trees and bulbs bloom, and then the flowers, bushes, shrubs, and vegetables all sprout and grow. One of sweetest spots to watch nature at work is in my garden and the forest surrounding it. I can feel the fairies nestled in the flowers and trees, and I know I am a part of nature as I work my gentle magic in my garden. I make every effort to work with nature, with the fairies and elves, to grow beautiful flowers and delicious vegetables and fruits.

The best way to attract the helpful elves and fairies into your life is to plant a fairy garden. You can plant one large garden with trees, flowers, and vegetables that fairies and elves particularly like, or you can plant separate smaller flower and vegetable gardens if you prefer. They will attract flower and vegetable fairies accordingly. If you only have a small space, you can plant flowers, certain trees, and some vege-tables in large pots, and create a fairy haven on your balcony, patio, or in a window box. Whenever possible, be sure to include some favorite fairy trees in your garden because they attract helpful elves.

When you plant your garden with love and care, the fairies will honor you with their presence and magical gifts. The simple pleasure of stepping into a fairy garden to touch and smell the fragrant flowers and herbs can reconnect you with the beauty of nature, in particular the elves, fairies, and nature devas.

Gardens reflect your unique tastes. They act as a magic mirror into fairyland. If you always keep in mind that the elves and fairies treat you in the same manner as you treat them, you will be blessed by their magical gifts. You will be working in harmony with nature and allowing her bounty to nurture and sustain you.

Fairy gardens provide inspiration. Magical beings float on the fragrant scent of flow-ers, and you can sometimes hear the soft laughter, joyful singing, and merry music they create on the afternoon breeze. Gardens offer a magical haven where you can better get in touch with the elf and fairy within yourself as well as become more aware of the changing seasons. When you are in your garden, it's important to listen to the fairy and elf messages, the messages of the nature spirits, so that your garden will thrive with the blessings of the gentle folk.

Be creative when you design your fairy garden. Use color harmonics to add balance to your garden; for example, red to bring more passion into your life, pink to bring more romance, and gold to bring you fairy riches. Include tiny fairy houses, bat and birdhouses, as well as bee boxes. These additions will charm and delight your elven and fairy friends. You can even create a grassy area just for fairy dancing and merry-making. Or if you own a few acres, you might dedicate a meadow with wildflowers to the unicorns, or a rock outcropping to the dwarves.

Fairy gardens are also the perfect place for a secret rendezvous, engagement, wedding, or handfasting (a fairy or pagan marriage, which is sacredly symbolic of the union of the divine mother and father). After all, the Fairy Queen Titania and Fairy King Oberon were married atop a small, mossy magic garden knoll surrounded by soft, fragrant white roses and sweet-smelling jasmine vines in full bloom. The elves and fairies that attended sat gently on the lemon verbena, with bouquets of lilies of the valley and forget-me-nots for the bride in their hands.

Fairy Tales and Legends

Most fairy gardens are more than a little extraordinary. In L. Frank Baum's 1911 fairy tale "The Sea Fairies," he described the fairy garden of the queen of the mermaids. It was a vast cavern in the sea, so great that the dome overhead looked like the sky. In the center of the immense cavern was a splendid coral castle. Surrounding the castle was a magical garden filled with beds of beautiful sea flowers, all in full bloom, and laid out with great care in artistic patterns. Gold and silver fish darted here and there among the flowers.

Remember that each and every fairy garden contributes to the natural beauty of our planet. For this reason, I feel that everyone needs to experience the joy of growing a garden. When doing so, we realize that we're part of nature, not separate from it. When you connect with the elves and fairies, you open yourself to the spirit of beauty and feelings of love and compassion. When the wind blows, it is your breath. When the tree gains strength, you gain strength. When the rosebud opens with beauty, you also open to your beautiful inner spirit.

Getting Things Ready

Begin by figuring out the best location for your fairy garden, the sweet spot. In music recording, the sweet spot is the ideal spot to put the microphone. It is the warmest, most resonant spot that captures the fullness of the sound. Use this metaphor when selecting your fairy garden spot. Choose the spot that feels right to you, one that has the best vibrations.

The sweet spot can be in your yard, on your balcony or patio, in front of a window box, or in the middle of several terra cotta pots. It needs to be a spot where there is the right amount of sun and shade to successfully grow the plants you have in mind. It should be a bright place to grow plants and trees that are desirable to friendly elves and fairies. It should be a spot conducive to feeling the soft breath of the elves and fairies on your skin.

A variety of items are available that you can add to your garden. Fairy garden motifs are rapidly gaining popularity in garden magazines, books, on the Internet, and in gardening stores. There are elf and fairy ornaments, winged fairies, garden gnomes, mermaid fountains, glass orbs, dragon weathervanes, and fairy wind chimes. You can paint fairies and elves on your flowerpots and add small stones that you have collected in nature. Bird feeders and birdhouses are the perfect selection, as are water ponds, birdbaths, and other water features.

> **Through the Ages**
>
> From inside comes a voice and from inside comes the scent. Just as one can tell human beings in the dark from tone of voices, so in the dark, every flower can be recognized by its scent. Each carries the soul of its progenitor.
>
> —From *Nanna, the Soul-Life of Plants* by Gustav Fechner (1801–1887), German scientist and mystic

When you tend your garden in a happy mood, your garden thrives in kind. You begin to communicate with nature around you, listening to its soft breathing messages. By working with the nature spirits, you can co-create your fairy wonderland and better know which plants to use for healing, dreaming, and making magic. Also, if there are problems with the plants, trees, or animals nearby, you are better able to listen to their cries for help and find a remedy.

Determining What to Plant and Other Practical Considerations

To determine what you want to plant, it certainly helps to become familiar with the flora and fauna of your area. Easy ways to do this are by checking out bird and flower books from your local library, or joining a garden or bird-watching club such as the Audubon Society.

Before you start planting your garden, sit down and relax in the space you have allocated. Commune with the flower, herb, and tree elves and fairies of each of the kinds of things you are planning to plant. Ask for instruction on how to create the best possible fairy garden, and how to help those plants and trees in it to flourish and grow strong.

Garden elves and fairies have a fondness for thyme, clover, and foxglove. To attract fairies to your garden, plant pansies, snapdragons, foxglove, forget-me-nots, roses, sunflowers, honeysuckle, yarrow, lilac bushes, as well as verbena, daisies, rosemary, thyme, and lavender. Planting bluebells is a way to attract dancing and singing fairies, and planting rosemary is a means of attracting the sea fairies and butterflies. Grow poppies to entice the helpful fairies into your dreams, and plant snapdragons to protect you from mischievous fairies. Remember to always leave a small section of your fairy garden uncultivated and wild in honor of your elven and fairy allies. Both cultivated and wild flowers appeal to fairies, as do flowers on what might be considered garden weeds. And every fairy garden needs some clover and a garden snake.

If space allows, be sure to plant a few fairy trees such as the apple in your fairy garden, too. In this way you will experience the power and wisdom of the elves as you sit with your back against a flowering apple or a budding oak.

If you have limited space—let's say a small patio, balcony, or window box—I suggest you plant flowers, vegetables, and trees specially suited to your environment and space. For example, plant lots of flats of blooming pansies in larger pots on your patio in the spring. Pansies like a mixture of shade and sun and are very hardy. Add miniature roses and rose trees if space allows. There are also miniature and drawf trees you can grow in small spaces. You can also grow vegetables; for example, large, deep pots planted with young tomato plants produce very well on sunny balconies. Call your local nursery to find out what grows best in your area and in the space you have available for gardening. Local nurseries and garden stores provide a wealth of information and suggestions to make your fairy garden a blooming success!

Wizardly Wisdom

The herb most associated with the fairies is the flowering herb thyme, which also attracts butterflies and bees. The fairy queen Titania in Shakespeare's *A Midsummer Night's Dream* sleeps in a bed of thyme, and Pilliwiggin in England is a wild thyme fairy. Wild thyme mixed with calendula flowers, rosewater, and hazelnut buds is an old English recipe for an elixir to help one see fairies. There is a copy of the original recipe in the Ashmolean Museum in Oxford. The best time for blending this mixture is at Beltane or Midsummer.

Every year I draw out where I want to plant the seeds of my vegetable garden. I like to rotate my crops so everything's in a different place each year, which has the interesting effect of making each garden unique. Another thing that happens to make each year unique is that after I plant my seeds, things always sprout that I didn't plant. The first year it was lettuce that appeared in little places throughout the garden. The next year it was melons, and the third year it was little white pumpkins that I used to decorate our home for the harvest celebration. These unexpected garden plants are gifts from the fairies and the divine Mother Goddess, popularly known as Mother Nature or Mother Earth.

Keep your soil healthy in your fairy garden and it will produce more vibrant foods, flowers, bushes, and trees. Become familiar with the type of soil you have and the weather zone you are in. Ask your local gardeners what flowers, herbs, vegetables, and trees grow best in your area. This will save you a lot of gardening grief.

One way to ensure fairy goodwill is to leave the first and last fruit of any harvest out for the fairies. You also can leave mead, sweets, or wine for your garden flower fairies, next to where fairy flowers grow. Be generous to them and they will bless your garden. When you plant elf and fairy flowers and herbs, say a simple, sincere blessing such as:

> May the elves and fairies bless this splendid flower (or herb) with fragrant beauty.

When you plant vegetable seeds and plants, bless them by saying:

> May the elves and fairies bless these seeds (or plants) with light and nourishment.

Likewise, when you plant a fairy tree, say a blessing such as:

> May the elves and fairies bless this tree with strength and wisdom.

For more specific blessings for relationships, wellness, and enrichment, for instance with the lavender deva, refer to my book *Empowering Your Life with Natural Magic* (see Appendix A).

Wizardly Wisdom

The best times to encounter elves and fairies in your garden are at dawn, noon, twilight, midnight, and during full moons and on Great Days (see Chapter 11). They are more likely to show themselves at these times. For example, you might feel the soft brushing sensation of a winged fairy at midnight on a warm summer's night during a full moon. Or you might glimpse a flower fairy out of the corner of your eye, drinking dewdrops from the flowers at dawn on Beltane morning.

Favorite Fairy Flowers

Elves and fairies adore the natural beauty of flowers. Some of their favorites have been named for them. For example, heritage roses such as the Fairy Rose with their mass of pink blossoms are the perfect selection for your fairy garden, as is Fairy's Petticoat, a pink clematis that requires a trellis. Other favorites are Pink Fairy's baby's breath, with its soft pink blossoms; plum-eyed daylilies called Fairy Jester; and miniature roses called Fairy Moss, with their deep pink flowers. Plant forget-me-nots and then run your hands over the full blooms to help you actually see the flower fairies.

Flowers will certainly please and delight your magical friends, and bring you, your family, and your friends hours of joy in your garden. Also remember to return all the flowers to the earth once they are spent in respect for elves and fairies. When you do so, say a simple thank you to the helpful flower fairies and elves.

Planting a Fairy Tree Garden

Trees embody the three worlds of subterranean (roots), middle earth (trunk), and celestial (branches and leaves). They are blessed and protected by the fairies and elves, and as such can be used as bridges to the Otherworld of fairyland.

There are many ways to gain rapport with the tree elves and fairies. For example, you can sit, meditate, sleep, or simply daydream beneath a favorite tree, inviting the elves and fairies to communicate with you. You can eat a piece of ripe fruit from a fruit tree, thus becoming one with the tree and its spirit. You can lean against a tree or climb the tree, sit in its branches, and sing a favorite song to draw the magic to you. You can also scatter pieces of the tree such as bark and leaves in your fairy ring as a way to attract helpful fairy and elf favors and insights.

Fairy tree gardens include the fairy trees that attract elves and fairies, especially tree dryads. Trees are alive with these divine spirits. The elves and fairies have always known this, but unfortunately mortals haven't. All trees have a nature spirit, most often called a tree wight or dryad. The dryad is unique to the kind of tree it inhabits, so oak dryads appear somewhat different than willow dryads; they more closely resemble oak trees than willows. For the most part, this holds true for all dryads.

Attract the helpful dryads by planting a few of the trees that are favored by fairies in your gardens. These include alder, apple, ash, beech, blackthorn, elm, hawthorn, hazel, and willow trees. You will be delighted with the shade, fruit, birds, and seasonal beauty of the trees, and you will be blessed with the divine favors of the tree spirits.

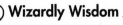

Wizardly Wisdom

I encountered an oak tree dryad in front of my home one evening at twilight. As I was walking by the ancient oak, a luminous woman flowed out of the tree trunk. She had greenish hair that flowed down past her feet. She was over eight feet tall, with brown skin. I stood perfectly still and asked her who she was. She told me she was the Lady of the Tree, and that she wanted me to cut back the small madrone trees that were crowding her branches. I promised I would do so, and she flowed back into the oak tree. Needless to say, I have a different view of that oak tree than I did before encountering its dryad!

Bringing in the Magic

You can enjoy the natural magic of fairy flowers, herbs, and trees all year long by bringing blossoms, sprigs, and boughs inside your home and workplace. Cut-flower arrangements bring fragrant beauty to every room of your home and to your workplace. You can arrange fresh vegetables in a basket on skewers and take the fairy basket to a party and share it with friends and family. You can create a horn of plenty at harvest time with fairy garden gourds, pumpkins, and ears of corn. You can share flowers, bulbs, and cuttings with people you care about so that they can start their own magical fairy gardens. You can also grow houseplants such as ferns to encourage the favors of the elves and fairies and add natural beauty to your living and working environments.

One fun and creative way to bring the magic of your garden onto your balcony, patio, or next to your front door is by making a living fairy wreath. You will need an 8-inch to 10-inch round wire frame, moss, wetted earth, copper wire, and plants. Jade and other succulents work best for this wreath. Put the moss down first around the wreath frame, and then lay the wetted earth on the moss. Use the copper wire to wind around the wetted earth and moss and frame so that you make a donut-shaped wreath. Wind the copper wire around the frame, moss, and wetted earth three times to secure everything in place. As you wind the wire around the frame, chant:

Three times wound and wound.

Fairy favors round and round.

Next, use a pair of tweezers to poke a small hole in the moss. Plant the small succulents, such as jade, into the moss. Poke them in well and they will root quickly. With each small plant you poke into the wreath, repeat:

Blessed be the fairies!

Cover the wreath with succulents. Water the living fairy wreath by placing it in a garbage can top or similar container filled with water. Let it soak for an hour. Remember, the succulents in your fairy wreath will not withstand freezing temperatures, so bring it indoors if the temperature drops.

The Least You Need to Know

- ◆ Fairy gardens put you in touch with the power of nature and elf and fairy energies, while beautifying your environment and creating a peaceful haven.

- ◆ When planting your fairy garden, first find the sweet spot—the spot that has the best energies for growing fairy and elven favorite flowers, vegetables, and trees.

- ◆ Determine what to plant by becoming familiar with the many fairy flowers and trees that are certain to attract friendly fairies and elves into your garden space.

- ◆ Keeping your soil and garden environment naturally healthy greatly pleases the fairies and elves and will draw their favors and gifts to you and your loved ones.

- ◆ There are many ways you can bring the beauty of the outdoors inside to enjoy all year round.

Part 6 Exploring the Magical Powers of Elves and Fairies

The last part of our elf and fairy adventure takes a look at the things associated with elves and fairies. This includes different elven and fairy foods and beverages, with a detailed list and some magical (and tasty!) recipes. Next, I tell you all about elven and fairy herbs, stones, and essences and how they can be used for medicinal and magical purposes. The book concludes with a series of exercises and techniques designed to help you connect with the elf and fairy energy within you. It's a way of bringing another level of depth to the life experience.

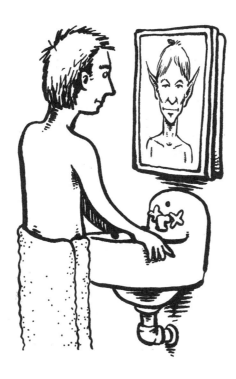

Chapter 21

Eat, Drink, and Be Merry

In This Chapter

- ◆ The foods and beverages elves and fairies like best
- ◆ Celebrate the magic of elves and fairies with a picnic party
- ◆ Have a fairy wedding and reception
- ◆ Some magical recipes to satisfy the elves and fairies in your home (and you!)

Traditionally, the exchange of food and beverages was a way for elves, fairies, and humans to cement their relationships. There is something sacred about food and drink in that they come from the divine creator as a means of sustaining our lives. Beyond this sacredness, food and drink have a magical quality that gives them the sensations of taste, texture, smell, and vitality. In a practical sense, food and drink give us vitamins and such to keep our physical bodies healthy, which in turn keeps our mental and spiritual bodies well.

This chapter contains a broad listing of elven and fairy foods and beverages as well as suggestions for having a fairy party and ideas for a fairy wedding. The section at the end of the chapter contains several good recipes for food and beverages that you could serve at your next fairy party or wedding, depending on your mood and who will be there.

Favorite Fairy Fare

Most friendly fairies are vegetarians. Fairy food favorites include beans and corn, mushrooms, cheeses, nuts, and seaweed, as well as roots, herbs, fruits, breads, cakes, ice cream, and pies. They have a fondness for beverages such as honeyed milk, cream, wines, beers, ales, meads, and teas. They are known to create magical displays of food at fairy banquets and feasts, with whimsical ice sculpture centerpieces. Fairy food is often shaped in the forms of trees, leaves, flowers, animals, birds, and butterflies.

> **Fairy Tales and Legends**
>
> The Oakmen in Beatrix Potter's *The Fairy Caravan* live in oak stumps with saplings. They are dwarflike men with red caps and noses who tempt intruders in their woods with appetizing foods that are actually made of fungi.

Because the fairy energy originated in the spirits of the old agricultural goddesses and gods of the earth, they controlled the ripening of the crops and the milk yields, and thus offerings were given to the fairies at regular intervals.

To attract elves and fairies to your home and garden, leave them food offerings—traditionally milk, fresh water, bread, and cheese. When you make them feel welcome and show them the proper hospitality by offering favorite foods, you're creating a bond of trust.

Elves and fairies like human food and drink. There are many tales of fairy theft of milk, butter, and grain. The Danish elves are known to steal bread dough, their particular fondness. Most fairies and elves like acorns, nuts, and berries, especially the berries from red-berried trees and bushes. Other foods they love are barley, candies, cakes, butter, milk, and honey.

> **Wizardly Wisdom**
>
> To befriend a pixie or sprite, go to a place where they live and call to them in a respectful way. When they come, keep them close by flattering them constantly and offering them gifts of acorns and sweets.

In England, people who befriend the elves and fairies leave offerings of sweet milk and bread on their stoves, or milk or cream in a saucer in the kitchen. To attract helpful, friendly elves and fairies and win their favors, put abundant food offerings on a plate or in a wooden bowl in your kitchen, just outside your door, or in your garden, backyard, or balcony. Remember that compost is a form of fairy offering in that the food is given back to the earth, home of the fairies. It also enriches the soil so you can grow more food.

More often than not, depending where you live, the food offering will still be there the next morning. The elves and fairies don't necessarily eat the food. Many times an animal (such as a bird) or an insect will eat the offering. This is a very good omen, as it might be a fairy or elf in another natural form enjoying your offering.

Favorite Elven and Fairy Foods and Beverages

Here's a summary of some elf and fairy favorites:

- ◆ **Apples and fruits**—Apple trees, like most fruit trees, are sacred to the elves and fairies. The fruit of the apple represents love, romance, fertility, healing, and immortality. Leave the first and the last piece of fruit on apple, peach, apricot, plum, pear, kiwi, cherry, and nectarine trees as an offering to the elves and fairies. Fruits left on the trees and not picked are often referred to as the pixie or fairy harvest.

- ◆ **Barley**—Sprinkle dry barley around your fairy ring and circle to draw earth fairies and elves to you as well as their favors and gifts. Barley is one of their main foods. This healing grain can also be put in small mounds or circles in your garden or yard to attract helpful fairies and to bring more abundance into your life.

- ◆ **Beer**—If you want to brew beer yourself, it's always best to get the blessings of the elves and fairies. Beer is made from fermented barley, a grain the fairies are particularly fond of. Be sure to leave the elves and fairies a bit of your beer or ale, for example when you are on a picnic in the woods, or offer a bit to a stream or river as you ask for the blessings of the helpful fairies. House elves and brownies also like a bit of beer!

- ◆ **Blackberries**—The elves and fairies particularly like blackberry wine, berries, and jam. Go blackberry picking on the days closest to Lughnassad, and eat them as you pick them, make cobbler or pie, or put them over vanilla ice cream.

> **Fairy Tales and Legends**
>
> In European myths, fairy islands of apple orchards were paradises of eternal youth. The legendary British Isle of Avalon (Isle of Apples) was in the West. King Arthur was taken there as he lay dying by Morgana, the ruler of nine fairy sisters who guarded the apples of the Otherworld. To the Celts the Land of Promise, Avalon, was an apple orchard where the trees were always in fruit.

- **Butter**—Fairies and elves enjoy creamy butter. Whether they are feeling sweet or sour often has a direct effect on the quality of the butter (fairies traditionally can spoil butter if they feel they've been mistreated). They love offerings of butter, cream, honey, and cakes, and will bestow their favors upon those who leave bits of their favorite treats on a small plate in the kitchen or on the doorstep.

- **Cakes and candies**—Elves and fairies have a soft spot for sweets, and they love offerings of bits of cakes and candies. They love all flavors and kinds of sweets. Sugar is one of the best ways to attract fairies.

Through the Ages

In *The Merry Wives of Windsor*, Shakespeare writes "God defend from that Welsh fairy, Lest he transform me to a piece of cheese!"

- **Cheese**—Most fairies and elves have a hankering for a bit of good cheese now and again. Leave a few small squares of your favorite cheese in your garden for the fairies, or a few bits in the forest or park for the elves.

- **Honey**—Wild honey is the fairies' and elves' favorite kind. They like the sweet taste of honey, and bees are sacred them. Leave a bit of honey in a bowl in your garden or yard as an offering. Coat toasted bread with honey and cover it with sunflower seeds. Put the bread out for the birds to eat to draw fairy and elf favors and gifts to you.

- **Juices**—Fruit juice is the nectar of the gods, so all kinds of tasty juices are favorites of the fairies and elves. Leave a small sweet juice offering for the fairies in your garden, or under a fruit tree, after toasting to their health and fortune.

- **Milk**—Fairies and elves absolutely adore milk, honeyed milk, and cream. If milk or cream goes bad or is spilt, then it is seen as an offering to the fairies. In Cornwall, England, no one is scolded for spilling milk because it is seen as a gift to the good people.

- **Mushrooms**—Small, winged fairies sometimes dine on toadstools and fairy butter made from tree fungi. By means of glamour, elves and fairies also make their own food from mushrooms and leaves.

- **Spices**—The spices the fairies and elves like the best are fragrant, tasty ones such as basil, thyme, rosemary, bay, and cinnamon. Scatter spices around your fairy ring and circle, and use the aromatic powers of spices to deepen your connection with the fairies when meditating, praying, or doing rituals.

- **Teas**—Fairies are fond of lavender, jasmine, chamomile, mint, rose hip, and vanilla teas. Encourage fairy encounters by drinking herbal teas that appeal to flower, garden, or woodland fairies you are trying to attract.

- **Vegetables**—The fairies particularly like corn, beans, tomatoes, peas, squash, carrots, celery, eggplant, lettuce, cauliflower, and cabbage. Make offerings of the first and last vegetables of the season to the fairies and elves. Leave the last corn stalk in your garden to honor them. When cooking vegetables, put a piece in the compost container as a fairy offering.

- **Water**—Being one of the essential elements of life, fairies are partial to pure and natural water without chemicals or additives, for example water from a clear mountain stream, fresh well water, or a bubbling artisan spring.

- **Wines and spirits**—All fairies and elves like wine and spirits, and often protect wine cellars, vintners, and distilleries. Leave a small offering of wine or spirits after you toast to the splendid health and magical powers of the fairies and elves.

> **Fairy Tales and Legends**
>
> On the Isle of Man, people believed that if fresh water was not left out for the fairies overnight, they would retaliate by sucking the blood of those sleeping in the house.

One word of caution: Never eat or drink anything offered to you by an elf or fairy! There are stories of mortals being carried away into fairyland, or held there if they ventured into a fairy hill and tasted fairy food or drink. Thomas the Rhymer, the legendary Scottish bard, was warned by the fairy queen about eating the apples in her garden. She told him if he ate fairy food he would never return to the land of the living.

Fairy Picnic Party

As you probably know, food always seems to taste better outdoors. So take your loved ones on a fairy picnic in nature, preferably by a stream, pond, lake, or other body of water (water enhances the experience). The experience is certain to bless and sweeten your lives with adventure and a little fairy magic!

Choose a sunny afternoon and invite one or more of your favorite people. Bring along some fresh flowers for your fairy ring, a picnic lunch with tasty fairy foods such as apples, peaches, grapes, cakes, candies, bread, and cheese, and fairy brews such as chilled sparkling cider, beer, ale, or a bottle of wine. Also bring plenty of water, a blanket, folding chairs, and a guitar or CD player if you want some music.

Before you spread out your blanket, set up your chairs, and lay out the food, draw a fairy ring and scatter the fresh flowers clockwise around it. As you do this, have everyone chant together:

> Friendly elves and fairies
>
> Bless our picnic party!

Set up your chairs and picnic inside the fairy ring. Savor each bite of delicious food and toast to the fairies and elves. Leave a few choice morsels as offerings to them. Enjoy each other's company, some music, stories, and the beauty of nature for an hour or two or three. Before you leave, give the offerings to the fairies and elves of the area. Be sure to pick up any trash and leave the spot as undisturbed and natural as possible.

Fairy Weddings

Fairy weddings involve the marriage of two people (humans). The weddings traditionally last seven days: the three days before the wedding day, the wedding day, and the three days after the wedding day. During the three days before the ceremony, the bride and groom go on a quest for each other. The quest set is traditionally something your beloved can reasonably accomplish in three days. The results of the quests of the bride and groom are presented at the wedding ceremony. For example, the bride sets the groom upon a quest for 100 red roses. He presents the roses to her before the wedding ceremony begins in an enchantingly loving and magical manner. Be creative and have fun!

If possible, perform the wedding ceremony outdoors in the woods, in a meadow, or somewhere in the splendor of nature. Draw a large fairy ring, ample enough to contain all of your guests and festivities. Invite the friendly fairies and elves into the ring. Even though you might not see them, you will know they are there with you by the caress of a fairy breeze, a flash of green light in the forest in front of you, or a song in the air that is and isn't there.

Draw a fairy circle for the wedding ceremony itself. Have fun and allow your whimsy and mischievous spirit to blossom. For example, the bride (referred to as the Fairy Queen) and the groom (referred to as the Fairy King) should dress in fairylike clothes. Also encourage the person who performs the ceremony and your guests to dress in a similar fairylike manner. Be sure to include music, singing, and dancing as these are activities the fairies especially adore. Remember that the fairies and elves especially like it when the wedding gifts are ones that are handmade or special in some way.

At the reception, decorate the space accordingly in a magical theme, and serve special fairy foods such as strawberries, apple pastries, breads, cheese, wines, and ciders. Include fairy ice sculptures and flowers.

Keep in mind, it's always a good idea to have someone other than the bride and groom cook and serve the food. Toast the bride (Fairy Queen) and groom (Fairy King) as well as the friendly fairy folk. Leave many offerings of the bits of wedding food and drink to the fairies and elves when the ceremony and reception are over. By doing so, you will most likely win their favors for many moons.

> **Wizardly Wisdom**
>
> There are several sites on the Internet that feature fairy wedding dresses, shirts, pants, swords, jewelry, and capes. Check out Visabella at www.visabella.com or The Noble Collection at www.noblecollection.com.

For an enchanting wedding night (and three days and nights after the wedding), do this fun and tasty fairy ritual. Draw a fairy ring around your wedding bed. Sprinkle rose petals around the ring and on your bed. Put a bowl of fresh strawberries or other berries in a bowl and put it on the bed. A loving gift the bride (Fairy Queen) and groom (Fairy King) can offer each other is to express their love for one another through a fairy strawberry offering on their wedding night. You can also do this anytime you'd like to reaffirm your loving bond with your beloved. The strawberry represents love, romance, passion, magical gifts, and good fortune. Feed your beloved one strawberry at a time, and say:

> Your love is enchantingly sweet and magical.

Have your beloved feed you one strawberry at a time, and repeat:

> And your love is enchantingly sweet and sublime.

Do this several times, leaving a few berries in the bowl as an offering to the fairies of love and romance. Enjoy the loving magic of the night!

Magical Recipes

The following fairy food and drink recipes are easy to make, fun, and tasty. Bring a little elf and fairy magic to others as you share these elf and fairy favorites with your family and friends.

Fairy Cinnamon Butter

> ½ cup confectioners' sugar
>
> ½ teaspoon cinnamon
>
> 1 stick butter, softened
>
> 1 tablespoon orange juice

Combine all the ingredients in a bowl and blend until completely mixed and creamy. As you do this, chant:

> Sweet magic come to me.
>
> Elves and fairies, blessed be!

Refrigerate the fairy butter and use within the next few days. Spread liberally on bagels, biscuits, muffins, cakes, and toast for a treat at breakfast or teatime.

Sweet Strawberry Fairy Potion

> 1½ cups ginger ale
>
> 1 cup fresh strawberries, hulled
>
> 1½ cups vanilla ice cream

Blend all the ingredients in a blender until smooth and creamy. As you blend the potion, chant:

> Sweet strawberry fairies so bright
>
> Bless this potion with magic light!
>
> So be it! Blessed be!

Serve in chilled glasses with green and red straws. Serves two.

Flower Fairy Honey

> ½ cup fresh pansy petals, rinsed, dried, and finely chopped
>
> 1 jar wild honey
>
> 1 pot warm water

Scoop out three teaspoons of honey and offer it to the flower fairies by leaving them a small offering. Next, warm the jar of honey by putting it in the pot of warm water. Add the pansy petals to the jar of honey. Hold it between your hands and say three times:

> Bees, flowers, and fairies
>
> With your magic, bless this honey.

Put the jar back in the pot of warm water, uncapped. Do not allow any water to get into the jar. Put the pot over low heat and simmer gently for about 30 minutes. Allow the honey to cool. Cap and store the flower fairy honey for 12 days before using to allow the flowers to steep. Add the honey to your tea or put it on biscuits and muffins. Make an offering of flower fairy honey to the flower fairies in your garden or yard by dripping a bit of the fairy honey on the ground. Use the honey within 30 days.

Fairy Nut Sweets

> ½ cup butter, softened
>
> ¾ cup light brown sugar
>
> ½ cup confectioners' sugar
>
> 1 teaspoon flower fairy honey (see previous recipe)
>
> 1 tablespoon vanilla
>
> 2 eggs
>
> 1 tablespoon fresh lavender flowers, washed, rinsed, and finely chopped
>
> 1¾ cups flour
>
> 2 teaspoons baking powder
>
> ½ cup roasted cashews, crushed

Preheat oven to 375 degrees. Cream together butter, sugars, and honey. Beat in the vanilla and eggs. Blend in the flowers, flour, and baking powder. As you are blending the ingredients together, chant this blessing to the fairies:

> Fairies sweet, blessed be!

Fold the cashews into the cookie dough. Grease cookie sheets and drop cookie dough on the sheet using a teaspoon. Bake for about 10 to 12 minutes. Cool and eat. Makes about 30 cookies.

The Least You Need to Know

- ◆ Elves and fairies have a fondness for certain types of human food and drink; to attract them to your home, offer some of their favorites.

- ◆ Plan a picnic party complete with a banquet of food and drink, and don't forget to invite the elves and fairies.

- ◆ Having a fairy wedding is an enchanting way for two people to join in holy matrimony.

- ◆ Fairy recipes offer a perfect way for satisfying your own hunger as well as winning favor with elves and fairies.

Chapter 22

Elven and Fairy Healing Herbs, Stones, and Essences

In This Chapter

- ◆ Why fairy herbs, stones, and essences are important
- ◆ Healing properties of fairy herbs
- ◆ Magical qualities of different types of fairy stones
- ◆ A fragrant array of elf and fairy essences

Within folklore, the fairies known as blue ladies taught shepherds about the medicinal uses of herbs. Elves and fairies long ago mastered the use of herbs, stones, and essences, employing them in not only healing, but also for magic. Through time, the elves and fairies imparted this information to the druids and others, and through time it has been written down in folklore and mythology.

In this chapter, you will gain a good background of the magical uses of these fairy herbs, stones, and essences, and learn how you can use them to enhance your health—and your life.

Why Are Herbs, Stones, and Essences Important?

Herbs, stones, and essences are nature's gifts to us all. Many of these gifts have healing as well as magical qualities. The essences, herbs, and stones can be used for fairy blessings, rituals, and mediation (see Chapter 16), to contact helpful elves and fairies, or to ward off harmful ones.

An example of why herbs are important, for instance, appears in Lady Wilde's book *The Ancient Legends of Ireland, Volume I*. There is a story about a girl who was enticed into a fairy dance on a fairy hill at Halloween. After dancing with the fairy prince, she was led to a magnificent fairy banquet. Just when she took a golden cup the prince handed to her, and was raising it to her lips, a man passed by and whispered, "Eat no food and drink no wine, or you will never reach your home again."

The girl refused to drink, and because of this, the fairies became very angry, and a great noise arose, and a fierce, dark man stood up, and said, "Whoever comes to us must drink with us." He took her arm and held the wine to her lips, so that she almost died of fright. Just at that moment a red-haired man came up, and he took her by the hand and led her away and said, "You are safe for this time. Take this herb, and hold it in your hand till you reach home, and no one can harm you." He gave her a branch of the plant called ground ivy. She took the branch and fled into the dark night. She heard footsteps behind her in pursuit. When she reached home she barred the door and went to bed. A great clamor soon arose outside, and voices were heard crying to her, "The power we have over you is gone through the magic of the herb, but wait until you dance again to the music on the hill, you will stay with us forevermore, and none shall hinder this." By and by, the girl wisely kept the magic branch of ivy safe, and the fairies never troubled her again.

As I pointed out in Chapter 12, herbs, stones, and essences can be used to attract fairy enchantment to you, or as in the previous example, to protect yourself from it. The herbs, stones, and essences listed in this chapter will give you information on both attraction and protection. But before delving into the lists, let's look at how to use these herbs, stones, and essences.

First, a Word of Warning

Be aware that some people might be sensitive to or have an allergic reaction to certain product ingredients. Be sure to consult a knowledgeable herbalist, acupuncturist, naturopathic or homeopathic professional, or physician *before* using herbs or essential oils in any form to treat a specific condition or illness, or if you are pregnant, epileptic, diabetic, or have a mental illness.

Before applying an herb or essential oil directly to your skin or adding it to your bathwater, do a patch test on a small area of skin to make sure you're not allergic to the ingredients. Most pure oils should be diluted before they are applied to the skin. Be sure to read any directions that come with an oil before using it. Essential oils are potent, and care must be taken when using them. If you have any adverse reactions, check with your health-care provider.

 On Guard!

Never use an herb, stone, or essence without first knowing its medicinal and magical properties. Use this chapter to familiarize yourself with each as you come into contact with it. Remember, everyone's body is different, and reactions to herbs and essences can vary.

Which Ones for What Occasion?

Each herb, stone, and essence has individual properties that make it unique. These properties can be both medicinal and magical, and they greatly vary from item to item. The greatest tool in using herbs, stones, and essences is knowledge. Knowing the medicinal and magical properties of different ones gives you insight into which herbs, stones, and essences to use for what occasion.

Elves and fairies are experts at helping nature grow and weaving new life into the world. Ask them to show you how to use elven and fairy herbs, stones, and essences to their full potential. Allow these magical beings to show you how to grow your dreams and find a wealth of joy and whimsy where the wild thyme grows.

Herbs, stones, or essences might come into your life in two main ways. One way is when you come into contact with an herb, stone, or essence for whatever reason, and because of the experience, choose to learn about it. The other way involves seeking an herb, stone, or essence to meet a particular need.

Often things come into your life at a time when you need them. I've often encountered a stone, and when I read about the medicinal and magical properties of the stone, I find the stone addresses certain issues in my life. An example is when my husband bought a ruby ring for me as a Christmas present. When I looked up the medicinal and magical qualities, two of them were strength and fertility, just the combination that I needed to finally get pregnant, something that my husband and I had been working on for over 11 years.

What Are Your Needs?

As the natural wisdom of elves and fairies is being rediscovered, many of us today are making efforts to live in harmony with nature. We are finally realizing that nature's gifts sustain our bodies, minds, and spirits in ways that are more like the good people of Irish folklore. We can slow down the aging process and become healthier in our daily lives.

When assessing your personal needs, first sit down with a sheet of paper and write what you think they are. You might want to break these needs down into separate categories, such as the following:

- ◆ Relationships—Your needs regarding the relationships in your life, including family and friends

- ◆ Health—Your needs regarding your current physical condition and overall health

- ◆ Livelihood—Your means of income, property, and amusement

When looking for herbs, stones, and essences to help meet some of your needs, search for ones that best fulfill these needs. Begin by using only one herb, stone, or essence, and assess how it affects you—physically, mentally, and spiritually. If you then want to combine another herb, stone, or essence to the first, add just one, and again assess the effect it has on your being as a whole. The problem with adding more than one at a time is that if you experience either a "good" or "bad" effect, you don't know which one caused the effect. By adding one at a time, you know what herb, stone, or essence is affecting your being in what way.

Nature's magical beings such as elves and fairies communicate directly with us through nature's color, smell, taste, sound, shape, and texture as well as its subtle energies. Use the fairy herbs, stones, and essences listed in this chapter in accordance with your needs. Always check with how you feel in your heart before drawing helpful elves and fairies to you with these powerful gifts from Mother Nature.

The following fairy herbs, stones, and essences are presented as keys for encouraging positive fairy encounters and enchanting elf and fairy dreams. Woodland, mountain, meadow, flower, garden, water, fire, winged, and house elves and fairies can all be lured into your life with natural herbs, stones, and essences.

Fairy Herbs and Plants

I encourage everyone to begin to grow and use fresh herbs, thereby cultivating a healthy connection to the fairies. You will be generously rewarded; fresh herbs have incredible flavor, wonderful aromas, and endless uses. Keep in mind that location, climate, and season all influence herb properties. Also remember when gathering herbs in nature or your garden to take no more than one third of the foliage of a plant. Always treat plants with respect, thanking them for their natural gifts.

> **Through the Ages**
>
> In *A Midsummer Night's Dream*, Shakespeare writes that Titania's bower is on "... A bank whereon the wild thyme blows, Where oxlips and the nodding violet grows, Quite over-canopied with lush woodbine, With sweet musk-roses, and with eglantine."

- **Aloe**—This fairy healing plant is easy to grow and attracts gentle and joyful earth fairies. Use its gel to relieve poison oak, sunburn, and burns.

- **Angelica**—Sprinkle this purifying herb around your fairy ring to encourage magical inspiration and enhanced creativity.

- **Basil**—Put fresh basil leaves and sprigs around your fairy ring and circle to attract helpful fairies, love, happiness, and good fortune. This herb of devotion and faith instills passion and awakens the fairy and elf essence within the moment. Basil can be used to ward off unwanted dragons as well.

- **Blessed thistle**—This purifying herb expands your awareness and helps you communicate with the elves and fairies of the Otherworld. It also can be used to rid your sacred space of negative energies and potentially harmful fairies and elves. Use this healing herb in a tea or capsule form to strengthen your memory and immune system.

- **Burdock**—Sprinkle bits of this herb around your fairy ring and circle or other magic space to promote harmony and rid the area of any unwanted or harmful fairies. Drink as a tea to help balance your body, mind, and spirit.

- **Catnip**—To make a simple fairy sleeping potion, stir a teaspoon each of catnip, lavender, and chamomile herb into a cup of boiling water, steep and strain, and sip. Playful feline fairies love this herb, and planting a patch of catnip in your garden or in a pot in your kitchen window encourages visits by your feline friends as well as your fairy friends.

- **Chamomile**—Drink chamomile tea before going to sleep to dream of the elves and fairies and the Otherworld. Sprinkle the herb, fresh or dried, around your fairy ring and circle to draw tiny winged fairies to you. Plant a living fairy ring using chamomile and lavender in your yard to encourage love and prosperity. A purifying cup of chamomile tea is perfect just before fairy meditation, too!

- **Clover**—Clover attracts all kinds of helpful fairies and elves. Tie a piece of two-leafed clover together with seven flowers such as roses (thornless) or daisies with a green ribbon. Hold the tied clover and flowers in your hands for a few minutes just before going to sleep and focus your mind on your image of fairyland. Tuck the bunch inside your pillowcase to promote dreams of fairyland. Clover juice mixed with rainwater applied to your eyelids helps you see the fairies. Clovers found by sacred streams make the most powerful charms to enable the user to sight elves and fairies. Three-leafed clovers are best for protection, and four-leafed clovers bring good fortune, riches, and second sight.

> **Wizardly Wisdom**
>
> Some herbs and plants act as protective charms. The strongest is the four-leafed clover, a traditional symbol of good luck, which reveals fairy glamour as well as helps you to see elves and fairies on full moons and fairy festival days.

- **Coriander**—Elves and fairies all delight in this herb of love, passion, desire, and prowess. Use it in cooking, or sprinkle the foliage around your fairy ring or circle to draw love and passion to you.

- **Dandelion**—Drink tea made from dandelion leaves to heal and energize you, or sprinkle the leaves, flowers, and puffballs around your fairy ring and circle to attract helpful garden fairies and elves. Offer dandelion wine to the fairies in your garden on the full moon by pouring a glass onto the earth and thanking the fairies and elves for their magical blessings and gifts. Pick a puffball on the day of a full moon. Make a wish and blow the puffball as hard as you can. The winged fairies of the wind will bring your wish to you.

- **Elecampane**—This herb is also known as elfswort and elfdock. Scatter it around your fairy ring and circle to attract helpful elves and fairies. Keep some in a small bag or pouch; hold it between your hands to strengthen the power of fairy blessings as you say them, or use it when you meditate on the Otherworld.

- **Eyebright**—Use this herb to see the unseen, for all eye ailments, hay fever, colds, and sore throats, and to more readily see the fairies and elves and to see past their illusion.

◆ **Flax**—Fairy flax is used to weave fairy clothes. This protective herb promotes healing and rids your fairy ring and circle of potentially harmful energies. Scatter a few flax seeds on your fairy ring and circle to encourage visits from helpful elves and fairies. Scatter a few seeds on your hearth to draw brownies and house elves to your home.

◆ **Garlic**—When you need to get rid of any nasty magical creatures or cruel kinds of fairies, the protective herb garlic is always useful. The fresh juice or herb is best for healing and boosting your immune system. Hung in bunches in your kitchen or over doorways, garlic promotes abundance, good fortune, success, and riches.

◆ **Marjoram**—Attract joyful, merry, and delightful garden fairies to your yard by growing marjoram in your garden. Use this fairy love herb in teas, potions, and cooking to encourage romance, love, marriage, and fertility.

◆ **Meadowsweet**—A favorite love and romance fairy herb, use meadowsweet to promote sweetness in your love life. It also encourages an open heart and helps to bring more passion, creativity, and blissful magic into each and every day.

◆ **Milkweed**—Blow milkweed pods into the wind to send a heartfelt wish to the elves and fairies. Plant lots of milkweed around your house to attract butterflies, and you are certain to have many fairy visitors. Put three milkweed tassels in a small pouch and tuck the pouch inside your pillowcase to promote enchanting fairy dreams.

◆ **Mint**—Drinking mint tea increases your mental focus and promotes dreams of fairies and elves. Put the fresh herb in a small pouch and tuck it inside your pillowcase for a couple of nights to encourage dreams of fairyland. Return the spent herb to the earth when you are done. Put fresh mint leaves around your fairy ring and circle to attract helpful garden fairies and winged fairies. Crush several mint leaves in your fingers and smell the fragrance for a few minutes before doing fairy blessings and meditations.

◆ **Mistletoe**—Carry a sprig of mistletoe with you as a natural talisman to keep you eternally youthful. Harvest mistletoe on the summer solstice or on the sixth night of the new moon at dawn or at dusk to empower your communication with the fire and tree fairies. A fairy and

CAUTION

On Guard! _____

Keep mistletoe away from children and pets. Never ingest the berries because they are poisonous.

elf activator herb, mistletoe attracts love, romance, and passion. Tie seven sprigs of mistletoe with a red ribbon and put the bunch under your bed to encourage magical dreams.

◆ **Mugwort**—Make a crown of mugwort and lavender on Midsummer's Eve and wear it to help see the fairies and elves on that night and encourage prophetic dreams. Mugwort is a protective herb; sprinkle it around your fairy ring and circle to repel harmful fairies. Wash your fairy stones with mugwort tea to cleanse them of any impurities.

◆ **Rosemary**—Drink in tea or take a rosemary herbal bath to encourage remembrance and fidelity, ensure magical protection, and uplift your mood. Sea fairies, winged fairies, and garden fairies all love the fragrance of rosemary because it attracts butterflies. Also called elfleaf, plant rosemary in your garden or flowerpots to invite helpful elves. Rosemary is the perfect love herb for fairy weddings (see Chapter 21); all kinds of fairies and elves are enchanted by its fragrance.

◆ **Sage**—Tie three sprigs of sage, rosemary, and lavender together with a white ribbon and put the bunch next to your bed to promote enchanting fairy dreams. Carry sage in a small pouch with you to see fairies and elves when in natural settings. Burn sage and cedar smudge daily to protect you and your home from harmful energies.

◆ **St. John's Wort**—Put this protective and healing herb next to your bed to promote blessed dreams of the fairies and elves. It is also known as ragwort and fairy's horse. Leprechauns bury their gold underneath the roots of this herb. On the Isle of Man, it is believed that if you step on St. John's Wort on Midsummer's Eve at sunset, a fairy horse will spring up out of the earth and carry you off until sunrise. When picking this herb, ask permission from the fairies, and use only your left hand.

Through the Ages

Wild thyme was used in brews to help see fairies dating from 1600. One recipe says that to see the fairies, make a mixture of spring water, wild thyme tops gathered on the side of a fairy hill or mound, and add a few pinches of grass from a fairy throne.

◆ **Thyme**—An elf and fairy favorite, any place that wild thyme grows is a sacred fairy spot. The Fairy Queen Titania made her bower on wild thyme and flowers. At midnight on Midsummer's Eve, the fairies dance on wild thyme beds. Thyme attracts bees and butterflies. Carry it in your pocket when walking in nature to see fairies and elves. Sprinkle thyme outside your doorstep, on windowsills, and other entryways to invite the helpful garden and winged fairies into your home and workplace. Folklore says that fairies hide their babies in wild thyme for safekeeping.

◆ **Vervain**—Called the Enchanter's Herb, use vervain for protective amulets and charms. Sprinkle it around your fairy ring and circle to encourage love, prophecy, and the bright blessings of the fairies and elves.

◆ **Yarrow**—This herb embodies the divine feminine and is one of the favorites of the fairies and elves. Weather fairies especially like yarrow. It helps heal colds, purifies, renews, and is commonly used for love charms and divination.

Fairy Stones

Like herbs, crystals and gemstones can be used as keys to the doorways to fairyland. You can meditate with stones, wear them in jewelry, and use them in rituals, blessings, and as fairy dream stones by sleeping with them under your pillow or by your bed. They boost your natural energy field and create a vortex of light conducive to elf and fairy communication.

When wearing or using stones set in jewelry, tools, or other implements, remember that elves and fairies don't like iron and steel. Use copper, silver, gold, lead-free pewter, and wood settings. For more information about crystals and gemstones, please refer to my book *The Pocket Guide to Crystals and Gemstones* (see Appendix A).

◆ **Amethyst**—Hold this protective and healing stone in your receiving hand (your left hand if you are right-handed) as you drift to sleep to dream of the enchanting land of the elves and fairies. Hold amethyst in your hands while in meditation, prayer, and divination.

◆ **Aquamarine**—Use this stone to attract water fairies. Hold it in your hands when you are near a body of water and sing (if you are in good voice) to the fairies to bring their blessings and inspiration to you.

◆ **Carnelian**—A fire and garden fairy favorite, use this stone to build strength, courage, creative fire, focus, passion, and motivation when working with the fairies and elves.

◆ **Citrine**—This mind-empowering stone attracts fire and earth fairies. Use it to protect you from potentially harmful fairies, for shape shifting, meditation, and as a fairy dream stone.

- **Clear quartz**—Quartz crystals or stones with quartz veins through them are sacred to the elves and fairies. Quartz is an excellent choice for healing, enhancing your second sight, protection, shape shifting, meditation, and divination.

- **Diamond**—A favorite stone of fairy kings and queens as well as gnomes and dwarves, diamonds attract colorful winged and earth fairies. Use this stone to draw clarity, truth, strength, and prosperity to you.

- **Emerald**—This stone attracts garden and forest elves and fairies to you. Wear an emerald to encourage healing, growth, and abundance, and to draw the spirit of nature to you.

- **Flint**—Use this stone, together with iron, to ward off potentially harmful fairies and elves.

- **Garnet**—Attract fire fairies with this colorful red gemstone. Use garnets to encourage friendship with elves and fairies, as well as romance, passion, faithfulness, trust, and virility in love.

- **Jade**—Use this gentle stone to draw garden and woodland fairies, harmony, peace, and wealth to you and your home. Jade can be used as an amulet or charm to rid your person and home of any harmful energy.

- **Malachite**—Hold this stone in your hand as you drift to sleep and intend to dream of the fairies, or tuck a small piece inside your pillowcase while you sleep to encourage enchanting dreams. This stone is an excellent choice to enhance shape shifting, for communicating with the elves and fairies, and to bring more abundance and wealth into your life.

- **Milky quartz**—Hold a milky quartz (also called fairy frost) stone in your receiving hand as you meditate in nature or as you drift to sleep to more easily connect with the elves and fairies.

- **Moonstone**—An elf and fairy favorite, use this stone to get in touch with your emotions and with the magic of full moons and fairy festival eves. This stone attracts good fortune, prophecy, fertility, creative inspiration, and divine gifts.

- **Rose quartz**—This stone encourages love, romance, passion, compassion, fertility, trust, and inspiration. The fairies and elves love this stone because it is the essence of love and faith.

- **Ruby**—A stone of fairy kings and queens, wear this stone to attract the fairy royalty. Use rubies to build your courage, personal power, and insight when working with the fairies and elves. It is also a stone of fertility.

◆ **Star sapphire**—Some say the fairies and elves came from the stars hundreds of thousands of years ago. As stardust beings, the fairies and elves love the radiant star within the star sapphire. Use this stone to attract celestial, water, and earth fairies as well as to stimulate your creative passion.

◆ **Staurolite**—Called the Fairy Cross, use this stone to connect with helpful elves and fairies. The Cherokee Indians say fairy crosses are the fallen tears of the little people, tiny fairylike spirits who are shy, timid, and help those who are lost in the woods find their way. Keep a cross as a good luck charm to protect you against harm, illness, accidents, and disasters, as well as to attract divine fairy gifts and messages.

Fairy Tales and Legends

As its name implies, Fairy Stone State Park, near Roanoke, Virginia, is home of the fairy stones. Legend has it that many hundreds of years ago, fairies danced around a bubbling spring of water in these woods, playing with wood nymphs and naiads, when an elven messenger arrived from a faraway place. He said that Christ was dead. When the magical creatures of the forest heard this, they wept and their tears fell on the earth in the form of beautiful crystallized crosses. These crosses are the fairy stones. They are brown staurolite, and are found in stones that have been subjected to extreme heat and pressure.

Fairy Essences

You can use fragrant fairy essences in the form of essential oils or scented mixed oils in baths, misters, diffusers, sachets, charms, incense, and on cotton balls, as well as for anointing candles. To anoint your body with oils, be sure to mix essential oil with a carrier oil such as apricot or olive oil to dilute them properly. Each essence has unique magical qualities and can be used separately or mixed with other compatible essences.

◆ **Amber**—Elves and fairies, along with dryads and dwarves, all adore amber. Use this tree resin to draw love, romance, passion, and divine love to you. Rub a bit of the resin in your fingers and roll it around until it dissolves. Anoint your wrists with the resin to promote second sight.

◆ **Basil**—This good luck fairy essence stimulates and uplifts you, promotes love, passion, and romance, as well as helps heal wounds. Put a few drops of the essential oil, made from flowering tops and leaves, into your bath to attract the flower and garden fairies.

On Guard!

Do not use cedarwood essential oil on infants or small children. Always first dilute this oil with a carrier oil, as cedarwood is very irritating to the skin.

◆ **Cedarwood**—This strong woodsy essence is a favorite of the forest elves and woodland fairies and is considered sacred throughout the world. Use it to promote harmony, peace, and tranquility.

◆ **Chamomile**—A flower, garden, meadow, and woodland elf and fairy favorite, attract magical beings with this sweet, enchanting, and fruity essence. Put a few drops on your pillowcase to encourage joyful fairy dreams. Take a fairy essence dream bath by mixing a few drops of chamomile essence together with a few drops of lavender and neroli essence in your bathwater and soaking for at least 10 minutes just before you go to sleep.

◆ **Geranium**—A healing essence that is a favorite of the flower and garden fairies, use geranium oil to encourage healing, playful harmony, and sweet abundance.

◆ **Honeysuckle**—Its intoxicating aroma lulls flower and woodland fairies into dancing, merriment, and delight. Bees, hummingbirds, and deer all love honeysuckles. The lapwing is associated with this flower. Anoint yourself with this floral essence blended with a carrier oil before meditation and prayer, and before sleeping to draw beauty, love, romance, and passion into your life.

◆ **Jasmine**—This sweet, floral essence encourages enrichment, enchanting dreams, hope, love, and romance. Use in small amounts to draw the flower and woodland elves and fairies to you.

◆ **Lavender**—The fragrant essence comes from the flowering tops and leaves of the lavender plant and can be used to promote fairy dreams, healing, joy, peace, love, and harmony. To dream of fairyland, sprinkle a few drops of the essence on your bedding and anoint yourself with a few drops of lavender essence before going to sleep.

◆ **Lemon**—This fresh, citrus essence is cleansing and purifying. It draws the fruit fairies to you and encourages joy, happiness, merriment, mischief, and whimsy.

- **Neroli**—To sweeten things up, perfume yourself, your bathwater, and bedding with a blend of neroli and lavender essences. Neroli is both floral and citrus and made from the flowers of the bitter orange tree. Use it to draw helpful flower and tree fairies to you. It encourages joy, love, romance, and faith.

- **Patchouli**—This rich, earthy, and musky essence is the perfect choice when you want to draw helpful flower, garden, and woodland elves and fairies to you. Anoint yourself with a few drops to encourage love, romance, compassion, enrichment, shape shifting, and amorous fairy encounters.

- **Pine**—Made from the dry twigs, needles, and cones, pine essence attracts tree fairies, dryads, and forest elves. This healing essence enhances creativity, love, fertility, stamina, and focus.

- **Rose**—Use this fairy favorite essence to attract flower, garden, and woodland elves and fairies. This gentle, sweet essence is healing. It promotes love, romance, passion, good luck, and joy. Use rose essence in your bathwater to stimulate your senses and divination abilities. Put a few drops of rose essence on your pillowcase to encourage enchanting nights and dreams.

- **Sandalwood**—This rich woodsy essence enhances shape shifting and healing, and attracts woodland elves and fairies. Use a few drops in your bathwater to promote joy, peacefulness, and harmony.

- **Ylang-ylang**—This strong, sweet, floral essence attracts the flower and garden fairies and elves. Use it to encourage love, romance, passion, fertility, and good fortune.

The Least You Need to Know

- Elves and fairies are masters in the art of using herbs, stones, and essences.

- Be sure to follow some simple precautions before using any herb or essential oil.

- Knowledge of the medicinal and magical properties of herbs, stones, and essences is a powerful tool to have in life.

- Choose a subject or need and learn what herbs fulfill it.

- Stones have energetic properties that affect your being on many levels.

- Essences act not only on your sense of smell but also on your sense of touch, because your skin absorbs them.

23

Connecting with the Elf and Fairy Energy Within You

In This Chapter

- Exploring the elf and fairy energy within and outside of your world
- How magic mirrors reflect the elf and fairy within you
- Working with elf and fairy energy to make your life magical
- An assortment of fun elf and fairy projects and exercises

Each of us has good days when we feel like Glenda the Good Witch— understanding, compassionate, and full of vitality—and bad days when we feel more like a banshee—screaming, wailing, and out of control. Like the elf and fairy within, we exhibit many of their characteristics just as they exhibit many of ours.

In this last stage of our magical adventure, we explore how elves and fairies mirror us. When we are good, they are good, and when we are bad, they are bad. In the end, we are both reflections of one another.

Recognizing the Energy Within

In the modern fairy tale *The Fairy Godmother*, author Lester Del Rey tells the story of a 12-year-old princess named Samantha who is forced by her parents to go stay with her severe, grumpy Aunt Hepzibah. In the process of getting ready to go she laments to herself, "And where is my fairy godmother in all this? I am supposed to have one, though nobody has told me anything beyond the fact that there is such a creature."

Every time she asked her parents about it, they told her to wait until she was older—something they told her about everything.

On the journey to her aunt's, Samantha's coach is held up by robbers. In the confusion, she escapes and begins making her way back home. She avoids other robbers on her way by hiding and not being seen. Eventually she makes it to a house, where a middle-aged couple lives. They take her in and feed and clothe her as if she was their own child. She chooses not to tell them who she is, but instead lives for a time with them, calling them aunt and uncle.

One day while helping Aunt Bessie in the garden, Samantha encounters a snake. Aunt Bessie is bit saving the girl. The aunt becomes gravely ill, and Samantha has to go fetch the doctor. On her way, she encounters a man in a black cloak with its hood pulled over his face, sitting on a rock by the crossroads. He asks her what she is running from, and she tells him she is fetching the doctor. In the ensuing conversation, he tells her he is a doctor of metaphysics and that he can help her. What he does is make time go backward, until the time just before the girl's aunt was bit. Only this time, the girl and her aunt call her uncle, who kills the snake.

The next morning her father, the king, arrives to bring her back home. He tells of how a man in black with a hood came to the back door of the palace, claiming to know where the princess was. After saying his thanks and arranging it so that the princess can visit her newfound aunt and uncle often, the king and princess begin the journey back to the palace. On the way, she asks him about her fairy godmother, whom he tells her bestowed two gifts to her when she was born. They were "necessitous imperceptibility" (not being seen when it's absolutely necessary) and "nonindulgent summoning" (calling something or someone up when it isn't just being self-indulgent). He describes the fairy godmother as looking young with golden hair, a bright blue dress, and iridescent wings that change color as she moves.

Before the two travelers reach the main road, the princess looks over into the shadows of the forest, and sees the image of the dark stranger. He puts his finger up to where his lips should be, motioning her to be quiet. Then before her eyes, he begins to loosen the cloak, and from behind the cloak comes the image of golden hair and a mesmerizingly beautiful face. Samantha sees the blue dress and the iridescent wings described by her father. Smiling, with her finger still touching her lips, the fairy godmother blows Samantha a kiss and then disappears.

I find this story interesting because of the way it plays with the image of the fairy godmother. It goes from being a man hidden and dressed in black to a beautiful woman in a blue dress with wings that change color as she moves. These are two vastly different images that allude to the idea that outside help and fairy godmothers can sometimes take many different shapes.

The girl in the story not only recognizes the elf and fairy energy around her, but she also learns to express it from within by learning to love someone else and being less self-indulgent. In this way, the story shows the interplay between the elf and fairy energy both inside and outside the individual. These energies from within and without often mirror one another.

Fairy Godmother Dream Ritual

This exercise is a dream ritual to put you more in touch with your own fairy godmother. Do this dream ritual on a warm spring or summer night, on or just before a full moon. Your fairy godmother can bring you dreams of joy, adventure, and sweet laughter. She will also magically bless you with delightful dreams of fairyland.

You will need some soft fairylike music, a cup of water, a white candle, and a notebook and pen.

1. Turn on some soft fairylike music. Create a fairy ring and fairy circle around your bedroom or sleeping area, and call in the fairy guardians as described in Chapter 16.

2. Take the cup of water, and sprinkle the water clockwise around the fairy ring, starting and ending at the east point.

3. Light the candle. Dedicate it to your fairy godmother by saying:

   May this light guide my fairy godmother to me tonight.

4. Sit comfortably with your notebook and pen on your lap, and breathe deeply in time with the soft music for a few minutes while focusing on the candle flame to center your awareness. Then write this question in your notebook:

   In what ways can I bring more magic into my life?

Continue to focus your attention on the candle flame. Keep watching the flame, and imagine contacting your fairy godmother. Think about what your ideal fairy godmother would be like. Continue breathing deeply to the music to more clearly visualize the details of your fairy godmother. Write these details in your notebook.

5. Now return your focus to the candle flame. Imagine your ideal fairy godmother stepping out of the candle flame and into the room with you. You feel a bright, expansive feeling, and you know magic is afoot. Imagine your fairy godmother speaking your name and smiling brightly at you. When she calls you by name, it might be more like a whisper or a thought. Keep breathing deeply, and ask your fairy godmother the question you wrote in your notebook. Repeat the question a total of three times. Each time you ask your fairy godmother the question, take a few minutes and write down any answers she gives you. The answers might come in words, thoughts, pictures, or sensations. Just be open to the communication and make a note of anything you receive without analyzing it too much.

   When you are done asking the question three times and have written down any responses, thank your fairy godmother, and blow out the candle.

6. As you drift off to sleep, leave the fairy ring and circle intact. Repeat over and over to yourself:

   Fairy godmother, dream with me tonight.

   In the morning, write down everything you recall about your dreams in your notebook. At this time, bid farewell to the fairy guardians by standing or sitting at the center of the circle, ringing the bell once, and saying:

   Fairy Watchers of all directions

   I bid you farewell.

   Please depart in peace and love.

   Thank you for your presence.

   Ring the bell once more, and say:

   Blessed be! Evo-He!

7. Pull up your fairy circle and ring. Face east and hold your power hand outward. Slowly turn in a counterclockwise circle. As you do this, imagine the blue-white light of the circle being drawn back up into your hand. Then do the same thing with the green light circle. Scatter the flowers in the ring. Next, erase the ring mark with the heel of your shoe or with your hand if you are doing this ritual outdoors. Do this in a counterclockwise motion. When you are done, face center, ring the bell once, and say:

Blessed be! Evo-He!

8. For the next 21 nights, as you are drifting to sleep, repeat the phrase over and over:

Fairy godmother, dream with me tonight.

I will remember my dreams in the morning light.

Continue writing down everything you recall from your dreams in your notebook. Refer to your notes for insights and messages that will help you bring more magic into your daily life.

Mirror, Mirror on the Wall

In the fairy tale "Snow White," the stepmother has a magic looking glass that always speaks the truth. Rather than using it for positive purposes, such as self-discovery and helping others, she uses it to promote her vanity by asking it every day "Who is the fairest of them all?" Because she uses the magic mirror for selfish and evil purposes, the stepmother meets a nasty end. As the story reads, "And when the stepmother saw the bride, she knew her to be Snow White, but could not stir from the place because of her anger and terror. For the dwarves had ready red-hot iron shoes, in which the stepmother had to dance until she fell down dead."

Fairy Tales and Legends
The story of Snow White begins with the queen spinning at her ebony-framed spindle on a winter's day. The needle pricks her finger, and three drops of blood spill out onto the pure white snow. From this, her daughter is conceived, and later when the girl is born, the queen dies. Snow White's skin was white as snow, her lips red as blood, and her hair black as ebony. White, red, and black are the traditional fairy colors. The story overall is a metaphor for the goddess, who dies every winter and is reborn every spring.

"Snow White" contrasts with the more modern fairy tale of *Harry Potter and the Sorcerer's Stone*, where the mirror of Erisad shows the greatest desire of the viewer's heart. At first Harry uses it to view images of his parents, to the point of being self-indulgent. But in the end Harry's true and good self comes out, and the mirror shows him the location of the sorcerer's stone, thus helping him to defeat darkness.

> **On Guard!**
>
> Beware of people who are overly vain. I once had a friend who was continually looking at herself in the mirror. I would be talking to her, and the whole time she would be seemingly mesmerized by her own image. Our friendship eventually ended when her vanity ultimately became more important than our friendship.

Mirrors are interesting because they are a reflection of what's in front of them. You can look at the reflection and learn from the experience or you can become enamored with your own beauty and stay stuck in the same spot for a lifetime. As with most things that have to do with elves, fairies, and magic, the choice is yours to make as to how you use the mirrors in your life.

Use the following exercises to explore how you can use mirrors for physical and spiritual transformation and to bring a little more magic into your world.

Mirror Magic

Mirrors are spirit carriers, which can act as magic entryways into the Otherworld of the elves and fairies. For this fairy mirror magic experience you will need a twig and flower crown (directions follow), jasmine scented oil, a white taper candle and candleholder, and an 8-inch-by-10-inch mirror (or larger).

Fashion a twig and flower crown by weaving slender twigs together, tying them with green and red metallic ribbon. Glue on flowers with a glue gun. Anoint the crown with several drops of the jasmine oil. Then anoint your wrists and ankles with the oil. Rub a little scented oil on the candle, and put it back in its holder. Wipe your hands thoroughly.

Prop the mirror up so you can easily see your reflection in it. Put the candleholder with the candle between your body and the mirror.

Light the candle, and then gaze into the mirror, focusing on your reflection while saying three times:

> Fairy without, fairy within.

> Inside out, outside in.

> Looking out, looking in.

Think about the fairy and elven qualities you have within yourself. Address the mirror and say three times:

> Fairy mirror, please show me

> My fairy and elven qualities.

Keep gazing at your reflection, focusing your attention on the fairy or elven qualities that you see in your face, your body, your light, for at least 10 minutes. Feel good about yourself, realizing the magic is within you. Put out the candle when you are done. Keep the mirror in a place where you will look into it now and again. Return the crown to the earth after the flowers fade.

Fairy Mirror Glamour

The best time to do this fairy mirror *glamour* is on a clear night under a full moon. You will need a silver-colored bell, a handkerchief, and a small handheld mirror.

Magical Meaning

Glamour is a magic spell whose intention is illusion or enchantment. Elves and fairies use glamour to hide themselves and their homes from humans, as well as to appear in many shapes and sizes.

1. Draw a fairy ring and circle and call in the fairy guardians as described in Chapter 16. Line your ring with small stones, preferably white.

2. Face the full moon. Ring the bell seven times, and say:

> Helpful fairies of east, west, north, and south

> Please hear this silver bell as it rings out.

3. Spread the handkerchief out on the ground in front of you. Put the bell on top of the handkerchief. Look at the moon for a few minutes, merging with its luminous light.

4. Hold the mirror in your hand so that it reflects the moon's light. Keeping the mirror angled toward the moon, take three steps slowly around the silver bell in a clockwise circle. As you do this, watch the reflected moonlight in the mirror shooting out over the area around you. As you move, chant these words over and over:

   Please bless me with full moon fairy glamour.

5. Keep moving in a clockwise circle, gradually increasing your speed, all the while chanting and watching as the moonlight fills the mirror. Now angle the mirror so the reflected moonlight spreads over your face and body. Breathe deeply and inhale the power of the beautiful, bright moonlight. Fill yourself to the brim with this lunar energy, and then run clockwise around the circle three times really fast.

6. When you are done, bid farewell to the fairy guardians by standing or sitting at the center of the circle, ringing the bell once, and saying:

   Fairy Watchers of all directions

   I bid you farewell.

   Please depart in peace and love.

   Thank you for your presence.

   Ring the bell once more, and say:

   Blessed be! Evo-He!

7. Pull up your fairy circle and ring. Face east and hold your power hand outward. Slowly turn in a counterclockwise circle. As you do this, imagine the blue-white light of the circle being drawn back up into your hand. Then do the same thing with the green light circle. Next, erase the ring mark with the heel of your shoe or with your hand if you are doing this ritual outdoors. Do this in a counter-clockwise motion. When you are done, face center, ring the bell once, and say:

   Blessed be! Evo-He!

Walking Between Worlds

The fairy realm mirrors our world but is just out of our range of perception and is normally invisible. The portals between worlds are wide open on the eves of Beltane, Midsummer, and Halloween. Because of this, these are also the best times to go walking between worlds: the mortal world and the Otherworld of the elves and fairies.

You will need some upbeat Celtic music or other dance music, a bowl filled with earth, a pinch of thyme, and seven small white stones.

Begin by turning on the music. Put the bowl of earth in front of you. Cover the top of the earth with the pinch of thyme, and then put the stones in seven points around the bowl as if they are the points of an elvenstar. As you do, say:

> To the woods and other land,
>
> With an elf and fairy in hand.
>
> Mind and spirit, now set free,
>
> Open the fairy door, so I may see.

Now close your eyes for a minute or so, and imagine descending a long, natural rock stairway into the earth. At the end of the stairs is a circular doorway. Imagine opening the door and stepping into the magical other land of the fairies. Enjoy yourself as you experience the delight of fairyland. Continue doing so for several minutes. Allow the candle to safely burn down and the music to continue playing as long as you like. When you are done, return the soil, thyme, and stones to the earth.

How to Work with Elf and Fairy Energy

After you have used the mirror to get a fairly accurate reflection of yourself and the surrounding world, you can begin making adjustments that make your world a little better. One of the best ways to do this is to begin working with the elf and fairy energy that is everywhere.

The elf and fairy energy within you is expressed by how you interact with your world, including nature. Depending on your actions toward the outside world, it then responds to you accordingly. This then sets up a pattern where each is continually responding to the other. Their interaction is a continual mirror, each reflecting the actions of the other. If you are positive toward the world, it has a tendency to be positive back.

The following exercises are designed to help you work with the energy of elves and fairies.

The Healing Fairy Well

Wells are often associated with fairies, and they traditionally act as portals into the Otherworld of the elves and fairies. You can reap the benefits of a healing fairy well any night. You will need lavender essential oil, rosemary essential oil, and 3 teaspoons of baking soda.

Draw a warm bath and put several drops of lavender oil into the water. As you do, say:

> Lavender fairies, please bless me with your healing energy.

Now add about three drops of the rosemary essential oil. As you do, say:

> Rosemary fairies, please bless me with your healing energy.

Add the baking soda, and stir the water a bit with your hand. Step into the bath and soak in the fragrant water for several minutes. Notice how the water feels as it envelops your body. Breathe out any tension, discomfort, discontent, or pain you are feeling into the scented water. Keep breathing deeply and relax even more.

Now close your eyes. In your mind's eye, imagine soaking in a magic well, a healing well of warm, soothing water in the Otherworld of the fairies. Imagine the warm, healing waters of the well absorbing all of your emotional, physical, and spiritual pain and discontent. Breathe deeply for a minute or two, releasing more and more painful memories and sensations into the healing fairy well. Now breathe deeply and easily for a few minutes until you feel lighter. When you are done bathing in the healing fairy well, step out of your bath, briskly towel yourself off, and apply a few drops of the lavender essential oil to your wrists and ankles (lavender is one of the few oils that is mild enough to be used without a carrier oil). As you do this, say:

> Helpful fairies, please bless me with your healing energy.

> **Fairy Tales and Legends**
>
> In Celtic, Greek, and Roman mythology, the well was a symbol of both healing and fertility. Celtic women would throw gifts into Coventina's Well, while asking for the blessing of the goddess of fertility and healing.

Fairy Within Ritual

On warm summer nights, the fairies come out to play. There is a sudden stillness and then you feel them, soft like butterfly wings, as they brush against your skin. A breeze stirs and you see a strange glow from out of the corner of your eye. Soft, enchanting laughter teases your senses, and you know magic is afoot.

For this ritual, you will need a bouquet of fresh flowers such as roses for your fairy ring, some lavender scented oil, and three 12-inch lengths of ribbon: one white, one red, and one black.

1. On Midsummer's Eve or on the full moon in June, when the weather is warm and inviting, do this ritual at twilight. Create a fairy ring and circle, and call in the fairy guardians as described in Chapter 16. Line your circle with the fresh flowers.

2. Anoint yourself with the lavender oil. Also anoint the three lengths of ribbon with some of the oil. Now take the three ribbons and begin to braid them together. Knot the ends. As you tie and knot the ribbons, repeat over and over:

   Fairy red, black, and white

   Reveal the fairy within me tonight.

3. Hold the braided ribbons in your hands. Tie a knot in the middle of the ribbons. As you do this, imagine the fairy and elf within you. Imagine all those fairylike qualities you express such as humor, adventure, and childlike enthusiasm. Now tie another knot, and keep imagining your fairy qualities—for example, flirtatious moments, sweet songs you sing, or those cozy, magic moments with your beloved. Tie a third knot, and think about the ways that your features resemble a fairy or elf. Put the knotted ribbons in a top dresser or desk drawer. Take them out whenever you want to get in touch with your inner fairy and elf.

4. When you are done, bid farewell to the fairy guardians by standing or sitting at the center of the circle, ringing the bell once, and saying:

   Fairy Watchers of all directions,

   I bid you farewell.

   Please depart in peace and love.

   Thank you for your presence.

Ring the bell once more, and say:

Blessed be! Evo-He!

5. Pull up your fairy circle and ring. Face east and hold your power hand outward. Slowly turn in a counterclockwise circle. As you do this, imagine the blue-white light of the circle being drawn back up into your hand. Then do the same thing with the green light circle. Scatter the flowers in the ring. Next, erase the ring mark with the heel of your shoe or with your hand if you are doing this ritual outdoors. Do this in a counterclockwise motion. When you are done, face center, ring the bell once, and say:

Blessed be! Evo-He!

Elven and Fairies Enchantment

You can do many things to bring the enchantment of elves and fairies into your life. The following exercises offer you ways of encountering and connecting with this enchantment.

Through the Ages

When the first baby laughed for the very first time,
The laugh broke into a thousand pieces,
And they all went skipping about,
And that was the beginning of fairies.

—J. M. Barrie, author of *Peter Pan*

Fairy Wings

Make your own set of fairy wings to get in touch with the fairy within. Use wire coat hangers for small wings. Bend them to look like fairy wings. Cover the hangers with stretchy white or pastel-colored nylons. Glue or stitch on sequins, feathers, and glitter. Use a sash to hold your wings on. If you prefer larger wings, use bendable wire for the frames. Cover the wire with netting fabric available at fabric shops. Then decorate them. Fairy wings are perfect for Halloween and costume parties, during playtime with your children, as a campy surprise at breakfast with your family, or anytime you want to get in touch with your inner fairy.

Oak Tree Dryad Encounter

Find a living oak tree in your yard, park, town, or nearby woods that you feel a connection with, admire, or notice. Scatter bits of twigs, leaves, and acorns in a clockwise circle around the base of the oak. As you do this, repeat three times:

> I am the oak tree,
>
> The oak tree is me.
>
> We are one.

Place both of your palms on the trunk of the oak, and repeat:

> I am the oak tree,
>
> The oak tree is me.
>
> We are one.

Close your eyes, take a deep breath in, still your breath for three heartbeats, and exhale completely. Continue breathing in this manner for a minute or two. Now in your mind's eye, imagine the dryad in the oak. Sense the spirit of the oak tree. Become one with the dryad spirit for a few moments and feel what it's like to be the dryad of the oak. Imagine your roots growing deep within the moist, fertile earth. Feel the solid strength of your trunk, and then sense your limbs stretching out into the skies. Imagine your leaves as your thoughts, which act as tiny receptors of light that transform the light energy into your renewed growth. Continue doing this for a few minutes. When you are done, thank the dryad by saying:

> Beautiful and blessed oak dryad,
>
> Many thanks for your presence.

Flower Fairy Encounter

When you dream about flowers in full bloom with flower fairies all about them, it indicates that happiness and joyful whimsy are coming your way very soon. You will need a package of annual flower seeds and a circle of earth for this flower fairy encounter. Anything from a flowerpot filled with earth to a circle of land in your garden will work.

Begin by making sure the soil is fertile and ready for the seeds. Add any fertilizer or compost as needed. Now take a few minutes to imagine what your flower circle will look like when it is in full bloom. Imagine planting the seeds, watering them, cultivating the circle, and watching the flowers bloom. Seeds represent new beginnings, and the sowing of them cultivates success and personal growth.

Hold the packet of seeds in your hands. Empower the seeds in the packet by saying three times:

> Seeds of flowers, seeds of fairy powers,
>
> Please bring beauty and happiness every hour.

Take the seeds out of the packet and hold them in your power hand for a few minutes. Once again, imagine your fairy flower circle in full bloom. Now carefully plant the seeds clockwise (sunwise) in your fairy circle. As you plant the seeds, repeat three times:

> Seeds of flowers, seeds of fairy powers,
>
> Please bring beauty and happiness every hour.

When you are done planting, water the seeds as needed. Imagine the circle being filled with bright blooms and flower fairies. Each day, visit your fairy ring and tend it as necessary, and be on the lookout for flower fairies. When your flower circle is in full bloom, enjoy its beauty and magic, and enjoy the happiness and joyful whimsy that cavorting with the flower fairies can bring you.

Fairy Cottage Garden

Plant this garden with your children in the spring or early summer. Set aside a spot in your yard, garden, patio, or balcony just for your children to grow fairy flowers and to make a fairy cottage. Use natural materials for your fairy cottage, as this pleases the garden elves and fairies. You will need a few packages of flower seeds and pots of living flowers. Make sure they are fairy favorites—for example, daisies, miniature roses, and lavender. You will also need a small cardboard box for the fairy cottage.

Plant the flowers and the seeds in the design you prefer. Design suggestions are an elvenstar (seven-pointed star), a circle, or a flower. As you are planting the seeds and flowers, sing or hum a favorite song.

After you have planted the seeds and flowers, make the fairy cottage. First cut a hole in the box for the door so you can put offerings into the cottage. Glue stones, bark, twigs, acorns, berries, tiny pine cones, leaves, sea shells, and flowers onto the sides. Then make a thatched roof for your fairy cottage by gluing grasses, pine needles, or tiny twigs onto the top.

To please the garden fairies, put a few offerings into the cottage for them, such as a small dish of milk, 12 sunflower seeds, and 3 small pieces of fruit. As you do, say:

> These offerings are in honor of the garden fairies.

Every few days, make an offering to the fairies by putting something tasty—for example, a piece of candy or cheese—in the fairy cottage (see Chapter 21 for more about favorite fairy food and drink). When you do this, repeat:

> These offerings are in honor of the garden fairies.

Wizardly Wisdom

As the earth's closest celestial neighbor, the moon potentially has more effect than any other planetary body. As a result, rituals are usually done either on the full moon or the dark moon (when there is no moon). The full moon in particular is the time when the lunar power is strongest.

Leprechauns, Lollipops, and Lucky Coin Magic

You can do this fun ritual with your children to draw the good luck of the leprechauns into your lives. You will need some soft fairylike music, some lollipops, a silver dollar, and a cup of water.

1. On the full moon, turn on some soft music. Better yet, if someone in your family is a musician, have her or him play a few songs to set the tone for the ritual. Harps, violins, guitars, flutes, pennywhistles, drums, pianos, and panpipes are all fairy favorites. Create a fairy ring and fairy circle, and call in the fairy guardians as described in Chapter 16. Line your ring with your favorite kind of lollipops.

2. Take a few deep breaths to center your awareness. If you are outdoors or by a window, gaze at the full moon for a few minutes. Now imagine both your good fortune and good luck growing. Drop the silver dollar into the cup of water. Say:

Silver coin, bright silver moon,

Bring me the good luck of the leprechauns.

Lucky coin, bright fortunate moon,

Bring me the good luck of the leprechauns.

3. Gaze at the coin in the water and continue to think about your good fortune and good luck growing stronger and brighter. Do this for a few minutes. Now gaze at the moon and continue thinking about your good fortune and good luck growing brighter and brighter like the moon.

4. When you are done, bid farewell to the fairy guardians by standing or sitting at the center of the circle, ringing the bell once, and saying:

Fairy Watchers of all directions,

I bid you farewell.

Please depart in peace and love.

Thank you for your presence.

Ring the bell once more, and say:

Blessed be! Evo-He!

5. Pull up your fairy circle and ring. Face east and hold your power hand outward. Slowly turn in a counterclockwise circle. As you do this, imagine the blue-white light of the circle being drawn back up into your hand. Then do the same thing with the green light circle. Erase the ring mark with the heel of your shoe or with your hand if you are doing this ritual outdoors. Do this in a counterclockwise motion. Collect the lollipops and eat them!

When you are done, face center, ring the bell once, and say:

Blessed be! Evo-He!

6. Take the lucky coin out of the cup of water and put it in your pocket, wallet, or purse. Pour the water in the cup on the ground just outside your front door to attract even more luck and wealth.

As our adventure comes to an end in terms of this book, it begins in terms of each of our lives. Go out and experience elf and fairy energy wherever you go, particularly in nature. Make a difference in the world by going out and bringing light to the dark land. This is the way of elves and fairies—kindness is repaid with kindness.

The Least You Need to Know

- Elf and fairy energy exists within each one of us.

- Mirrors are practical tools for providing insight into who you are.

- By working with elf and fairy energy you can achieve anything you want.

- Elves and fairies are excellent ways to bring magic and creativity into your life.

Appendix A

Recommended Reading

Anderson, Rosemarie. *Celtic Oracles*. New York: Harmony Books, 1998.

Baum, L. Frank. *The Sea Fairies*. Chicago: The Reilly and Lee Co., 1911.

Baumgartner, Anne. *A Comprehensive Dictionary of the Gods*. New York: University Books, 1984.

Bettelheim, Bruno. *The Uses of Enchantment: The Meaning and Importance of Fairy Tales*. New York: Vintage Books, 1975.

Birzer, Bradley J. *J. R. R. Tolkien's Sanctifying Myth*. Willington, DE: ISI Books, 2003.

Blair, Nancy. *Amulets of the Goddess*. Oakland, CA: Wingbow Press, 1993.

Bolen, Jean Shinoda, M.D. *Goddesses in Everywoman*. New York: Harper & Row, 1984.

Bonwick, James. *Irish Druids and Old Irish Religions*. New York: Dorset, 1986.

Bord, Janet, and Colin Bord. *Mysterious Britain*. London: Paladin Books, 1974.

Briggs, K. M. *The Fairies in English Tradition and Literature*. Chicago: University of Chicago Press, 1967.

Buck, Pearl S., ed. *Fairy Tales of the Orient*. New York: Simon & Schuster, 1965.

Bulfinch, Thomas. *Bulfinch's Mythology*. Garden City, NY: Garden City Publishing Co., Inc., 1938.

Cabarga, Leslie. *Talks with Trees*. Los Angeles: Iconoclassics Publishing Co., 1997.

Campbell, Joseph. *The Power of Myth*. New York: Doubleday, 1988.

———. *Transformation of Myth Through Time*. New York: Harper & Row, 1990.

———. *The Masks of God, Vol I–IV*. New York: Penguin Books, 1977.

Carroll, Lewis. *Alice's Adventures in Wonderland* and *Through the Looking Glass*. Philadelphia: John C. Winston Co., 1923.

Carr-Gomm, Philip. *The Druid Way*. Rockport, MA: Element Books, Inc., 1993.

Creasy, Rosalind. *The Edible Herb Garden*. Boston: Periplus Editions, 1999.

Crosse, Joanna. *Encyclopedia of Mind, Body, Spirit, and Earth*. Boston, MA: Element Books, 1998.

Crowley, John. *Little, Big*. New York: Perennial, 2002.

Cunningham, Elaine. *Elfshadow*. Renton, WA: Wizards of the Coast, 2000.

Darling, Benjamin. *Shakespeare on Fairies and Magic*. Paramus, NJ: Prentice Hall, 2001.

Day, David. *Tolkien, The Illustrated Encyclopedia*. New York: Simon & Schuster, 1991.

Diamond, Denise. *Living with Flowers*. New York: William Morrow and Company, 1982.

Dubois, Pierre. *The Great Encyclopedia of Faeries*. New York: Simon & Schuster, 1999.

Eliade, Mircea. *Shamanism.* Bollingen Series: Princeton, New Jersey, 1964.

Ellis, Peter Berresford. *The Druids.* Grand Rapids, MI: William B. Eerdmans Publishing Co., 1994.

Evans-Wentz, W. Y. *The Fairy Faith in Celtic Countries.* New York: Citadel Press, 1990.

Evslin, Bernard. *Heroes, Gods, and Monsters of the Greek Myths.* New York: Random House, 1966.

Farmer, Philip José. *The World of Tiers.* New York: St. Martin's Press, 1996.

Ford, Patrick K., Translator. *The Mabinogi and Other Medieval Welsh Tales.* Los Angeles: University of California Press, 1977.

Frazier, Sir James George. *The Golden Bough.* New York: The Macmillan Company, 1935.

Froud, Brian. *Good Faeries, Bad Faeries.* New York: Simon & Schuster, 1998.

Froud, Brian, and Alan Lee. *Faeries.* New York: Harry N. Abrams, Inc., 1978.

Gannon, Linda. *Creating Fairy Garden Fragrances.* Pownal, VT: Storey Books, 1998.

Gantz, Jeffrey. *Early Irish Myths and Sagas.* New York: Penguin Books, 1982.

Gaster, Theodor, ed. *The New Golden Bough.* New York: The New American Library, 1959.

Gimbutas, Marija. *The Goddesses and Gods of Old Europe.* Berkeley, CA: University of California Press, 1982.

———. *The Language of the Goddess.* San Francisco: Harper & Row, 1989.

Glassie, Henry, ed. *Irish Folktales.* New York: Pantheon Books, 1985

Graves, Robert. *The White Goddess.* New York: Faber & Faber, 1966.

Green, Miranda J. *Dictionary of Celtic Myth and Legend.* London: Thames and Hudson Ltd., 1992.

Grimal, Pierre, ed. *Larousse World Mythology.* London: Paul Hamlyn, 1965.

Harland and Wilkinson. *Lancashire Legends, Traditions.* Wales: LLanerch Press, 1993.

Haviland, Virginia. *Favorite Fairy Tales Told in Denmark.* Boston: Little, Brown, and Co., 1971.

———. *Favorite Fairy Tales Told in Greece.* Boston: Little, Brown, and Co., 1970.

———. *Favorite Fairy Tales Told in Italy.* Boston: Little, Brown and Co., 1963.

———. *Favorite Fairy Tales Told in Sweden.* Boston: Little, Brown and Co., 1966.

Jacobs, Joseph, collected by. *Celtic Fairytales.* New York: Dover Publications, Inc., 1968.

Jacobs, Joseph. *European Folk and Fairy Tales.* New York: G. P. Putnam's Sons, 1916.

Jay, Roni. *Gardens of the Spirit.* New York: Sterling Publishing Co., 1998.

Jung, Carl G. *The Archetypes of the Collective Unconscious.* Princeton, NJ: Princeton University Press, 1990.

Knight, Sirona. *Celtic Traditions.* New York: Citadel Press, 2000.

———. *Dream Magic.* San Francisco: HarperSanFrancisco, 2000.

———. *Empowering Your Life with Dreams.* Indianapolis: Alpha Books, 2003.

———. *Empowering Your Life with Natural Magic.* Indianapolis: Alpha Books, 2004.

———. *Empowering Your Life with Wicca.* Indianapolis: Alpha Books, 2003.

———. *Exploring Celtic Druidism.* Franklin Lakes, NJ: New Page Books, 2001.

———. *Faery Magick.* Franklin Lakes, NJ: New Page Books, 2002.

———. *Goddess Bless!* Boston, MA: Red Wheel, 2002.

———. *Greenfire: Making Love with the Goddess.* St. Paul, MN: Llewellyn Publications, 1995.

———. *Moonflower: Erotic Dreaming with the Goddess.* St. Paul, MN: Llewellyn Publications, 1996.

———. *The Pocket Guide to Celtic Spirituality.* Freedom, CA: Crossing Press, 1998.

———. *The Pocket Guide to Crystals and Gemstones.* Freedom, CA: Crossing Press, 1998.

———. *The Witch and Wizard's Training Guide.* New York: Citadel Press, 2001.

Knight, Sirona, et al. *The Shapeshifter Tarot.* St. Paul, MN: Llewellyn Publications, 1998.

Le Guin, Ursula. *A Wizard of Earthsea (Earthsea Trilogy, Book 1).* Spectra, 1984.

Leach, Maria, ed. *Standard Dictionary of Folklore, Mythology, and Legend.* New York: Funk & Wagnalls Co., 1950.

Leodhas, Sorche Nic. *Sea-Spell and Moor-Magic.* New York: Holt, Rinehart, and Winston, Inc., 1968.

Linn, Denise. *The Secret Language of Signs.* New York: Ballantine Books, 1996.

Long, Jim. *Making Herbal Dream Pillows.* Pownal, VT: Storey Books, 1998.

Macnamara, Niall. *Leprehaun Companion.* New York: Barnes & Noble Books, 1999.

MacRitchie, David. *Fians, Fairies, and Picts.* London: Norwood Editions, 1975.

Manning-Sanders, Ruth. *A Book of Dwarfs.* New York: E.P. Dutton & Co., Inc., 1964.

———. *A Book of Ogres and Trolls.* New York: E.P. Dutton & Co., Inc., 1972.

Markale, Jean. *The Celts*. Rochester, VT: Inner Traditions International, 1993.

———. *Merlin: Priest of Nature*. Rochester, VT: Inner Traditions International, 1995.

———. *Women of the Celts*. Rochester, VT: Inner Traditions International, 1986.

Matthews, John. *King Arthur and the Grail Quest*. London: Cassell, 1995.

———. *Taliesin: Shamanic and Bardic Mysteries in Britain and Ireland*. London: Aquarian Press, 1988.

McCaffrey, Anne. *Dragonriders of Pern*. New York: Del Rey, 1988.

Mercatante, Anthony. *The Magic Garden*. New York: Harper and Row: 1976.

Molyneaux, Brian Leigh, and Piers Vitebsky. *Sacred Earth, Sacred Stones*. San Diego, CA: Laurel Glen Publishing, 2001.

Monaghan, Patricia. *The Book of Goddesses and Heroines*. St. Paul, MN: Llewellyn Publications, 1990.

Monmouth, Geoffrey of. *History of the Kings of Britain*. New York: E.P. Dutton & Co., 1958.

Morris, Jan. *A Matter of Wales*. London: Oxford University Press, 1984.

Murray, Margaret. *The God of the Witches*. London: Oxford University Press, 1970.

Opie, Iona, and Peter Opie. *The Classic Fairy Tales*. London: Oxford University Press, 1974.

Palmer, Roy. *The Folklore of Warwickshire*. Totowa, NJ: Roman and Littlefield, 1976.

Partridge, Eric. *A Short Etymological Dictionary of Modern English Origins*. New York: The MacMillan Co., 1958.

Paterson, Helena. *Handbook of Celtic Astrology*. St. Paul, MN: Llewellyn Publications, 1995.

Penwyche, Gossamer. *The World of Fairies*. New York: Godsfield Press, 2001.

Philip, Neil. *Fairy Tales of Eastern Europe*. New York: Clarion Books, 1991.

Rector-Page, Linda. *Healthy Healing*. Sonoma, CA: Healthy Healing Publications, 1992.

Rees, Alwyn, and Brinley Rees. *Celtic Heritage, Ancient Tradition in Ireland and Wales*. New York: Grove Press, 1978.

Rhys, John, M. A. *Celtic Folklore, Welsh and Manx*. New York: Benjamin Blom, Inc., 1972.

Ross, Anne. *Pagan Celtic Britain*. New York: Columbia University Press, 1967.

Scalora, Suza. *The Fairies*. New York: HarperCollins, 1999.

———. *The Witches and Wizards of Oberin*. New York: HarperCollins, 2002.

Sitchin, Zecharia. *When Time Began*. Santa Fe, NM: Bear and Company, 1993.

Smith, Sir William. *Smaller Classical Dictionary*. New York: E.P. Dutton, 1958.

Spence, Lewis. *The History and Origins of Druidism*. New York: Samuel Weiser, Inc., 1971.

Squire, Charles. *Celtic Myth and Legend*. Franklin Lakes, NJ: New Page Books, 2001.

Starhawk. *The Spiral Dance*. San Francisco: HarperSanFrancisco, 1979.

Stepanich, Kisma. *Faery Wicca, Book One*. St. Paul, MN: Llewellyn Publications, 1994.

———. *Faery Wicca, Book Two*. St. Paul, MN: Llewellyn Publications, 1995.

Stephens, James. *Irish Fairy Tales*. New York: Collier Books, 1962.

Stern, Marina T. *Fairy Folk*. York Beach, ME: Red Wheel, 2002.

———. *The Fairy Party Book*. York Beach, ME: Red Wheel, 2003.

Stewart, R. J. *Celtic Gods, Celtic Goddesses*. New York: Sterling Publishing Co., 1990.

———. *Creation Myth*. Rockport, MA: Element Books, 1989.

———. *Earth Light*. Rockport, MA: Element Books, 1992.

———. *The Elements of Prophecy*. Rockport, MA: Element Books, 1990.

———. *The Living World of Faery*. Glastonbury, Somerset: Gothic Image Publication, 1995.

———. *Merlin Through the Ages*. London: Blandford Books, 1995.

———. *The Power Within the Land*. Rockport, MA: Element Books, 1992.

Stewart, R. J., and Robin Williamson. *Celtic Druids, Celtic Bards*. London: Blandford Press, 1996.

Tolkien, J. R. R. *The Hobbit*. New York: Ballantine Books, 1937.

———. *The Lord of the Rings (50th Anniversary Edition)*. Boston: Houghton Mifflin Co., 2004.

———. *Tree and Leaf*. Boston: Houghton Mifflin Co., 1965.

Valiente, Doreen. *The Rebirth of Witchcraft*. London: Robert Hale, 1989.

———. *Witchcraft for Tomorrow*. New York: St. Martin's Press, 1978.

Wheeler, Post. *Hawaiian Wonder Tales*. New York: The Beechhurst Press, 1953.

Wilde, Lady. *Ancient Legends, Mystic Charms and Superstitions of Ireland*. New York: Lemma Publishing, 1973.

Worwood, Valerie. *The Complete Book of Essential Oils and Aromatherapy*. New York: New World Library, 1995.

Yeats, W. B., ed. *Fairy & Folk Tales of Ireland*. New York: Macmillan Publishing Co., 1983.

Glossary

Alfatofrar   The Norse term for elf magic or any enchanting effect.

Alfheim   Upper world home of the light elves in Norse mythology.

angels   Like fairies, these heavenly guardians, ministering spirits, and messengers act as intermediaries between the divine and the mortal.

animism   The belief that everything, whether animate or inanimate, has a soul or spirit. This spirit has life beyond the physical form, and as such, connects the physical world with the spiritual realm.

archetypes   Universal themes that are common within the human experience, such as mother, father, lover, and dreamer; the building blocks of not only the unconscious mind, but also the collective unconscious. Psychologist Carl Jung believed that these are the elementary ideas upon which all myths are based.

Asgard   Upper world home the Norse Gods.

Avalon   The British Isle of Apples, also called Avalon, was in the West. King Arthur was taken to Avalon as he lay dying by Morgana, the ruler of nine fairy sisters who guarded the apples of fairyland.

Beltane   The fairy and elf May Day festival, which is May 1.

blessing   A ritual used to hallow or consecrate by spiritual rite or word. A blessing is an approval or encouragement that is conducive to your happiness and well-being.

Celts   The Celts were a group of Germanic tribes that gradually migrated west and up north through Scandinavia. The Celts eventually settled in present-day Ireland, Scotland, Wales, England, and the western coast of France.

coomlaen   An Elven steed.

devas   Nature spirits who work with and give direction to the elemental energy and embody the essential energy and spirit of the plant species that they are associated with. *Deva* is a Sanskrit word that means "a being of brilliant light."

Dreamtime   The Aboriginal mythology with similarities to elves and fairies. It refers to the time before memory when ancestral spirits roamed the earth and in the process formed its natural features.

Earth Mother   A mother goddess who is the embodiment of the earth, and thus represents all of the earth's qualities and holds its combined wisdom.

eddas   Narrative poems of Norse mythology that are the stories of the Norse gods and goddesses, along with the origin of the world and everything in it, including elves and dwarves.

Eildon Tree   Another name for hawthorn, a sacred tree of elves and fairies.

elementals   Beings that spring from the basic elements and are creators of form. As such, they work as a connecting point between creative energy and physical form.

elements   The basic elements are earth, air, fire, water, and spirit.

elvenstar   The seven-pointed star also known as the fairy star.

elves   Magical beings with extraordinary powers who are associated with natural settings. They are called the white spirits, Elves of Light, the firstborn, the speakers, the elder (eldar) people, and the folk of the wood.

enchantment   Elven and fairy magic and glamour. *See also* glamour.

fairies   Magical creatures with supernatural powers who embody the many aspects of nature and life.

fairy circle   A bridge of light that ties the human and fairy worlds together into one. Often seen as a ring of flowers or grass.

fairy garden   A garden planted with the flowers and trees that are favorites of the elves and fairies.

fairy guardians   Helpful spirits who protect the elemental gates of your sacred space. They are also called the Watchers, as they watch the thresholds of the seven directions and remain in place until you bid them farewell.

fairy kings   The Gods of Irish tribes, often consorts to the fairy queens. They continue to defend the Irish clans.

fairy magic   The extraordinary state of being when you leave the ordinary world and enter the magical realm of the fairy.

fairy queens   The goddesses of Irish tribes. To this day, many of these fairy queens still guard the Irish clans and families. These magical ladies are the source of creation and sovereignty of the land.

fairy ring   A ring made by fairies. Also an energetic ring you can make for communing with the fairies by using a string and flowers, seeds, stones, leaves, or twigs.

fairy tale   A story involving fantastic forces and magical beings such as elves and fairies.

fairyland   An Otherworld that often mirrors the mortal world. A land filled with magic and magical beings doing ordinary and extraordinary things. No one ever ages, gets sick, or goes hungry in this magic place.

Findhorn   An eclectic community in northern Scotland, where fairy magic and organic gardening have worked together to produce some extraordinary results.

focals   Items in ritual that are used to give focus and energy to a ritual or work of magic.

folklore   The traditions, beliefs, and customs of a culture, preserved within its myths, legends, folk stories, proverbs, and other oral forms of folk art. It is also the study of folk cultures.

Gebo   The Norse rune that symbolizes the basic exchange in life in regard to giving and receiving. Written like an *X*, it represents two lines (the giver and the receiver).

gentry   The preferred name for elves and fairies.

geomancy   An ancient, holistic, integrated system of natural science and philosophy used to keep human activity in harmony with natural geometric patterns of nature.

glamour   A magical or enchanted illusion that elves and fairies use to hide themselves from humans.

Great Days   Also called the Sabbats, the Great Days are the names that the ancient Celts gave to times of the year when the sun and the earth are aligned in particular positions, specifically the solstices, equinoxes, and cross-quarter days.

heirloom seeds   Varieties of seeds that have been cultivated through generations of plants.

instant karma   When the result of your actions comes back to you very quickly. Elves and fairies fit these criteria because they use magic, which has a tendency to change things quickly.

Irish mythology   The tales of the five invasions of Ireland that happened in different periods of Irish history, the most relevant to the fairy being the Tuatha De Danann.

Jotunheim   Home of the giants who came into creation with Ymir in Norse mythology.

karma   The concept that everything we do in life builds up either good or bad consequences, depending on our intentions and actions.

leprechaun   A type of fairy usually associated with elves; both have a traditional tie to shoemaking.

living traditions   Spiritual traditions that view everything as being alive with spirit and continually evolving, much like nature, and just like fairy tales and mythology.

Lughnassad   Occurring at the beginning of August, this time of celebration signals the end of summer and beginning of fall. *Lughnassad* literally means "Lugh's wedding feast." Also called Lammas.

magic   The experience of something extraordinary, unseen, or unknown—an enchantment, or glamour. After you experience the magic, your perception is permanently altered.

meditation   A relaxed and altered state of awareness in which you are open to other realms of being, leading to personal and divine insights.

Midgard   Middle Earth, the world of mortal humans.

Midsummer's Eve   The eve just before the summer solstice, which is one of the primary elf and fairy festival days. Also called St. John's Eve.

morphogenic field   Rupert Sheldrake's theory that an energetic field of resonance or vibration is just beyond the spectrum of normal human perception.

Mother Goddess   Often viewed as the sole deity from whom all growing things come.

mythology   The collective myths and legends of a particular people, displaying their perception of power and order in the world.

New Age   A New Age approach to fairies involves viewing fairies as part of other earth energies, such as nature devas, and working with these energies. This is integrated into New Age practices that include things such as channeling, organic gardening, and working with herbs, oils, crystals, and gemstones.

Nifelheim   Home of the frost giants or hoarfrost in Norse mythology.

Norse   The combination of Germanic tribes who moved northward and settled in the area now known as Scandinavia—Sweden, Denmark, and Norway.

Otherworld   The invisible land, the fairyland paradise. A world where the natural laws of the universe don't necessarily apply. The land of immortality and home of the divine.

peri   A Turkish word that means "fairy" or "beautiful girl."

perilous realm   Another name for the fairy realm.

pixie   A type of fairy.

pixilated   A term used to describe someone who has been affected by the elves and fairies.

polarities   The positive, negative, and neutral energies of the universe.

power hand   Your dominant hand (your right hand if you are right-handed); the hand you use to direct energy or power.

prophecy   The ability to predict events before they actually occur. The word itself means to "speak," as prophecy frequently blends elements of prediction, forecasting, and divination. Also thought to be of a psychic and spiritual nature, many prophecies are considered messages from the divine.

quest   A transformative journey of body, mind, and spirit.

rath   A fairy fort or mound, often surrounded by a ditch.

receiving hand   Your left hand if you are right-handed. The hand you use to receive energy or power.

ritual   The enactment of a myth, enactment referring to the life act you are engaged in. A proscribed way of doing something.

runes   Each rune is a magical symbol that represents cosmic energies at work in the universe. Each of the 24 runes in the Elder Futhark provides a doorway into fairyland.

sacred geometry   Also known as the language of light and the language of creation, sacred geometry revolves around the idea that energy moves in universal patterns, which influences the form of everything, including our DNA.

Samhain   Halloween, when the veil between the mortal and fairy worlds is at its thinnest and is most easily lifted.

second sight   Also called clairvoyance or extraordinary perception, the ability to perceive things beyond the range of ordinary perception.

shape shifting   The ability to change form at will.

sidhe   Pronounced *shee*, the Irish word for fairy.

sleeper kings   Ancestral kings whose energy and knowledge waits to be summoned by future generations.

spirit   The energy that connects all the elements together. Everything has a spirit that makes it magical. Spirit is considered the fifth element, or sometimes the union of all the other elements. This union forms the divine quintessence.

staurolite   A powerful fairy stone also called the Fairy Cross.

Svartalfheim   Norse home of the dwarves in the lower world.

Tir-na-n-Og   The home of the Celtic gods and goddesses, the Land of the Blessed, and the divine land of immortality. Its name means "country of the young," a reference to the fact that age and death have no power there.

tradition   The passing of information, beliefs, and customs from one generation to another. Traditions are continually evolving and being reinvented to remain viable.

Tuatha De Danann   The tribe of the goddess Danu (Anu) that invaded Ireland by coming down from the skies and creating a thick mist on May Day morning.

Vanaheim   World where the Vanir, the ancient nature gods and goddesses in Norse mythology, live.

wizard   A magician who controls the elements.

wormhole   A path through which one can move through the time/space continuum, which uses the natural folds of space to move great distances at a very fast rate. They are avenues to the Otherworld of fairyland.

wyrrd   In Norse spiritual traditions, a magical energy where everything is interconnected. Rune masters use this energy when they use the runes to look into the future.

Y Tylwyth Teg   The Welsh name for fairies. It translates to "the fair folk or family." In the longer version, "y Tylwyth Teg yn y Coed," means "the fair family in the wood."

Yggdrasil   In Norse mythology, the World Tree whose branches held the nine worlds: three worlds above (includes the light elf world), three worlds in the middle (includes Middle Earth), and three worlds below (includes the dark elf world).

Yule   The Great Day or Sabbat occurring at the winter solstice, usually on or around December 21. This time of celebration lives on in our current holiday of Christmas.

Index

T